AF386855

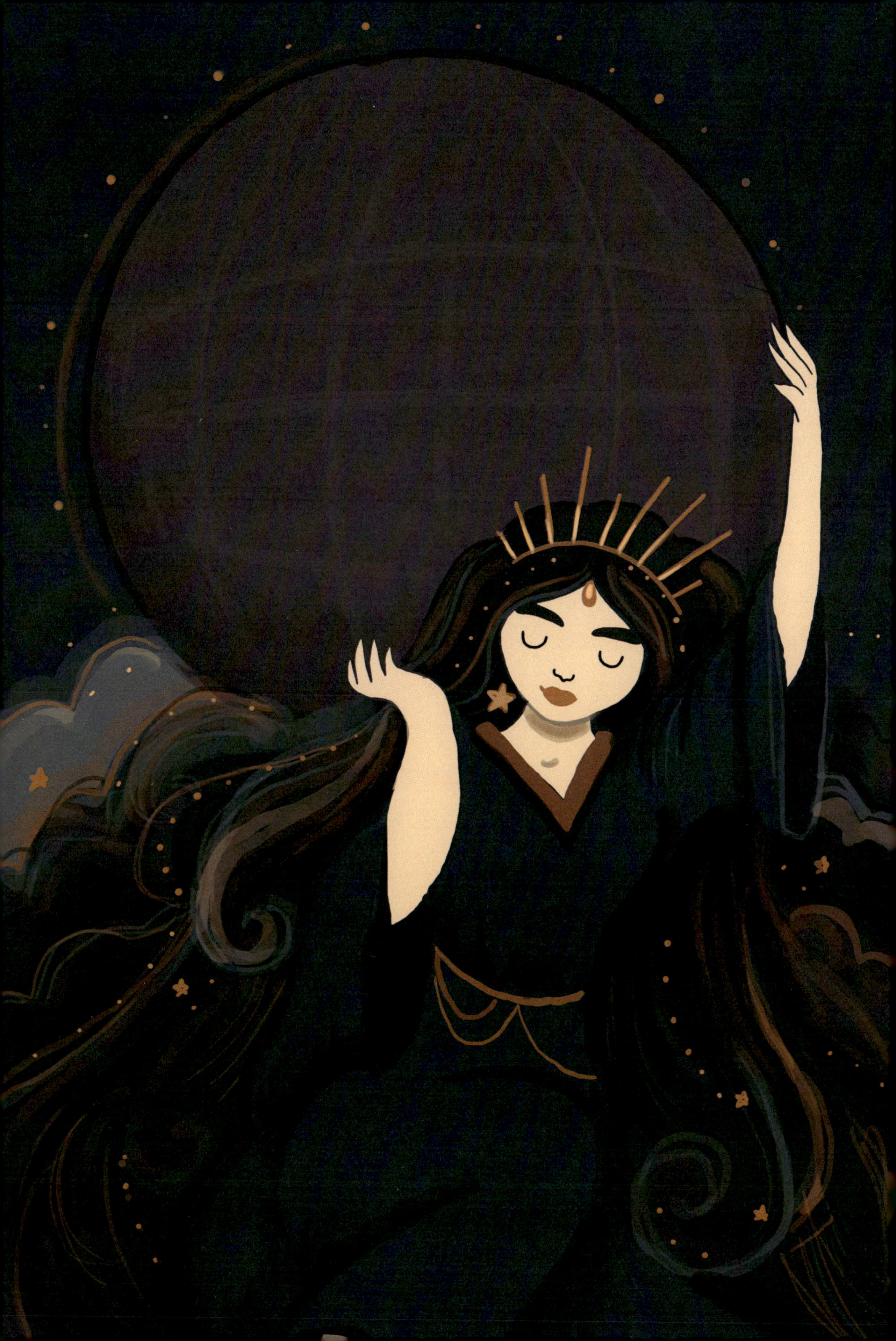

THE
GODDESS
ATLAS

THE GODDESS ATLAS

An Illustrated Guide to Female Deities, Myths, and Sacred Feminine Stories from Around the World

Anette Pirso and Israel Gonzalez

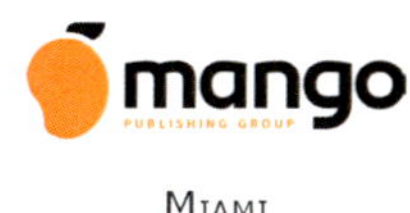

Miami

The Goddess Atlas: An Illustrated Guide to Female Deities, Myths, and Sacred Feminine Stories from Around
the World

Library of Congress Cataloging-in-Publication number: 2025942901
ISBN: (hc) 978-1-68481-885-3, (ebook) 978-1-68481-886-0
BISAC category code: OCC036050 BODY, MIND & SPIRIT / Goddess Worship

"For the goddesses forgotten by time, and
the ones still waiting to be remembered."

—Anette Pirso

"For love, lore, and literature: my three graces."

—Israel Gonzalez

TABLE *of* CONTENTS

Preface   13

Áine   15

Akhilandeshvari   17

Amaterasu   19

Anahita   21

Angrboða   23

Aphrodite   25

Arianrhod   27

Artemis   29

Artio   31

Asibikaashi   33

Atabey   35

Athena   37

Bast   39

Baubo   41

Berehynia   43

Boann   45

Brigid   47

The Cailleach   49

Ceridwen   51

Chang'e   53

Dakini   55

Dali   57

Danu   59

Demeter   61

Dodola   63

Durga   65

Eir   67

Elen of the Ways   69

Erinyes   71

Eris   73

Eve   75

Feronia   77

Flora   79

Freyja   81

Frigg   83

Gaia   85

Guan Yin   87

Hathor   89

Hecate   91

Hel   93

Hera   95

Hestia   97

Hlín   99

Iara   101

Iðunn   103

Inanna   105

Iris   107

Isis   109

Ix Chel   111

Justitia   113

Kali   115

Konohanasakuya-hime   117

Lada   119

Leto   121

Lilith   123

Maeve   125

Mariang Makiling   127

Mbaba Mwana Waresa   129

Medeinė   131

Medusa   133

Milda	135
Mokoš	137
Morana	139
The Morrígan	141
Nehalennia	143
Neith	145
Nephthys	147
The Norns	149
Nótt	151
Nyx	153
Oizys	155
Oshun	157
Oya	159
Pele	161
Persephone	163
Rán	165
Santa Muerte	167
Sedna	169
Sekhmet	171
Selene	173
Sif	175
Sigyn	177
Skaði	179
Sól	181
Tuuletar	183
Uzume	185
Valkyries	187
Vesna	189
White Buffalo Calf Woman	191
Yemaya	193
About the Authors	194

PREFACE

Welcome to *The Goddess Atlas*. With this book, we hope to provide an introduction to the rich and varied goddesses from cultures across time. This is by no means an exhaustive study, but rather a curated selection of better- and lesser-known goddesses, as understood by both modern perspectives and historical contexts. In these pages, we explore their enduring legacies and the stories that have shaped our perceptions of them.

The goddesses presented here are arranged simply in alphabetical order, not according to any hierarchy of importance or popularity. It is worth noting that, while mythology offers a multitude of interpretations, the prevailing portrayal of goddesses often relegates them to supporting roles within larger narratives, frequently introducing them through their relationships with male counterparts rather than highlighting their own unique accomplishments, domains, or inherent powers. We reject this male-centric narrative and aim to bring these goddesses into the limelight. We also acknowledge that not all these figures would be seen as "goddesses" by those who revered them; however, we honor their power and impact on their followers by including them in this powerful group.

Though this book contains ninety entries, it is crucial to remember that this represents only a small fraction of the countless female deities who have been venerated throughout world history. The sheer number of goddesses who have held significance for various cultures underscores the enduring human impulse to recognize and honor the divine feminine in its myriad forms.

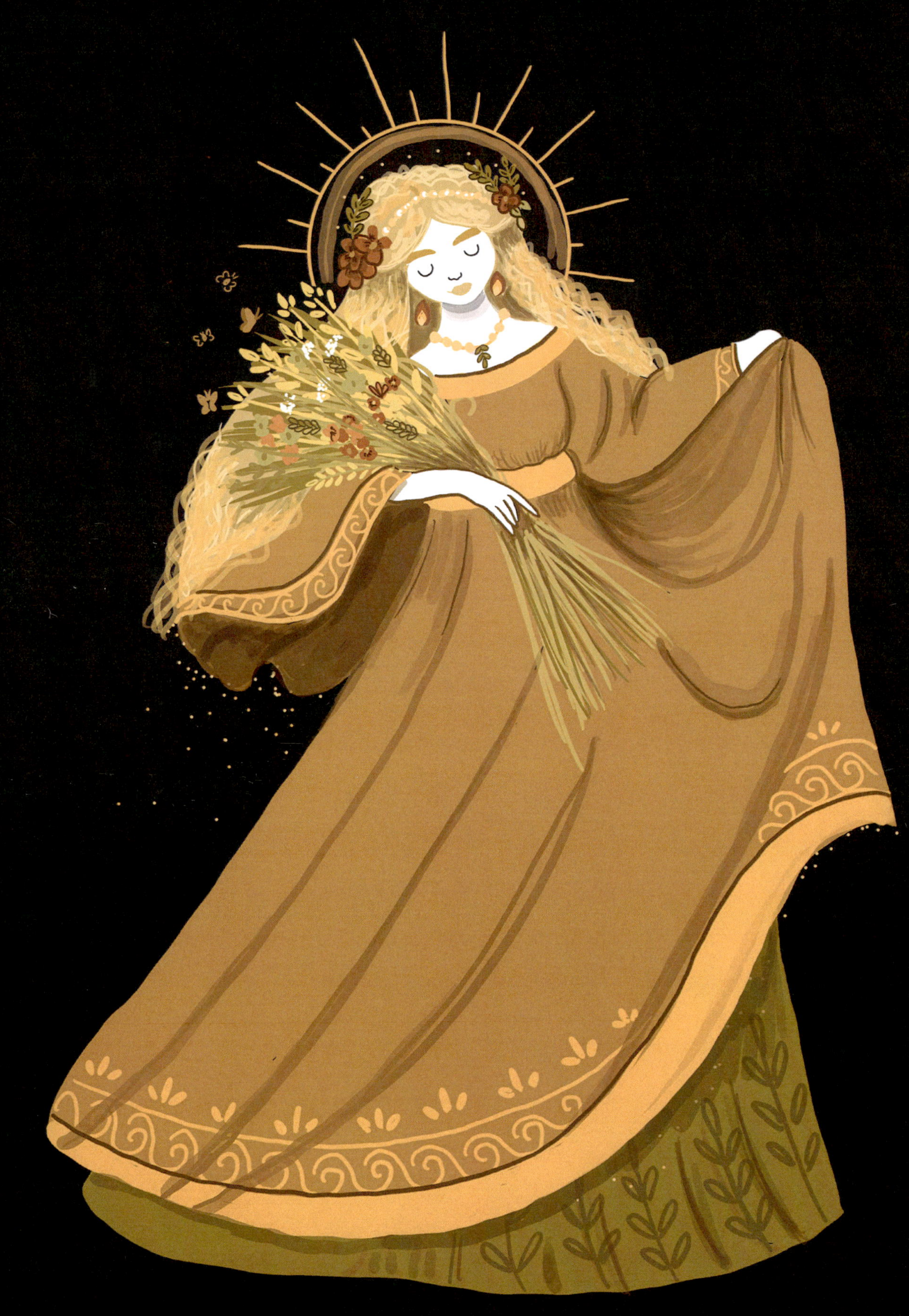

ÁINE

Celtic mythology honors well over 400 distinct deities, each representing various aspects of Iron Age life. Within the myriad legends that span the centuries of Celtic lore, one goddess often stands apart from the others: Áine. Often referred to as Ireland's *Magna Mater*, or "Great Mother," Áine (*awn-yah*) is the Celtic embodiment of independence, taking lovers as she so desires while simultaneously keeping a careful eye over the thriving summer crops. She wears a crown of meadowsweet (a sacred herb in ancient Celtic rituals) and granted the plant its distinctive, fragrant aroma.

Medieval texts declare Áine to be the daughter of the sea god Manannán, yet her name is closely associated with the fieriness, radiance, and brightness of the sun. "Áine" is also thought to be derived from the complementary root word Án, used in Ireland to praise someone as being "brilliant or delightful." The province of Munster in southern Ireland is home to Áine's sacred hill, Knockainy, where she is said to reside within a castle that was promised to her until the end of the world.

This promise can be traced back to a poem, thought to have been written between 1080 and 1120 CE, in which five tribes of great warriors sought to win the hill for themselves, spurred on by various gods.

According to the poem, Áine secured her claim to Knockainy by mediating the conflict between the five warrior tribes by using her magic to divide the land after they agreed to her terms, thereby ending widespread bloodshed and establishing her dominion over the eastern side of the hill. The lake of Lough Gur, renowned as the site of one of Ireland's oldest known stone circles, as well as the Paps of Anu, breast-shaped mountains thought to be the physical embodiment of Áine herself, are also under the protection of this ancient goddess.

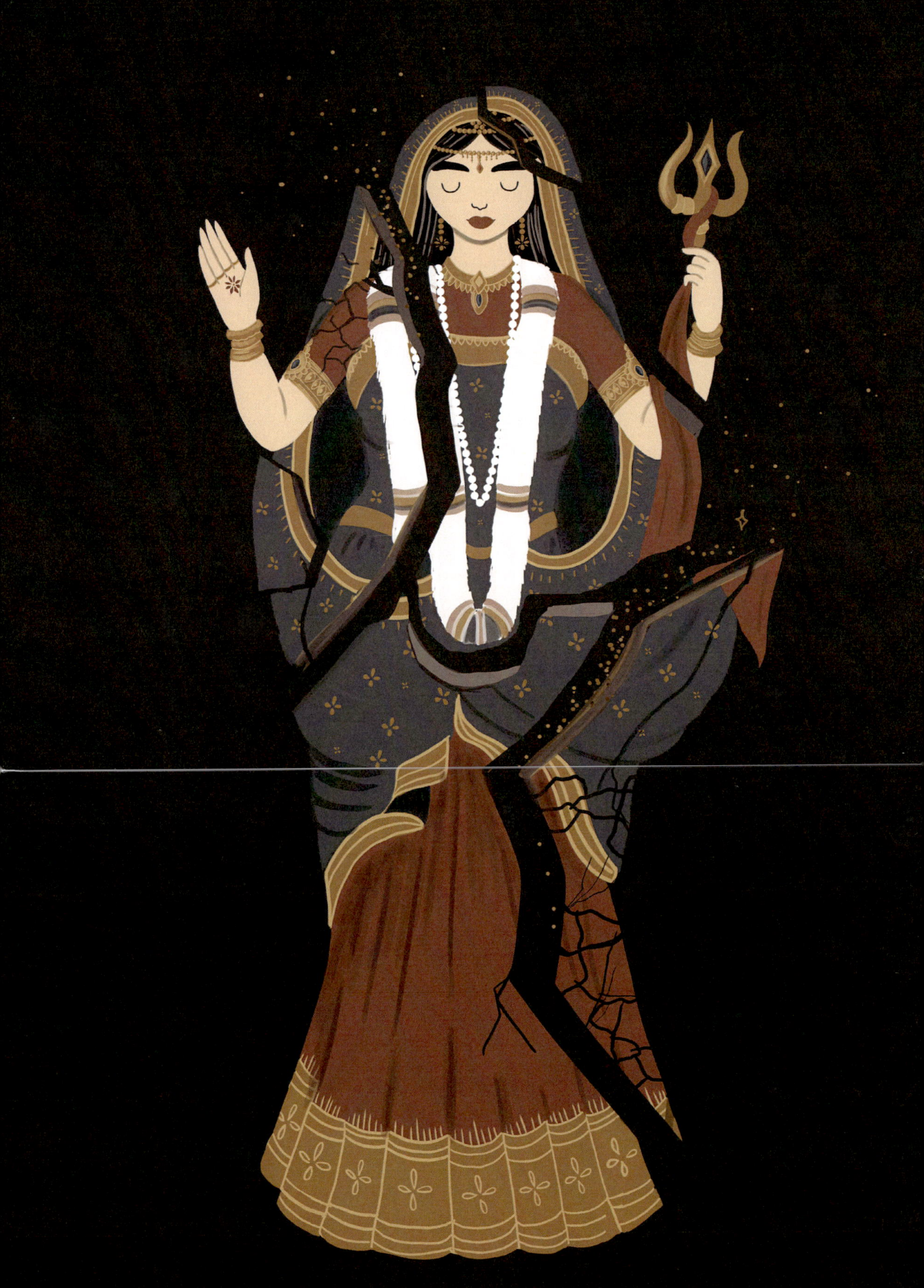

AKHILANDESHVARI

"O GODDESS, YOU WHO DWELL IN ALL BEINGS IN THE FORM OF POWER."

—*DEVI MAHATMYA,* CHAPTER 5, VERSE 13

Within the Shaktism sect of Hinduism, tradition states that all Hindu goddesses are a unique manifestation of the supreme goddess Mahadevi, also known as Adi Parashakti or Abhaya Shakti. Shaktism, one of the major Hindu denominations, is represented by the core philosophy that the entirety of our metaphysical reality is both governed and metaphorically personified by the supreme goddess. Of these various archetypes, it is Akhilandeshvari (*ah-kee-lahn-dehsh-vaa-ree*) who teaches that in order to be complete, we must first be incomplete.

Unlike many goddesses with well-documented historical origins, Akhilandeshvari's presence is more subtle, woven into the philosophies of Shaktism and embodied in specific temples. One of Akhilandeshvari's primary abodes is the Jambukeswarar Temple in Thiruvanaikaval, where she resides alongside her consort, Shiva. Here, she is revered as a form of Adi Parashakti, the primordial cosmic energy. However, Akhilandeshvari's name holds a deeper meaning. While *Akhila* signifies "complete," the name's meaning shifts dramatically in *Akhilanda,* forming the phrase "never not broken." Scholars interpret it as a double negative, emphasizing the inherent brokenness or imperfection of the universe. This resonates with *Shakta Tantra,* which views the microcosm, our humanity, as a reflection of the macrocosm, the universe. Our own experiences of suffering and impermanence are mirrored in the ever-changing, impermanent nature of the cosmos.

Akhilandeshvari represents profound understanding and acceptance of life's inherent challenges. Iconographically, she is often depicted with a serene smile, wielding a trident: a symbol of her power and connection to Shiva. She rides a crocodile, navigating the turbulent currents of existence. This imagery underscores her role as a guide through life's difficulties, similar to Durga, another powerful goddess associated with overcoming hardship. She is sometimes considered part of the *Trishakti,* a powerful triad alongside Meenakshi and Kamakshi. Together, they represent the totality of the divine feminine, encompassing creation, preservation, and destruction.

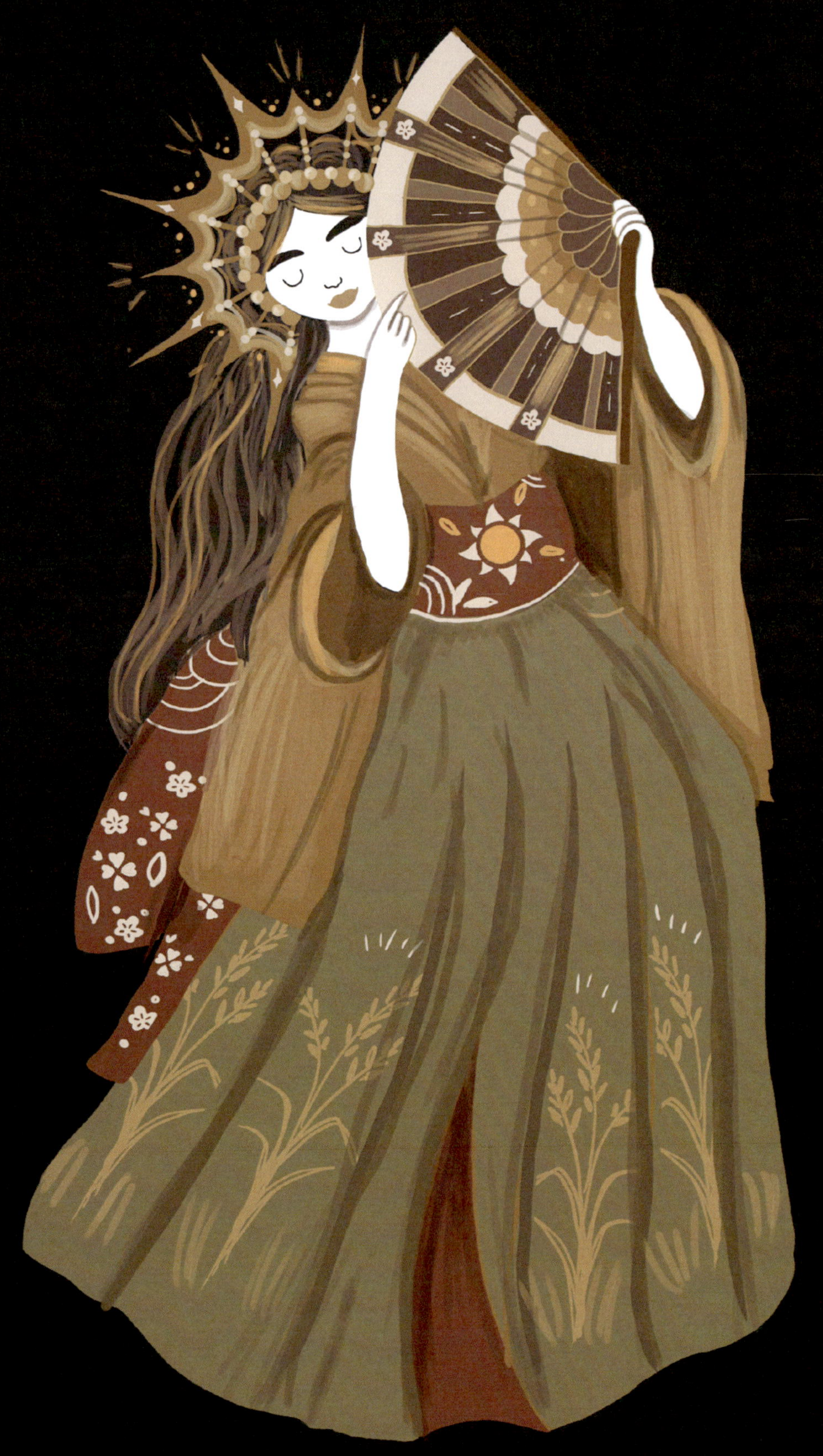

AMATERASU

"NOW, WHEN HIS AUGUSTNESS IZANAGI-NO-MIKOTO WASHED HIS LEFT EYE,
THERE WAS PRODUCED THE GREAT AUGUST DEITY."

—*KOJIKI,* BOOK 1

Amaterasu (*ah-mah-teh-rah-soo*), shorthand for *Amaterasu Omikami*, is the supreme deity of the Shinto religion and the ancestral goddess of the Japanese imperial family. She is revered as the ruler of *Takama-ga-hara*, the Shinto realm of the heavens, and her brilliance sustains the natural world, fostering growth and prosperity. Amaterasu is mentioned in the *Kojiki* and *Nihon Shoki*, the two oldest chronicles of Japanese history. These texts tell the story of Amaterasu's birth and her role in the creation of Japan.

According to the legend, Amaterasu was born from the left eye of the god Izanagi after he cleansed himself of the impurities of the Underworld, imbuing her with the life-giving power of the sun. A pivotal myth, recorded in the *Kojiki*, describes Amaterasu's withdrawal into a cave due to her brother Susanoo's destructive actions, leading to the world's immersion in darkness. The other deities eventually lured her out with a clever plan involving a sacred mirror and lively performance, thereby restoring light and order to the cosmos.

In Shinto mythology, Amaterasu is said to have given the Japanese people the gift of rice cultivation, and she is worshipped as the protector of their harvests. She is also a reminder of the close connection between the Japanese people and their natural environment. Amaterasu has played a significant role in Japanese culture and history for centuries. The Japanese imperial family, known as the "unbroken line of emperors," claim direct descent from Amaterasu, which helps to legitimize their rule. She has also been a source of inspiration for Japanese art and literature and been depicted in countless paintings, sculptures, and poems. Modern Japan continues to revere Amaterasu as a symbol of Japanese national identity. The Ise Shrine, her central place of worship, is renowned both as a popular tourist spot and a highly significant Shinto shrine in Japan.

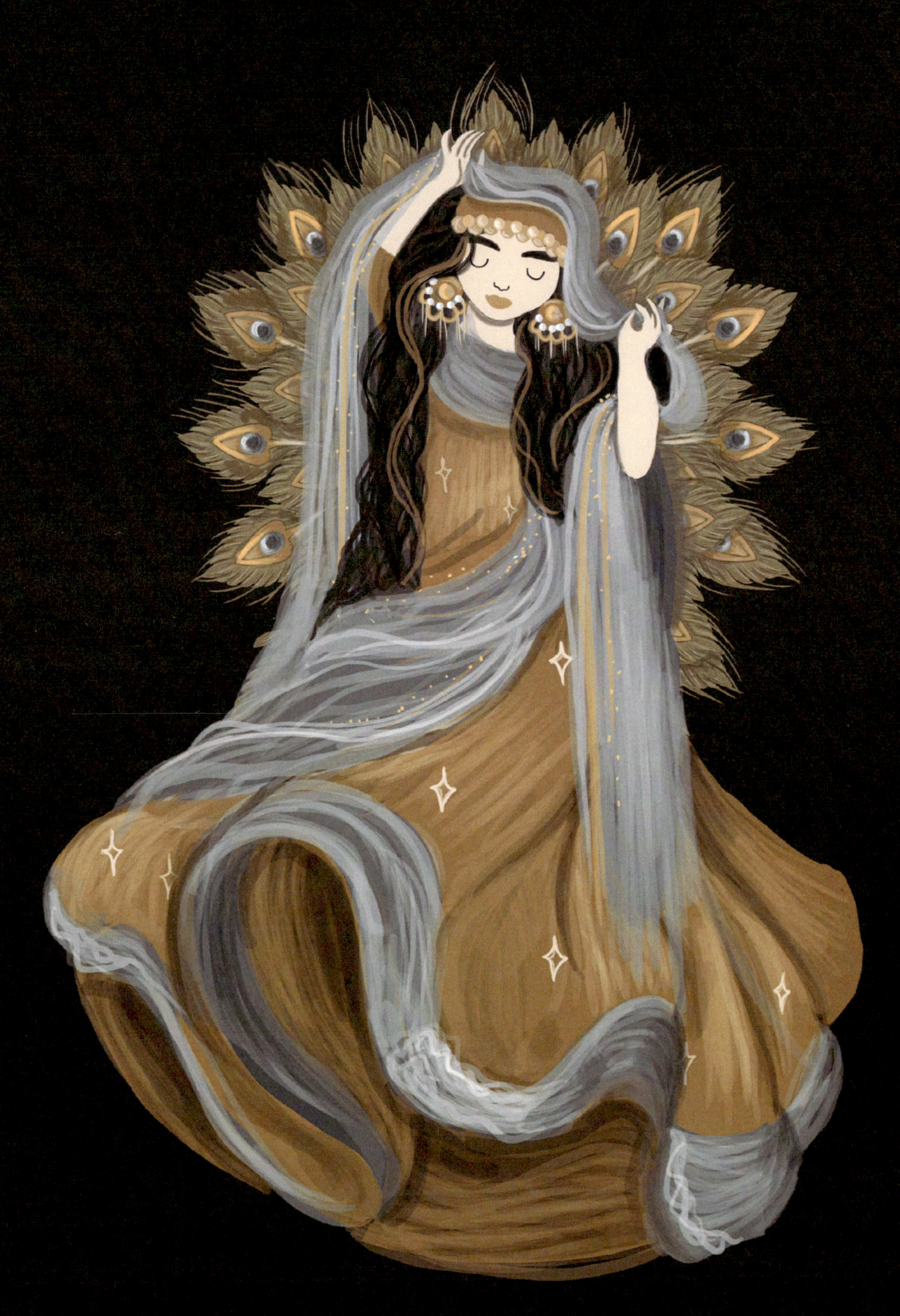

ANAHITA

"…THE UNDEFILED, THE MIGHTY ONE, THE TALL OF FORM, THE WELL-SHAPEN,
WHO WEARETH A GOLDEN MANTLE."

—*AVESTA,* YASHT 5, VERSE 128

Anahita (*ah-nah-hee-tah*), great goddess of ancient Iran and Armenia, rules over the waters of fertility, wisdom, and healing. While often associated with kingship and sovereignty, Anahita was also worshipped by people within all social classes, with temples and shrines being found throughout the Persian Empire. Her origins can be traced back to the Indo-Iranian pantheon, where she was known as "Aredvi Sura Anahita." Worship of Anahita was introduced into Iran by the Medes, and she would soon become one of the most significant deities of the Persian Empire (550–330 BCE).

Anahita was depicted as a tall and beautiful woman adorned with a golden crown and embroidered cloak. She traveled upon a great chariot drawn by four horses, meant to represent the wind, rain, clouds, and hail. As she was believed to preside over all of Earth's water sources, shrines dedicated to Anahita were typically located along rivers or springs, where her followers would pray for successful harvests with offerings of fruit and flowers.

This association with water extended beyond the physical realm, as Anahita was seen as a source of moral and spiritual purity as well. Later Zoroastrian texts depict her battling against the forces of evil, particularly drought and disease. Offerings of wine, considered a symbol of sacred purification, were often made in her honor.

After the fall of the Persian Empire, the goddess Anahita was adopted into the Zoroastrian pantheon. Modern Zoroastrianism considers her to be a *Yazata*, or divine being, and she has retained her dominion over the waters of the earth. Zoroastrians also believe that Anahita works to maintain the order and balance of the universe, providing humanity with healing and protection. The rise of Islam in the seventh century CE brought a halt to her worship within Iran, yet the legacy of Anahita survived through popular culture and folklore.

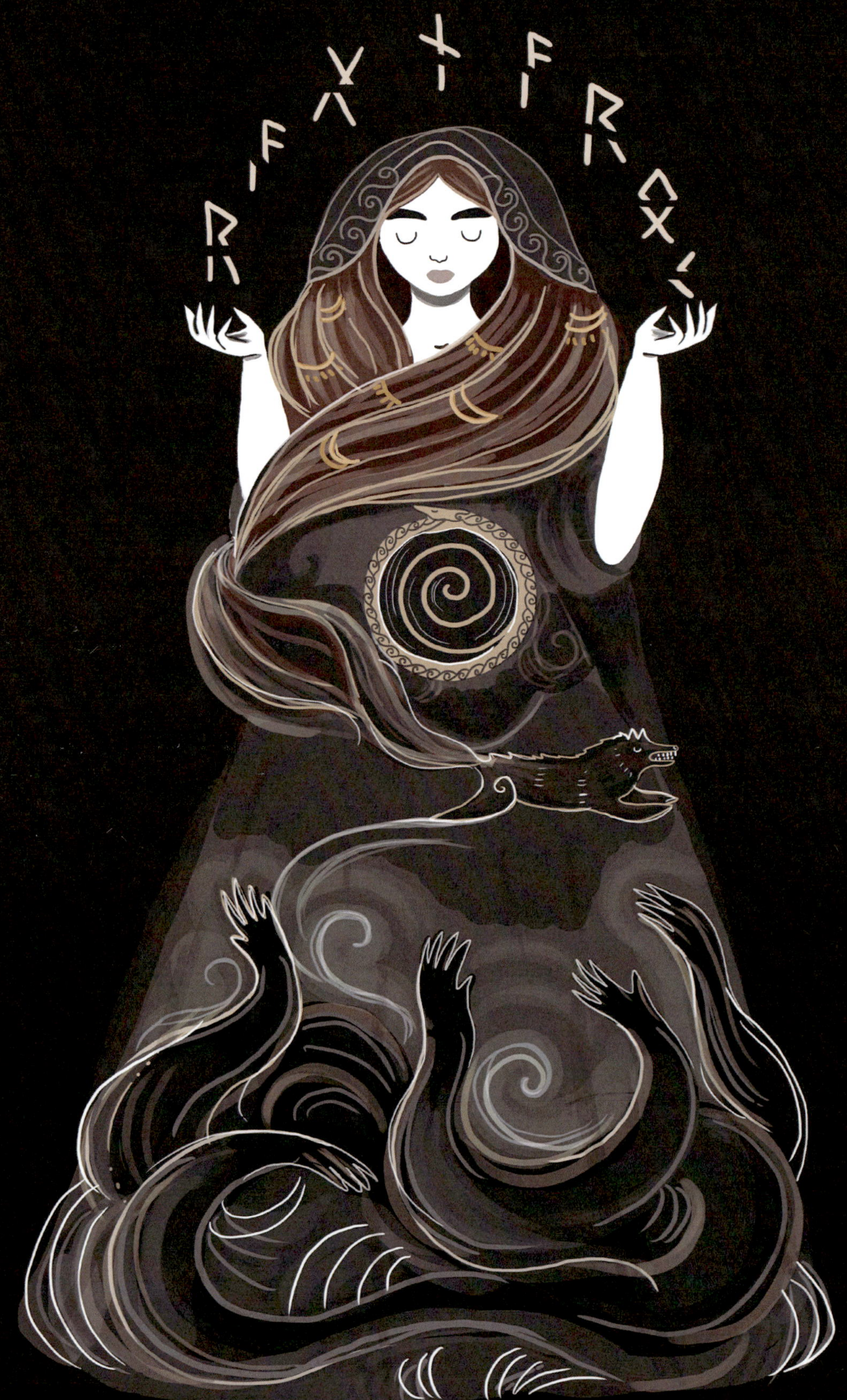

ANGRBOÐA

"FROM THY WOMB CAME THE LADY OF DEATH, DARK MISTRESS OF THE SHADES."

—**THE ORDER OF THE HORAE,** *THE PAGAN BOOK OF HOURS*

Though her mythos may be less thoroughly chronicled than some deities, Angrboða (*ang-grboh-thah*) remains an integral figure within Norse mythology. Ragnarök, the death and rebirth of the cosmos, would never have come to pass without her monstrous children, yet her place within the Eddas is still being debated by scholars to this day. Angrboða's true identity remains a mystery; she is frequently described as a witch, a giantess, a troll-queen, a werewolf, or even a member of the Vanir pantheon. At times, she was attributed to be all of the above or none at all.

The name *Angrboða* translates through Old Norse as "she who offers sorrows" or "the one who brings grief," yet this translation does not completely define her. She was a goddess of death and destruction, but also life and birth. As a conjurer of storms, she was known as the Hag of the East Winds, capable of steering ships to their doom upon the seas. When described as a giantess, she was called the Hag of the Iron Wood, simultaneously existing as a witch and shapeshifter as well. However, her most recognizable role was her time spent as a wife to the trickster god Loki and mother to three distinctive children destined to transform life itself.

Angrboða gave birth to the goddess of the dead Hel, the great wolf Fenrir, and the world serpent Jörmungandr. Upon learning of their connection to the inevitable Ragnarök, Odin sought to divide and imprison them far away from one another. Despite Fenrir's and Jörmungandr's fates being linked to the deaths of both Odin and Thor, Angrboða would forever continue to be a ferociously loving mother to her children.

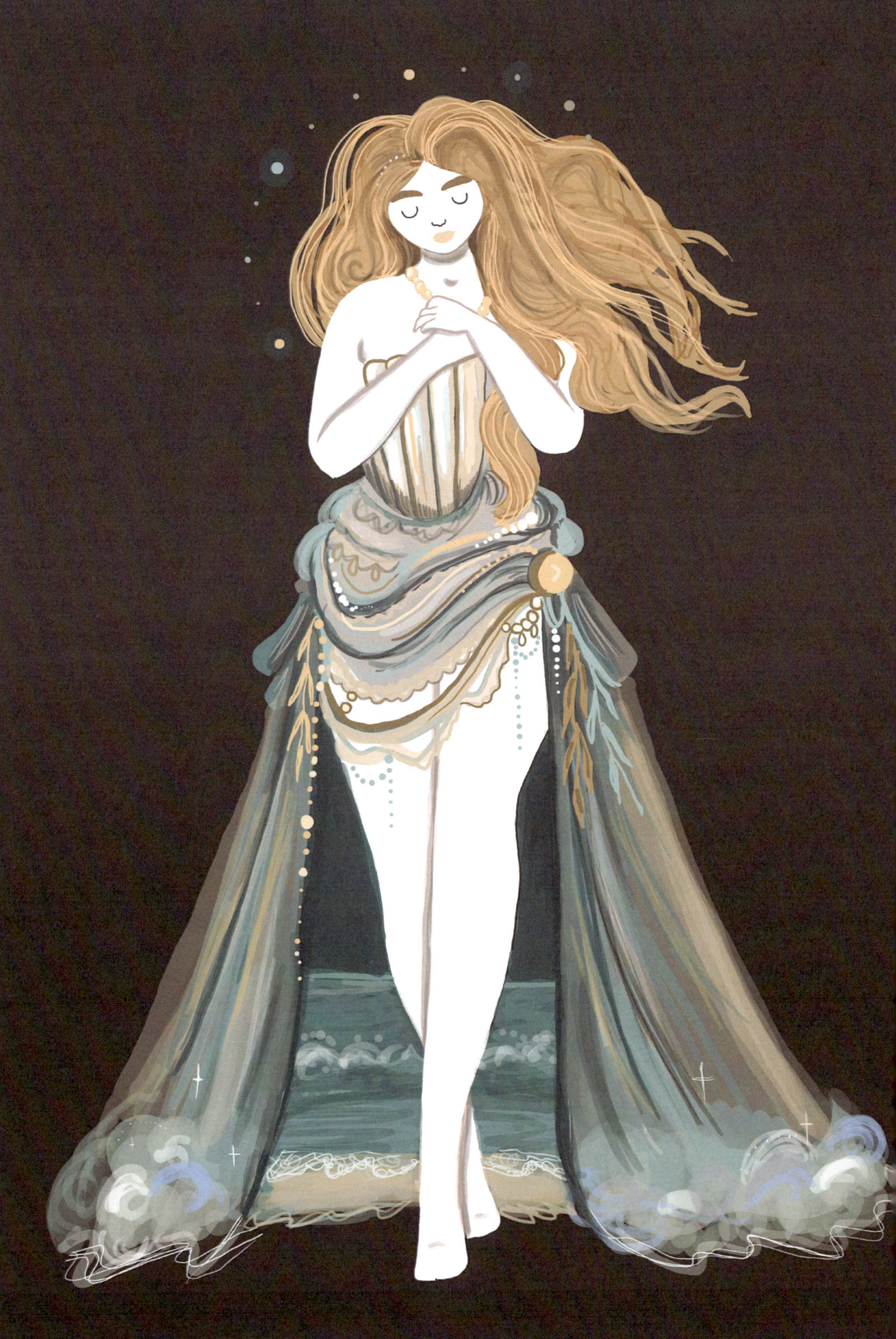

APHRODITE

"…TELL ME THE DEEDS OF GOLDEN APHRODITE KYPRIA, WHO STIRS UP SWEET PASSION IN THE GODS AND SUBDUES THE TRIBES OF MORTAL MEN."

—*HOMERIC HYMNS,* HYMN V ("TO APHRODITE")

According to the classical narrative of her origins within Hesiod's *Theogony*, Aphrodite (*af-ruh-dahy-tee*) famously emerged from seafoam following the death of the sky god Uranus. As the Greek goddess of sex, love, and beauty, she was said to be completely irresistible to any who laid eyes upon her, be it god or mortal. Although she was adopted into the Greek pantheon, historians trace her worship under various names throughout ancient Mesopotamia and Phoenicia before the rise of the Greek Empire.

Such was Aphrodite's irresistible beauty that, to prevent constant strife among the gods for her affection, Zeus arranged her marriage to Hephaestus, the god of blacksmiths. Despite this arrangement, Aphrodite's independence and autonomy regarding her affections remained a prominent aspect of her character. Her relationships, notably with Ares, the god of war, resulted in several offspring, including Eros (also known as Cupid), reflecting her connection to both love and strife. Aphrodite also played a role in instigating disputes. This influence is famously illustrated by her role in the lead-up to the Trojan War, specifically through her promise of Helen's love to Paris, as recounted in Homer's *Iliad*.

Although predominantly recognized for her dominion over infatuation and attraction, Aphrodite was also acknowledged as a protector of ancient seafarers. Due to her association with Venus, the planet that shines the brightest in the night sky (which is also the name of her Roman equivalent), she provided an invaluable point of reference for those voyaging across the oceans. Artists and sculptors frequently looked to Aphrodite for inspiration, and she became a common fixture at temples in the form of statues and paintings. She was most often depicted nude, either standing in the company of birds and marine life or lying on her side within large clam shells adorned with flowing fabrics.

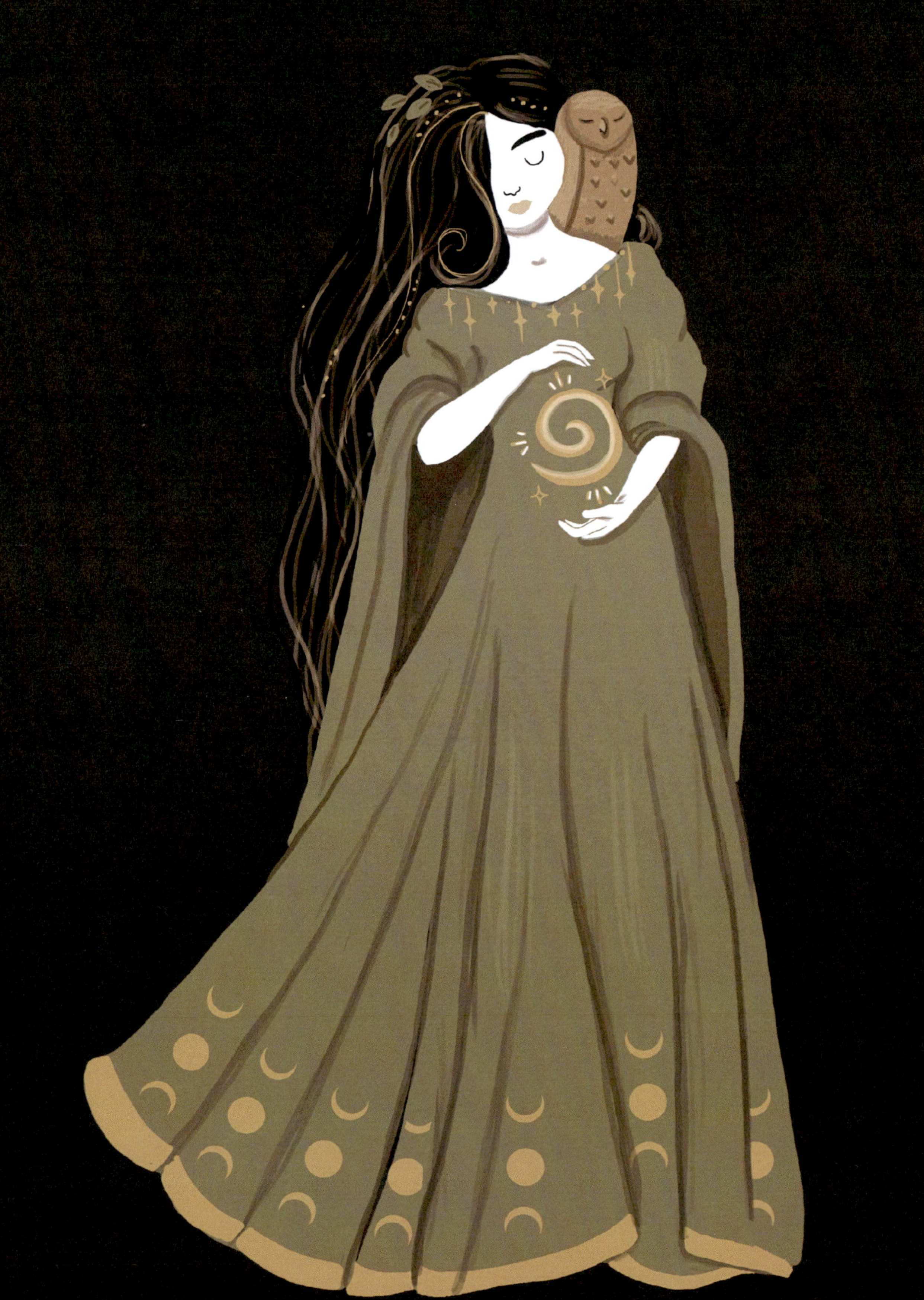

ARIANRHOD

"COMPLETE IS MY CHAIR IN CAER SIDI... THREE UTTERANCES, AROUND THE FIRE, WILL HE SING BEFORE IT, AND AROUND ITS BORDERS ARE THE STREAMS OF THE OCEAN."

—*BOOK OF TALIESIN* XIV, "SONG BEFORE THE SONS OF LLYR"

Recognized by many names and virtues, the moon-mother goddess Arianrhod (*ah-ree-ahn-hrohd*) is an extremely prominent figure within Celtic and Welsh mythology. Ancient Celts counted their days in relation to the night, establishing lunar calendars based upon the travels of the moon and stars. As the "Goddess of the Silver Wheel," she not only embodied the essence of the moon, but also held the distinction of escorting the dead to their final resting place of *Caer Sidi*, the Otherworld. Arianrhod would act as a guide to fallen warriors who were slain in battle, taking them upon her Oar Wheel ship to be delivered to *Emania*, the Moonland.

Arianrhod additionally rules over magic, reincarnation, and weaving. Legend states that she would enchant the thread of fate upon her wheel to create all that was to come to fruition. Another, extended version of her title was the "Silver Wheel that Descends into the Sea." In these two manifestations, the quintessential symbols of divine feminine are represented: intertwining the creation of life, necessary death, and the eventual rebirth. Arianrhod symbolized the "Mother" aspect of the Welsh Triple Goddess, with Blodeuwedd as the "Maiden" and the Morrígan as the "Crone."

The most prominent source for Arianrhod is the *Mabinogi*, a collection of myths believed to be compiled from between the eleventh and fourteenth centuries CE. Arianrhod possesses a certain otherworldliness, residing in the otherworld Caer Sidi, sometimes referenced as the constellation Corona Borealis. This association with the heavens connects her to the cycles of the stars and the moon, potentially reflecting an earlier veneration of her as a celestial deity.

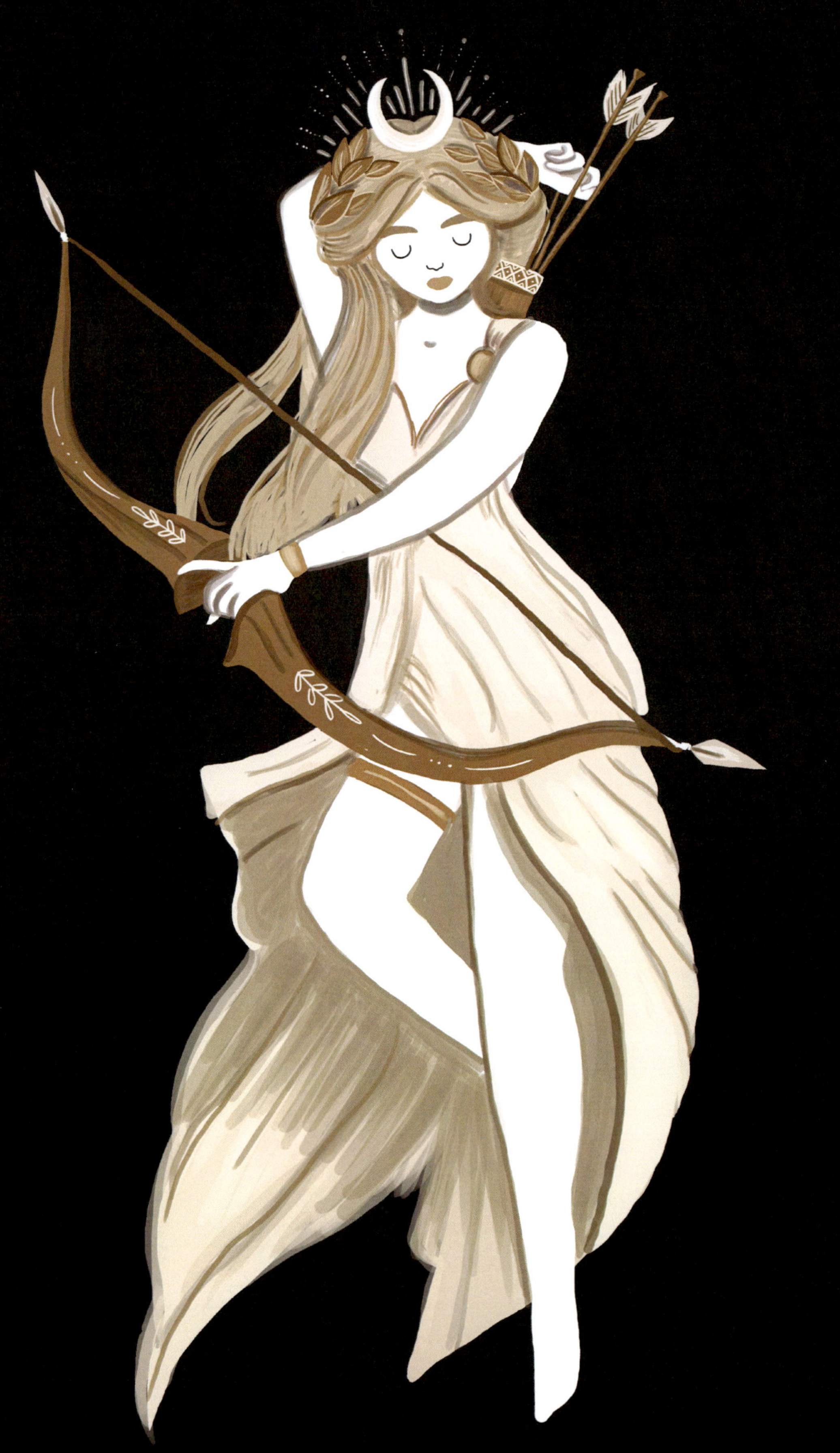

ARTEMIS

"…GLORY OF ARCHERS, WHO DELIGHTS IN THE CHASE, TWIN SISTER OF APOLLO,
SHE WHO FOSTERS HINDS IN GRASSY DELLS AND SWIFT-FOOTED LIONS."

—*HOMERIC HYMNS,* HYMN XXVII ("TO ARTEMIS"), LINES 1–3

Greek goddess and daughter to Zeus, Artemis (*ahr-tuh-miss*) embodied the untamed wilderness, the thrill of the hunt, and the nurturing aspects of nature. Yet, Artemis wasn't solely a symbol of the wild: she was also a staunch protector of women and young girls. She blessed pregnancies with swift, painless childbirth, even going so far as to assist her own mother with the delivery of her twin brother Apollo mere moments after her own birth. Widely recognized as the goddess of the hunt, Artemis fundamentally embodied the spirit of the wilderness. This encompassed the raw power of untamed mountains, the serene mystery of ancient forests, and the freedom of open, uncultivated lands, each reflecting a facet of her wild nature.

Artemis is an example of one of the oldest figures within the iconography of our past, seen throughout hunting societies all over the world: the mistress of wild game. In ancient Greece, she was often referred to as *Potnia Theron*, or "the lady of wild things." Early depictions of Artemis portray her as a young huntress, often wearing a short tunic and wielding a bow and arrow. Her association with the hunt linked her to wild animals, particularly the bear, boar, and deer. This connection wasn't merely symbolic; Artemis was believed to oversee the natural balance of these creatures, ensuring their populations remained healthy without unchecked predation.

The worship of Artemis, in her various forms, can be traced as far as Bactria in the east (modern-day Afghanistan) to Iberia in the west (modern-day Spain) and was widespread throughout ancient Greece. Sanctuaries dedicated to her were found in major cities like Ephesus and Brauron, where she was associated with protecting girls from illness. Her image adorned pottery, sculptures, and coins as a constant reminder of her presence in the lives of those who worshipped her.

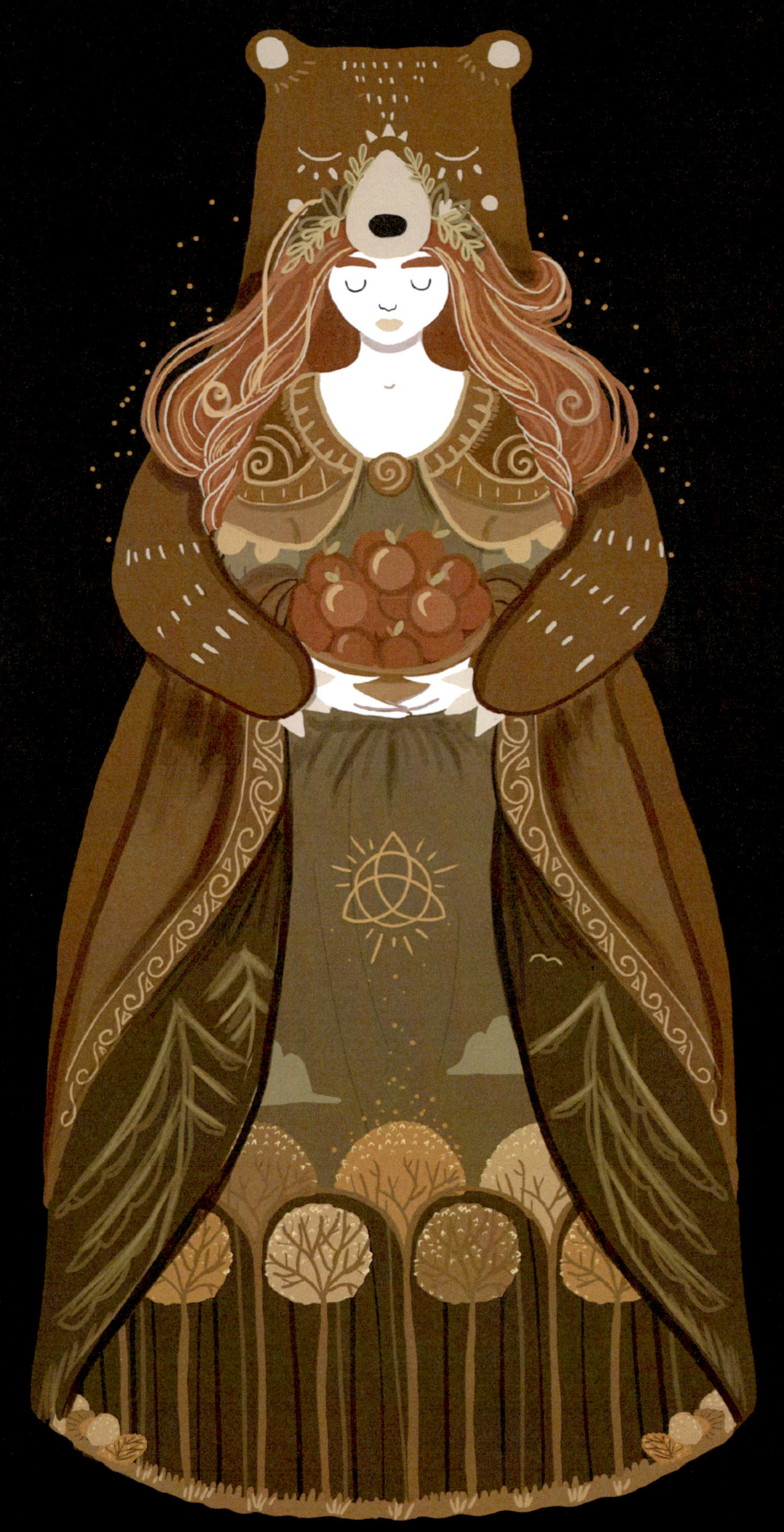

ARTIO

"...REVOLVING FOREVER AS CONSTELLATIONS AROUND THE POLE STAR,
AXIS MUNDI OF THE HEAVENLY VAULT."

—JOSEPH CAMPBELL, *HISTORICAL ATLAS OF WORLD MYTHOLOGY* (1988)

Artio (*ahr-tee-oh*), the "She-Bear," is the illusive Celtic goddess of abundance and wildlife. With a name that traces back to the Gaulish *Artos* and Welsh *Arth*, both meaning "bear," the goddess Artio was known for her power to seamlessly transition between the physical forms of a bear and a human. This dual nature likely informed her multifaceted symbolism: the raw, untamed power of the wilderness embodied by the bear coupled with the intelligence and connection of the human world. While little is actually known regarding her origins, Artio was presumably brought into Europe along with the Celtic Helvetii tribe who made their way to Switzerland around 440–450 BC.

The only known surviving image of Artio comes from a silver votive plaque found at the sanctuary of Bern-Münsingen in Switzerland. The plaque depicts a seated woman with a bear crawling over her lap. The woman is holding a basket of fruit in one hand and a cornucopia in the other. The cornucopia is a symbol of abundance and prosperity, and Artio was likely associated with these qualities. The bear was a sacred animal to the Celts and was seen as a symbol of strength, courage, and fertility.

The naming of the constellations Ursa Major and Ursa Minor, or *Great Bear* and *Little Bear*, are considered to be indications of ancient European bear worship. However, it's important to remember that the Celts were not a monolithic group, and their religious beliefs varied from region to region. That being said, Artio's widespread worship across the Celtic world, despite limited surviving evidence, confirms her significant place in their religion and mythology.

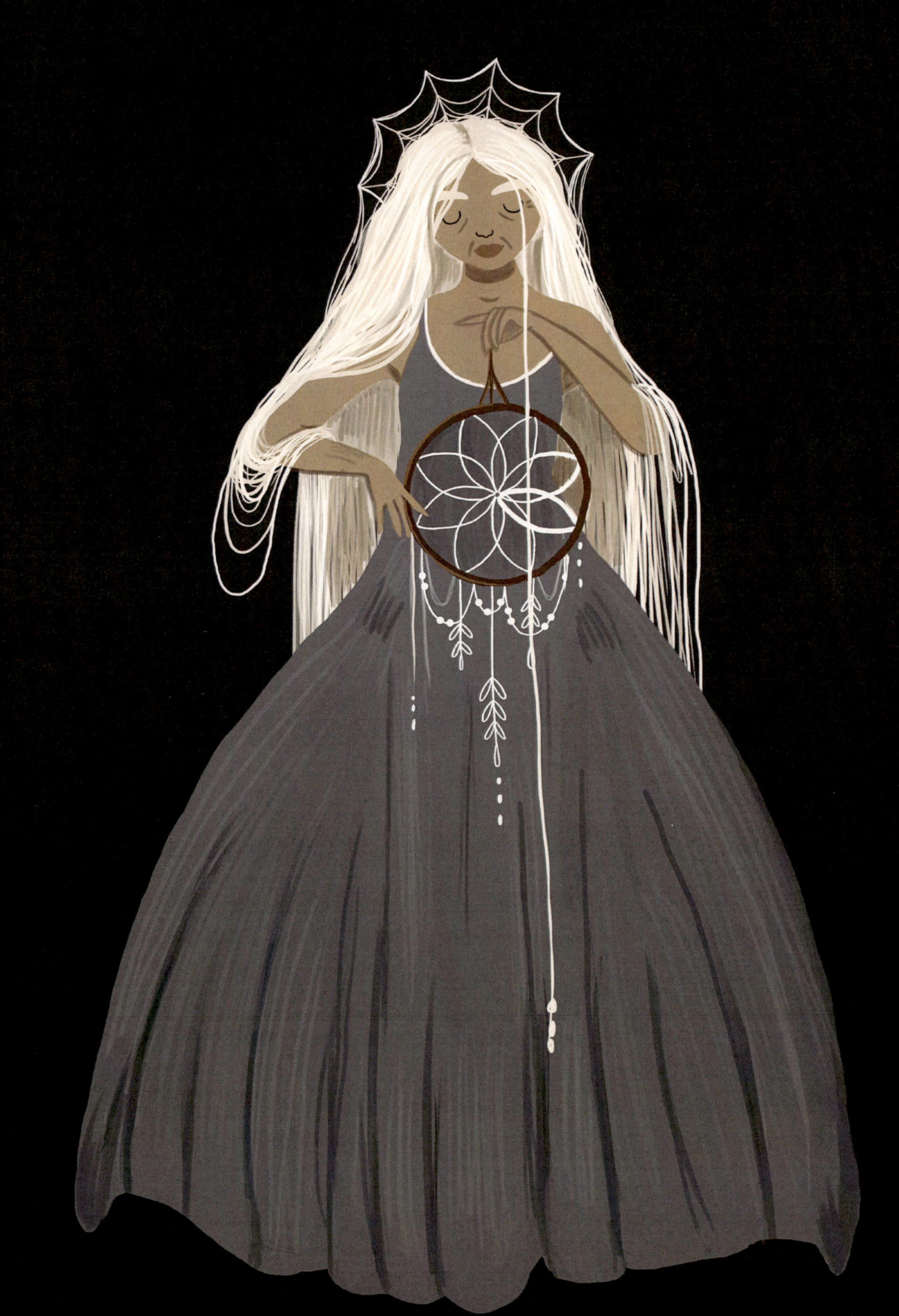

ASIBIKAASHI

"...SAFEGUARDED BY HER SACRED WEBS THAT CATCH EVIL AND MISFORTUNE."

—THOMAS PEACOCK AND **B. CORBINE,** *OJIBWE WAASA INAABIDAA:*
WE LOOK IN ALL DIRECTIONS (2009)

Passed down through generations of Ojibwe storytelling, the legend of Asibikaashi (*ah-see-bih-kah-shih*) tells of a great "Spider Woman" who would help bring the sun back to her people. She takes special care of Ojibwe people, deterring nightmares through the use of the dreamcatcher, a web of woven material hung above the bed. While the exact origins of Asibikaashi are shrouded in the mists of time, understanding her role sheds light on the enduring traditions of the Ojibwe people.

Legends depict Asibikaashi as a pervasive protector and caretaker, sometimes with the responsibility of placing the sun in the sky each morning to ensure life-giving energy. Recognizing the increasing geographic dispersal of the Ojibwe people, Asibikaashi's protection was extended as Ojibwe mothers and grandmothers wove their own dreamcatchers. These sacred objects became imbued with her protective magic, thereby safeguarding the dreams of future generations even from a distance.

The dreamcatcher's design reflects Asibikaashi's essence. The circular hoop represents the cyclical nature of life and the intricate web acts as a filter, capturing negativity while allowing positive dreams to pass through the central hole. Feathers, often attached in various ways, symbolize lightness and the carrying away of bad dreams by the morning light. Asibikaashi's legacy extends beyond the dreamcatcher. She embodies the enduring role of women in Ojibwe society. Mothers and grandmothers, like Asibikaashi, are seen as protectors and nurturers. They safeguard the well-being of their families, weaving a metaphorical web of love and support.

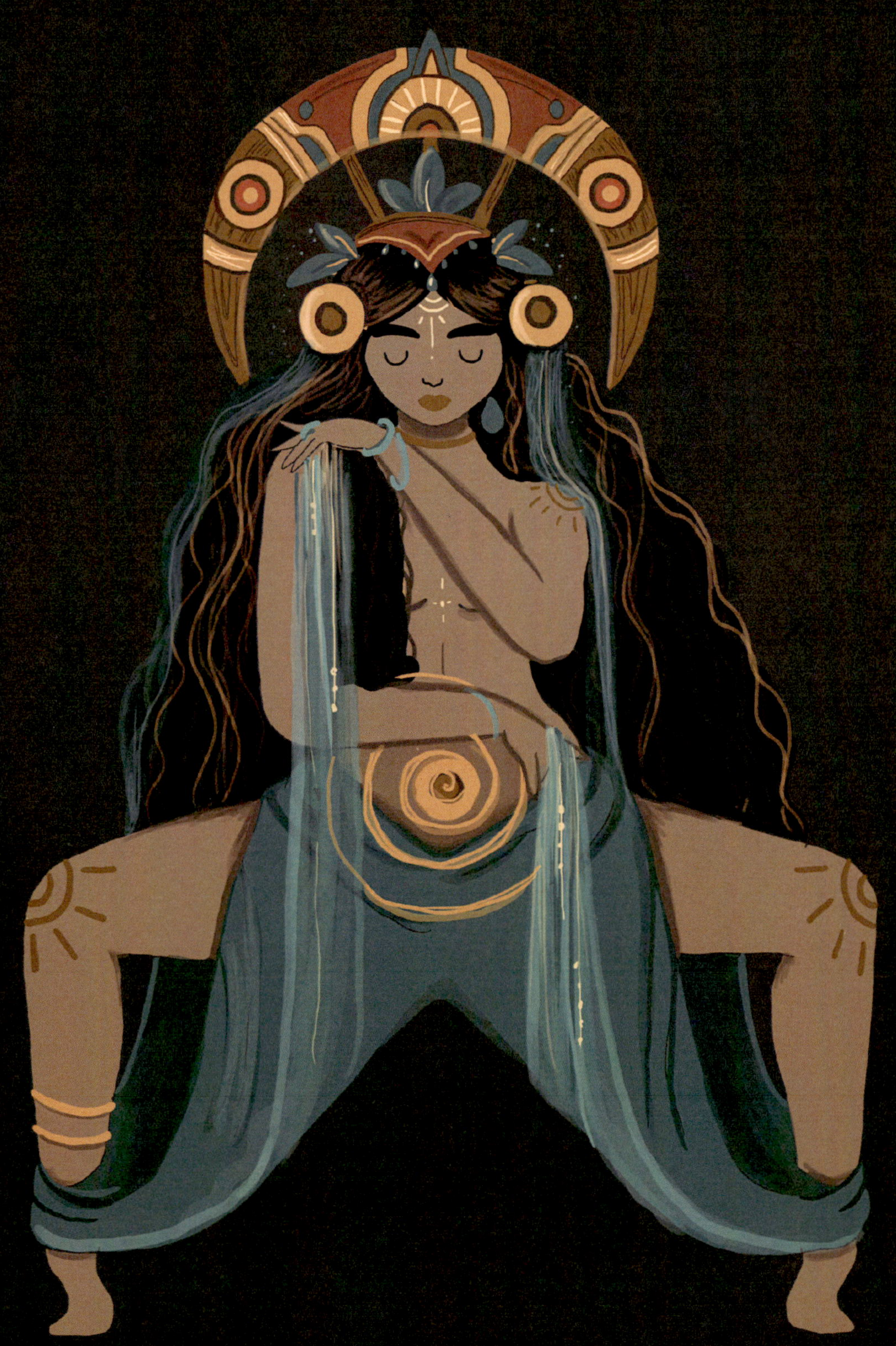

ATABEY

"...THE GODDESS OF THE WATERS AND OF THE EARTH,
AND THEY BELIEVED THAT FROM HER CAME ALL PEOPLE."

—**FRAY RAMÓN PANÉ** (1498)

The island nations of the Caribbean, long before the arrival of the Europeans, were home to diverse and vibrant cultures. Among these were the Taíno, indigenous people inhabiting much of the Greater Antilles, including Cuba, Hispaniola (today Haiti and the Dominican Republic), and Puerto Rico. Their spiritual beliefs were complex and polytheistic, with a pantheon of deities called *zemis*. At the heart of their cosmology stood the figure of Atabey (*ah-tah-bay*), the supreme mother goddess whose domains encompassed the moon, fresh waters, fertility, and childbirth.

Atabey's origins are deeply rooted in Taíno creation myths. In these narratives, she is centrally depicted as the primordial mother, often described as emerging from the vast cosmic sea. Her son Yúcahu, known for his rebellious nature, was banished from her presence which triggered childbirth pains and the first humans to emerge. Atabey was often represented as a squatting female figure, often adorned with serpentine and frog-like imagery. Frogs, due to their life cycle, symbolized both birth and transformation. Snakes and water imagery alluded to fluidity, renewal, and the connection between the earthly and the Underworld. Atabey was also linked to the moon, with its cycles of waxing and waning reflecting the natural rhythms of pregnancy and life itself.

Zemis, like Atabey, occupied a central role in Taíno religious practices. They were embodied in physical representations sculpted from wood, stone, cotton, or shells. These were not merely representations but were believed to contain the spirit of the deity. Offerings of food and precious materials were made, along with rituals involving song and dance to beseech the gods for protection, fertility, and balance within the natural world. Atabey, as the ancestral mother, was likely invoked for blessings upon women, childbirth, and the abundance of life-giving resources.

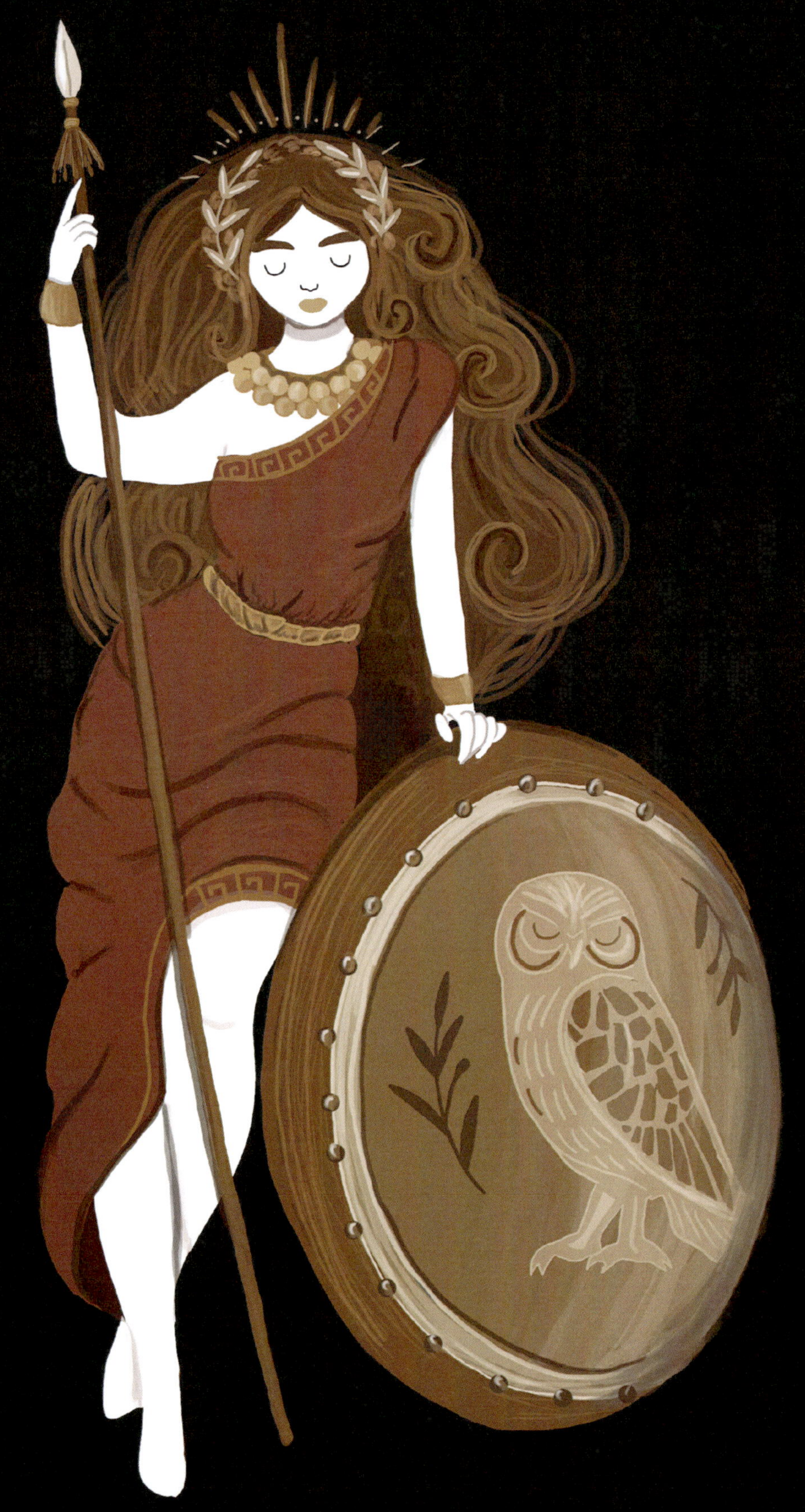

ATHENA

In the intricate tapestry of Greek mythology, Athena (*uh-thee-nuh*) embodied wisdom, strategic warfare, and the importance of justice. A daughter of Zeus born fully formed and armored from his head, her unique origin story established her intellectual prowess and martial strength. Athena is also deeply entwined with the arts that represented the pinnacle of civilized society. She is the patroness of craftspeople skilled in weaving, pottery, and other such arts. Revered across ancient Greece, Athena held a particularly potent position as the divine protector of Athens, the city that bears her name and where her legacy endures.

Athena's dominion over wisdom translated into an association with reason, intellectual pursuits, and astute judgment. She is the goddess to whom heroes like Odysseus turned for guidance, their cunning strategies and plans mirroring her own sharp wit. This aspect of Athena aligns with the philosophical currents of ancient Greece, particularly the emphasis on logic and rational thought that flourished in Athens. Yet, Athena is more than just a thinker. She is also the goddess of methodical warfare, unlike her bloodthirsty brother Ares, who represents war's brutality. Athena's role is that of the protector, embodying the controlled and deliberate use of force in the defense of the city-state. It is her intellect that informs her victories on the battlefield. She represents the Greek approach to warfare, which heavily emphasized the use of strategy and cunning.

The Parthenon, a magnificent temple perched upon the Athenian Acropolis, serves as the most enduring tribute to Athena. The temple, with its intricate sculptures depicting scenes from her life and battles, is a testament to her deep veneration. The Panathenaic Festival, a grand celebration held in her honor, further illustrates the centrality of Athena to Athenian civic and religious life.

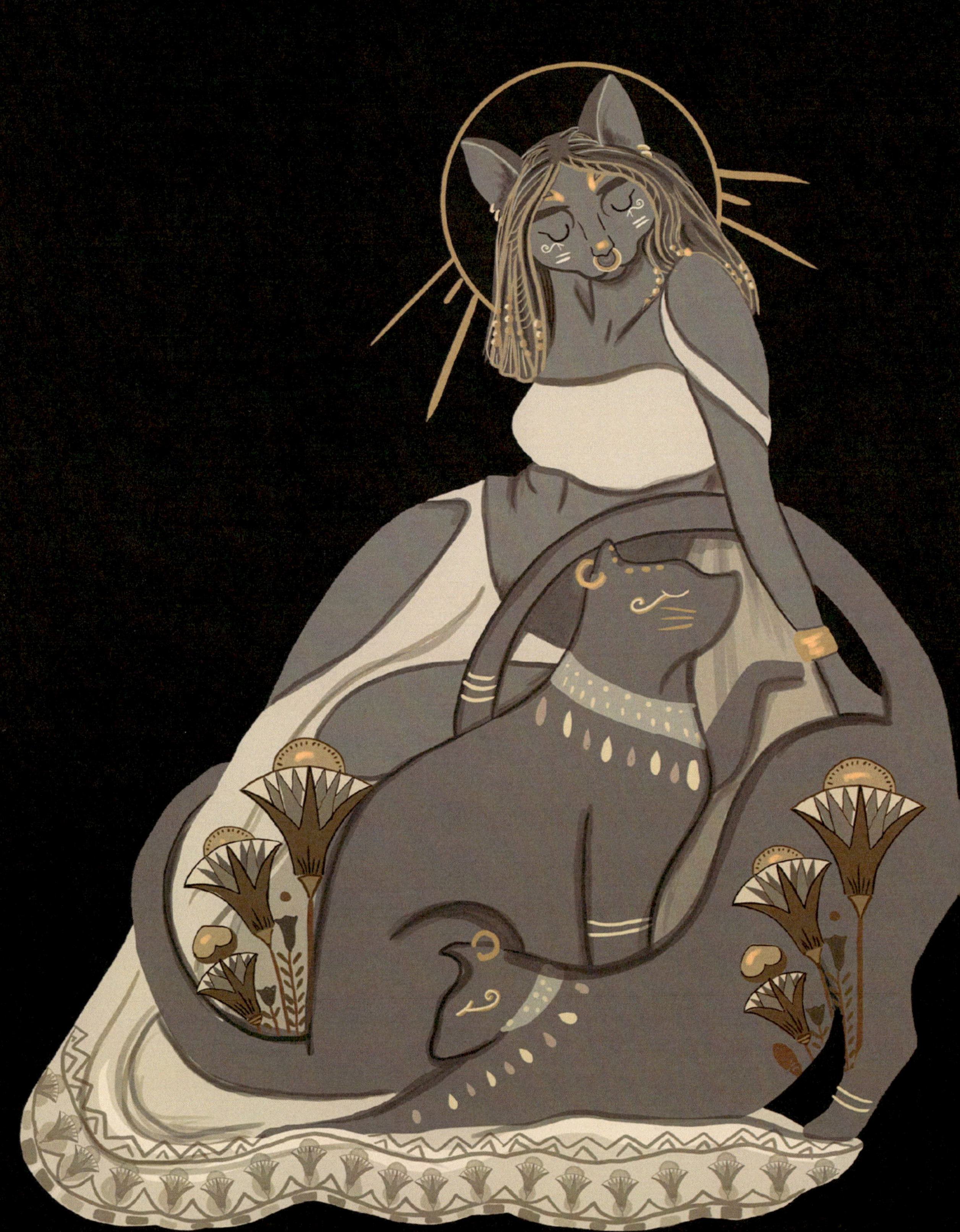

BAST

"HAIL, BAST, WHO COMEST FORTH FROM THE SECRET PLACE,
I HAVE NOT DEALT DECEITFULLY."

—*THE BOOK OF THE DEAD,* NEGATIVE CONFESSION 13

The Egyptian pantheon contains well over 2,000 different deities. Of that vast archive, few were as widely beloved as the feline goddess Bast. Also known as Bastet, Bast (*Bahst*) was worshipped for her power over sex, fertility, music, childbirth, and healing. Originally depicted as a lioness, akin to the warrior goddess Sekhmet, she was eventually represented as a domesticated cat. She is one of many deities associated with the *Eye of Ra*, an ancient force manifested through the solar feminine side of Ra, yet Bast was often referred to as the "eye of the moon" as well.

Bast was originally thought to have been widely worshipped throughout Egypt around 950 BCE; however, the earliest known paintings of the cat goddess can be traced back to nearly 3000 BCE. Her representation as a cat is entwined with the role of the domestic cat throughout ancient Egypt. Highly revered and often deemed akin to royalty, cats proved useful in the deterrence of the rats (which would eat and contaminate food stores) and even dangerous animals such as cobras.

The majority of Bast's cult worship was focused within the city of Bubastis, which can be transliterated in Egyptian as the "House of Bastet," firmly laying the groundwork for a central hub of the feline goddess's veneration. An annual festival was held in Bubastis that centered on the celebration of female sexuality and healing, tenets of the power Bast held within Egyptian society. Women upon boats traveled up the river Nile shouting and dancing along with women along the shore. This was seen as not only a ceremony of revelry, but also a strengthening of the bond shared amongst the women of Bubastis.

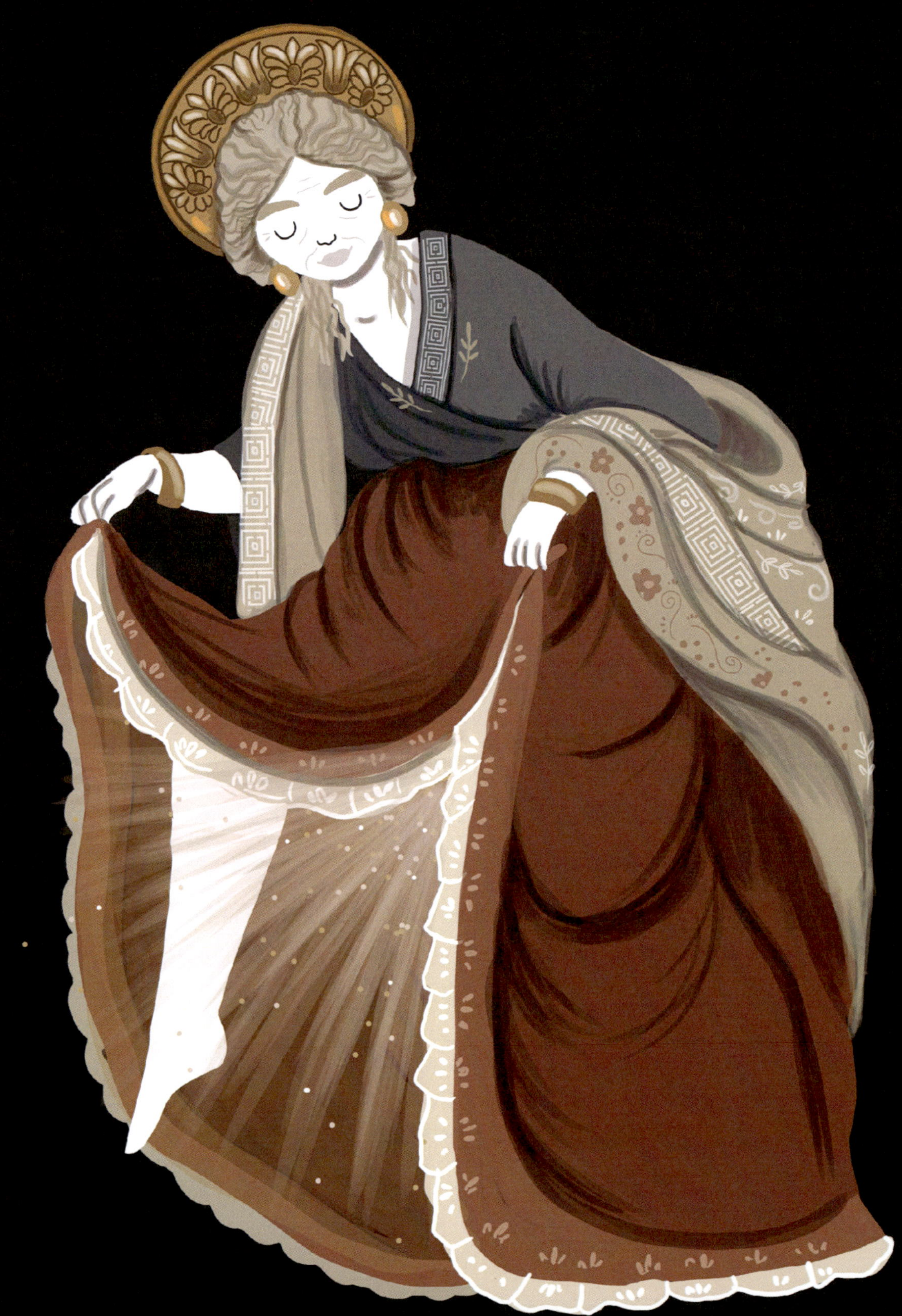

BAUBO

"...THEN TAKING UP HER GARMENTS, SHOWED HER SECRET PARTS TO DEMETER."

—**CLEMENT OF ALEXANDRIA,** *PROTREPTICUS,* CHAPTER II

Baubo (*bah-boh*) is the unabashed Greek goddess of the belly-laugh whose primary act of power hinges on a simple gesture—revealing her most intimate parts. At first glance, this imagery might provoke amusement, perhaps even a degree of shock. Yet beneath the surface of Baubo's seemingly crude display lies a profound symbolism deeply connected to the cycles of life, fertility, and the transformative power of feminine energy.

The story of Baubo is primarily known through fragmentary references rather than a complete narrative. One of the most significant sources is the Homeric Hymn to Demeter, dating back to around the seventh century BCE. In this hymn, the goddess Demeter, consumed by grief over the abduction of her daughter Persephone, wanders the earth searching for her lost child. An old woman named Iambe (who some scholars believe to be Baubo under a different name) attempts to cheer her up by lifting her skirt to reveal her genitalia, causing Demeter to break out in laughter. This display, known as *anasyrma,* held sacred significance within the Eleusinian Mysteries, an ancient Greek religious cult centered at Eleusis. Demeter's laughter signifies a release from her sorrow, a momentary spark of joy, and a possible turning point in her acceptance of her daughter's new role in the cyclical nature of life and death.

The late nineteenth-century discoveries at Priene yielded some of the most famous terracotta figurines depicting Baubo. Headless, the figurines nevertheless have faces on their abdomens. These figures emphasize an abstract portrayal of the female anatomy, with exaggerated genitalia as the central focus, thereby accentuating sexuality and fertility.

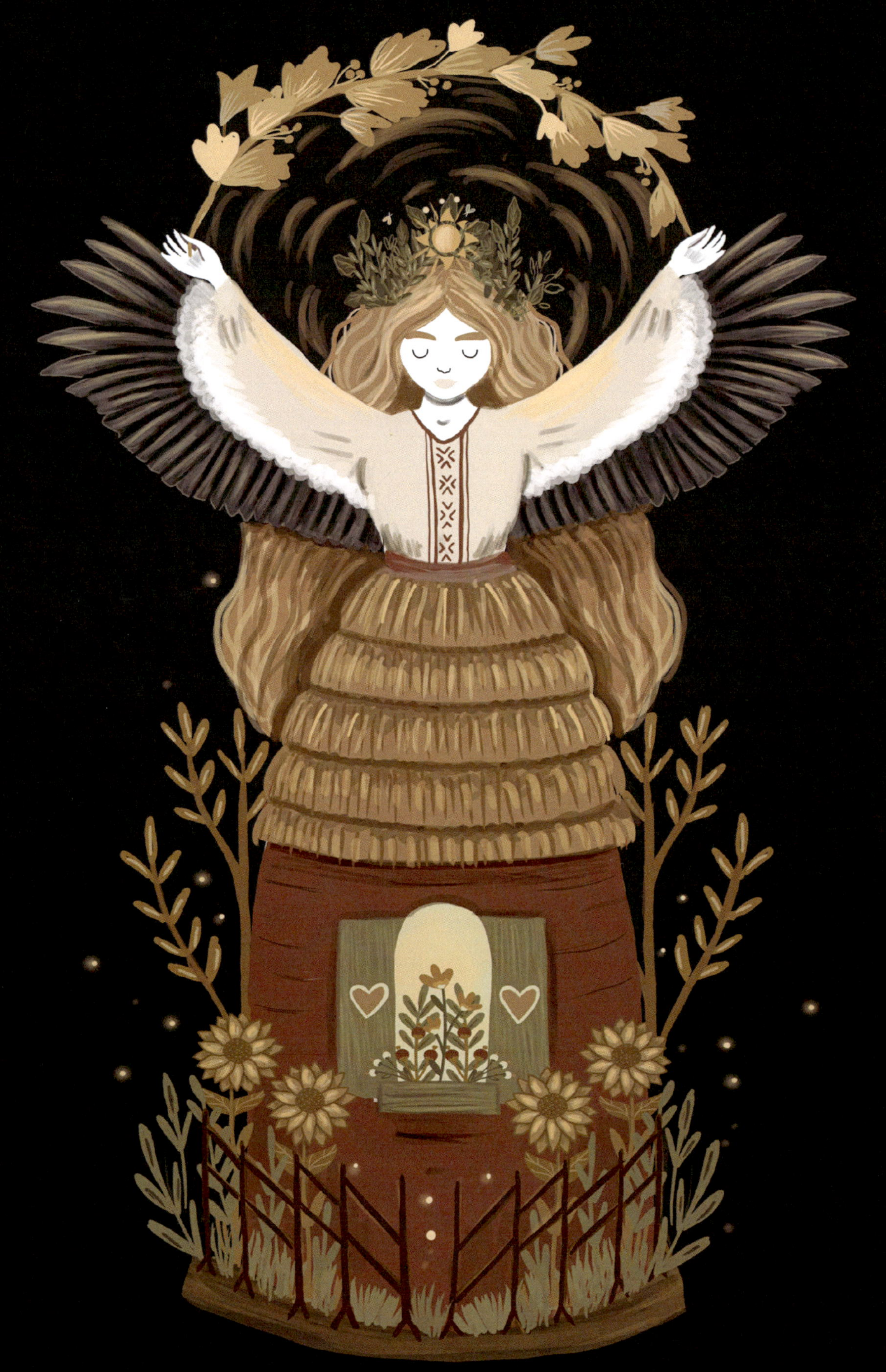

BEREHYNIA

"...THE PRESERVER OF LANGUAGE AND NATIONAL IDENTITY."

—MARIAN J. RUBCHAK, "IN SEARCH OF A MODEL: EVOLUTION OF A FEMINIST CONSCIOUSNESS IN UKRAINE AND RUSSIA" (2001)

Often depicted within Slavic mythology as a stately maternal figure, the goddess Berehynia (*beh-reh-hin-yah*) is venerated as a protector, a life-giver, and an embodiment of the fertile earth. Many scholars believe the roots of Berehynia stretch back to the Neolithic era, a time when the concept of a "great mother goddess" was widespread across many ancient cultures. A supreme female deity was often associated with fertility, the natural world, and the cyclical nature of life and death.

The name "Berehynia" itself may hold clues to her origin. The root word *bereg* in the Slavic languages means "shore" or "riverbank." This suggests a strong connection to water, a life-giving force in both the natural world and ancient belief systems. It's possible Berehynia began as a patroness of rivers and lakes, with her protection and blessings extending to the communities that depended upon these sources of water. Despite a lack of concrete evidence from early Slavic written records, Berehynia's presence endures in folklore, embroidery, and traditional rituals. These sources paint her as a benevolent figure, a guardian of the home, protector of women and children, and a force connected to the rhythms of the agricultural year.

With the adoption of Christianity in Slavic lands, it's likely that Berehynia's role underwent a transformation, a process common to pre-Christian deities. Some scholars suggest her aspects may have been absorbed into the veneration of the Virgin Mary and female saints. Regardless of the exact path of her evolution, Berehynia remains a fascinating deity for modern scholars and those interested in Slavic heritage. She represents the enduring respect for the feminine within Slavic culture: the power of motherhood, the bond with nature, and the resilience of traditions that echo through the centuries.

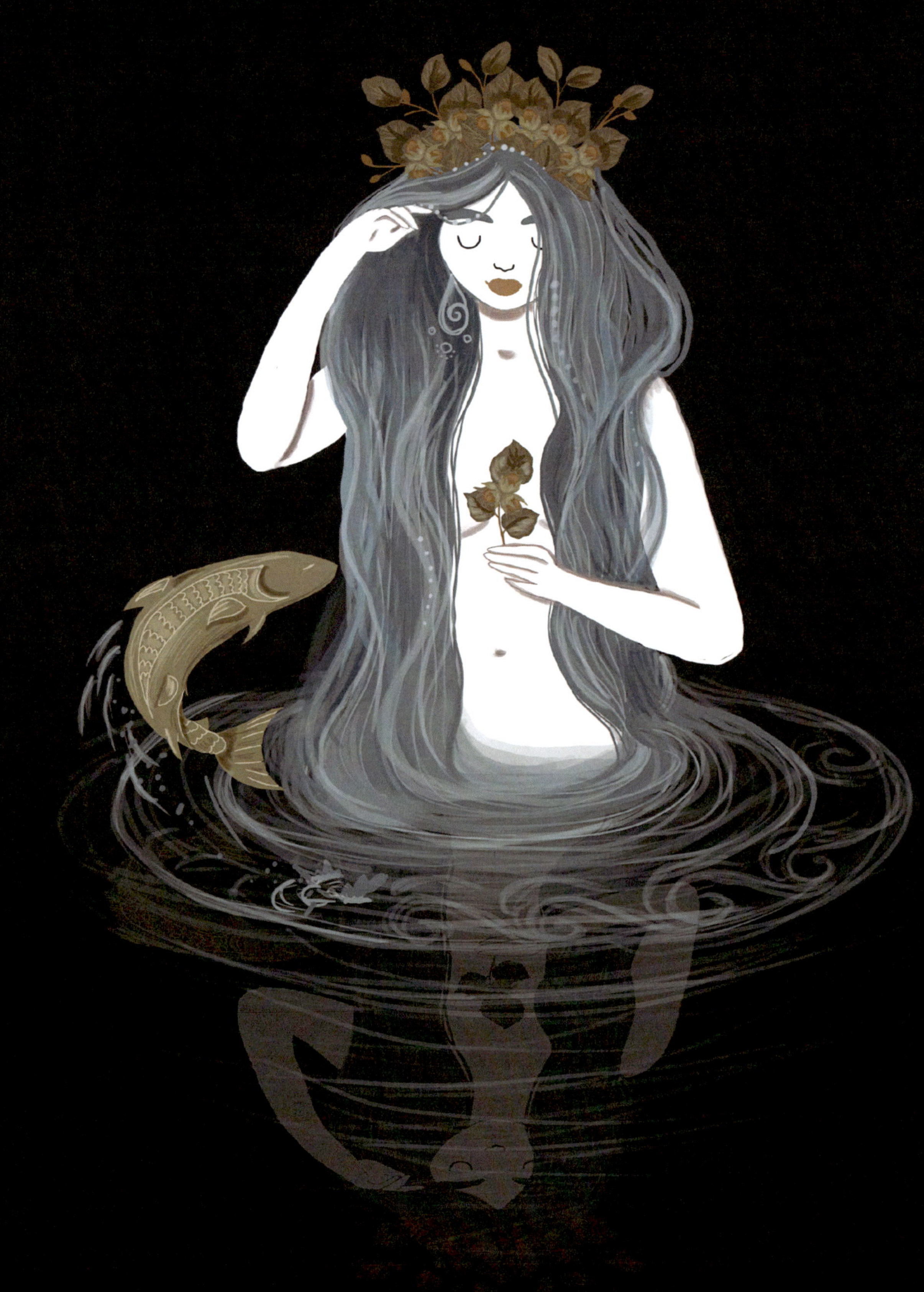

BOANN

—*METRICAL DINDSHENCHAS,* "BÓINN I"

Boann (*boh-uhn*), Irish goddess of fertility, inspiration, and the flowing waters, embodies the transformative power of the natural world and the hidden depths of knowledge. Her name has been indelibly linked to the River Boyne and remains as a link to Ireland's Celtic past. Boann's parentage is often traced to the Dagda, a powerful god within the *Tuatha Dé Danann*, the supernatural race of deities within Irish mythology. She is depicted as the wife of Elcmar, although a clandestine affair with the Dagda results in the birth of her most famous son, Aengus (also known as Oengus), the god of love, youth, and poetic influence.

The most well-known myth surrounding Boann centers on the creation of the River Boyne. The legend tells of a forbidden well, the Well of Segais, or the Well of Wisdom, guarded by nine magical hazel trees that drop crimson nuts of knowledge. It's said that salmon within the well feasted upon these nuts, absorbing their wisdom. Driven by curiosity and a desire for this forbidden knowledge, Boann defies the well's restrictions. It is said the well's waters surged forth in rebellion, chasing Boann and ultimately forming the great River Boyne, which carries her name. This myth highlights Boann's association with both the pursuit of knowledge and the untamed power of natural forces.

Her connection to the Well of Wisdom underscores her role as a source of profound knowledge and poetic inspiration. As one of Ireland's most important rivers, the Boyne's name is another a testament to the goddess's enduring legacy. Moreover, the valley of the Boyne holds *Brú na Bóinne*, a UNESCO World Heritage Site, home to ancient megalithic passage tombs like Newgrange, further intertwining the river with ancient spiritual significance.

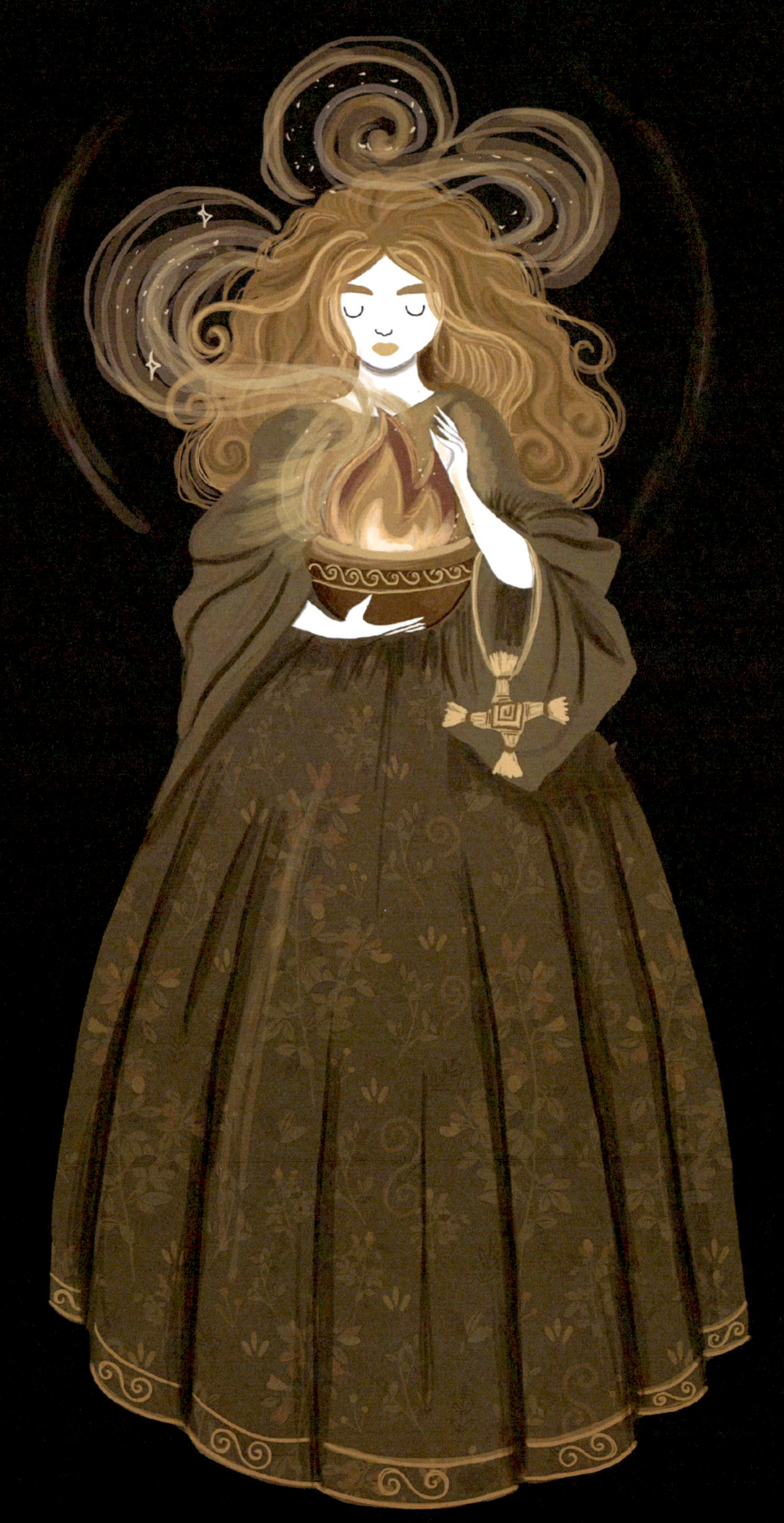

BRIGID

"HOLY MAIDEN BRIGIT, RADIANT ARROW OF FLAME, NOBLE FOSTER-MOTHER OF GODS."

—ALEXANDER CARMICHAEL (TRANSLATOR),
CARMINA GADELICA (1900), "GENEALOGY OF BRIGIT"

Few deities perform as many roles for their followers as does Brigid (*brigg-id*), the "exalted one." As one of the more widely known goddesses of Celtic mythology, Brigid held a mastery over a number of aspects including poetry, smithing, healing, fertility, and wisdom. The word *bride* is derived from her name and even carries with it the proto-Indo-European root meaning "to rise," which parallels her many descriptions as a goddess of the dawn. However, Brigid was also a goddess steeped in contradictions. Not only was she the patron deity of motherhood and love, but she was also the embodiment of fire.

Ninth-century monks portrayed Brigid as "the goddess whom poets adored," and often depicted her walking through the initial stirrings of spring that coincided with her feast day on the first of February, also known as the pagan celebration of Imbolc. In Ireland, she was one of the *Tuatha Dé Danann*, a race of gods and goddesses who were believed to have inhabited Ireland before the arrival of the Celts. Some sources say she had two sisters, also named Brigid, but this may have been an archaic expression of her representation within the separate forms of the Triple Goddess. One of her many symbols is "Brigid's cross," a four-pointed cross made of woven plants. These were placed over doorways to invoke Brigid's protection from evil forces that may seek to enter a home.

Many ancient deities are severely altered when absorbed by Christianity; however, the unique essence of Brigid was able to survive this transitional process. Instead of becoming an entirely new entity, she evolved into "Saint Brigid" and retained many of her original aspects. In the form of Saint Brigid, she was seen as the guardian of sacred flames and watched over the female priestesses and nuns who maintained them in her honor.

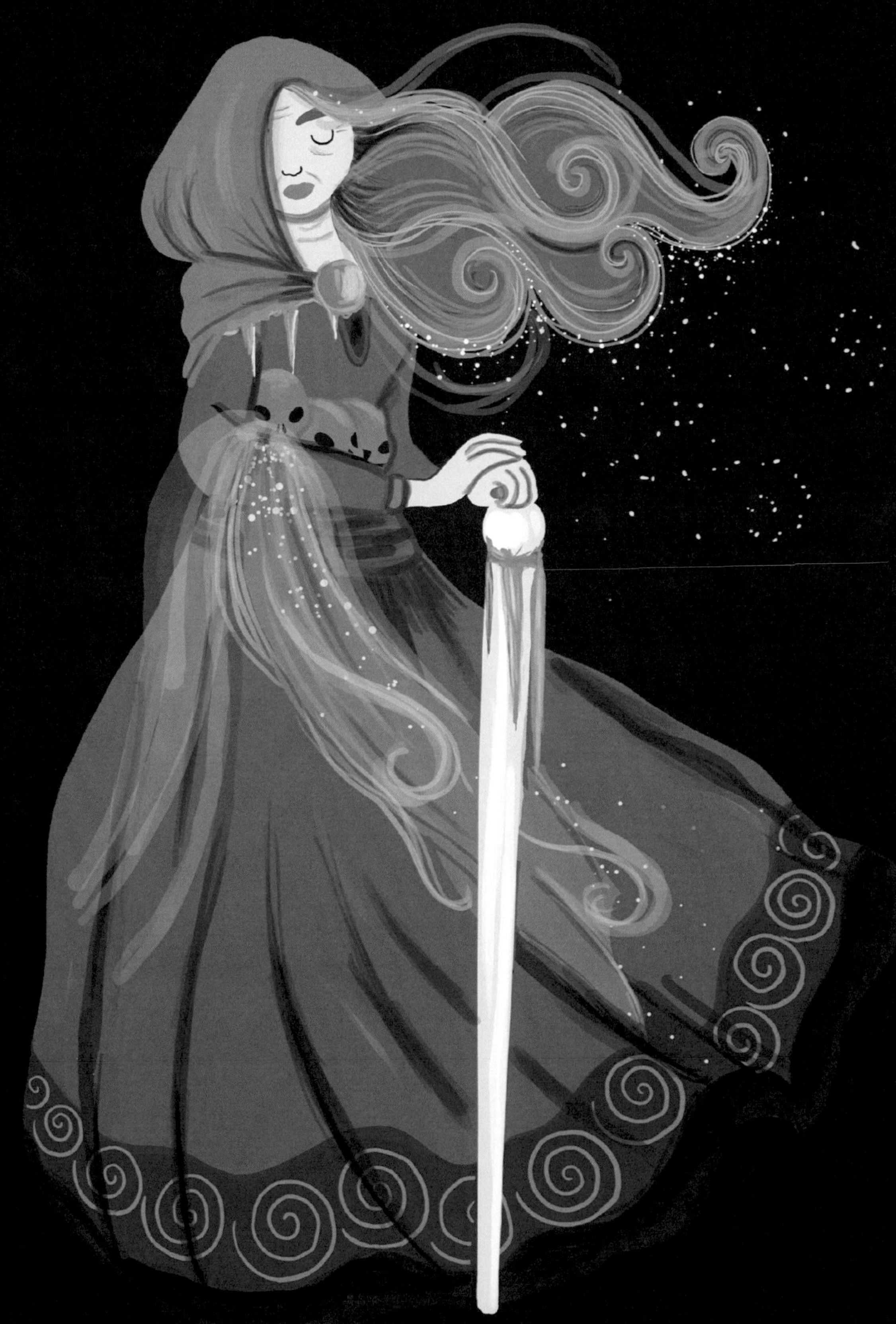

THE CAILLEACH

—**Gearóid Ó Crualaoich,** *The Book of the Cailleach: Stories of the Wise-Woman Healer* (2004)

Often known as the "Queen of Winter" or the "Veiled One," the Cailleach (*kal-yuhk*) is one of the many great Celtic ancestor deities. She is the goddess of the colder months and determines how long each winter season will last before Imbolc returns, bringing warmer weather. The word *cailleach* in the Scottish and Irish Gaelic languages translates to "old woman," stemming from the typical description of the goddess as an immortal elderly woman. The intentions of the Cailleach vary from tale to tale, keeping true to her natural and wildly destructive tendencies.

The Cailleach is intrinsically linked to the ever-shifting forces of nature. She is often associated with winter, storms, and the barrenness of the land. Legends tell of her herding deer, bringing blizzards, and shaping mountains and lochs with careless footsteps or with stones dropped from her apron. On February 1 (Imbolc or the traditional start of spring), it is said she gathers firewood to extend the winter. If the weather is fair, it means she has plenty of fuel and winter will endure; a stormy day signals the approach of milder weather. Yet, the Cailleach is not solely a figure of harshness. She is also credited with sowing the seeds of spring, ushering in milder temperatures, and bringing fertility back to the land. Her cyclical nature reflects the endless transformations found within the natural world.

In some stories, the Cailleach is connected to ideas of sovereignty over the land. The recurring motif of transformation in her myths, such as petrification and shapeshifting, highlight a deep spiritual resonance with specific locations, such as Beinn na Caillich on the Isle of Skye and ancient megalithic sites, suggesting a connection to ancestral beliefs.

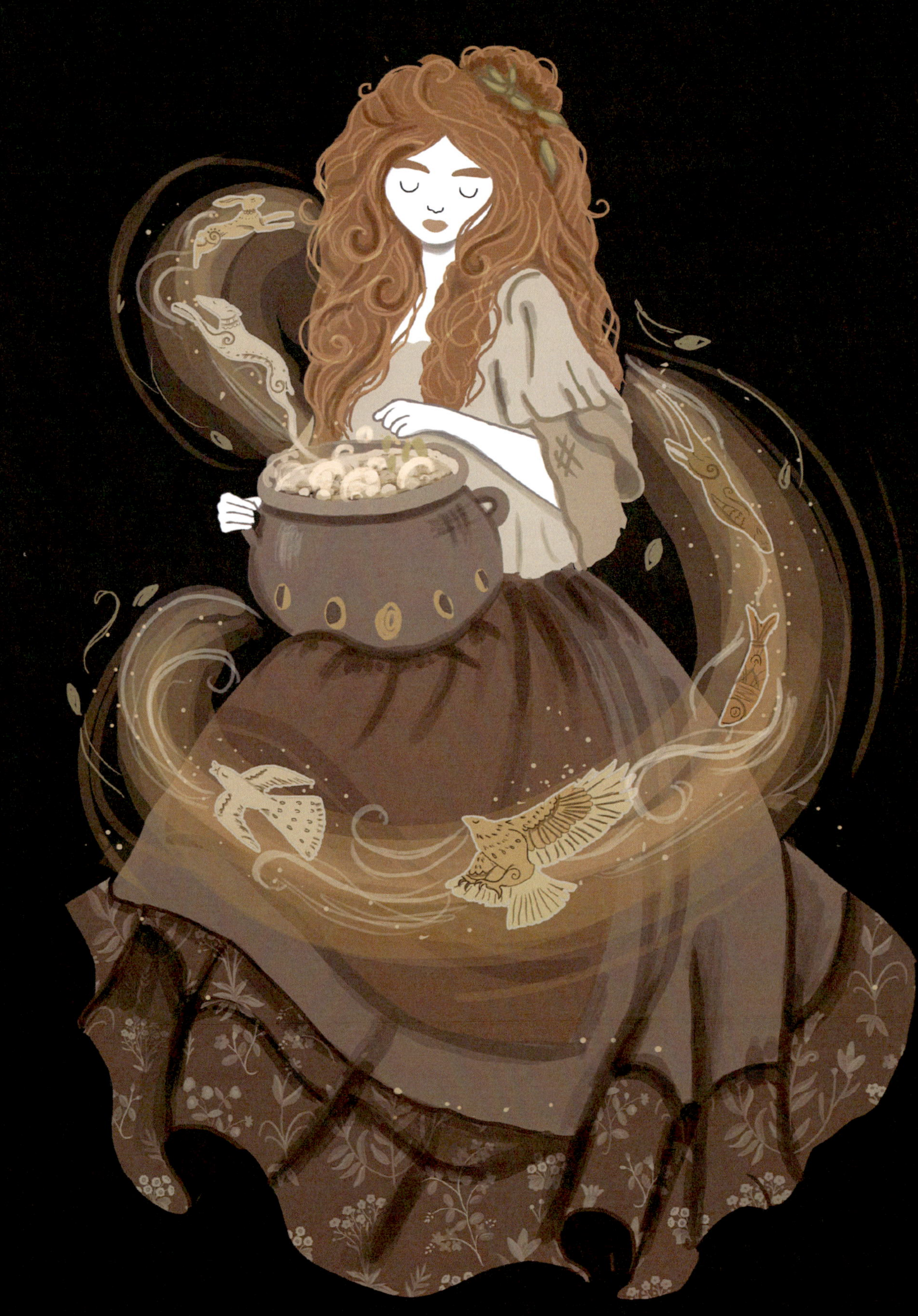

CERIDWEN

"SO SHE RESOLVED, ACCORDING TO THE ARTS OF THE BOOKS OF THE FFERYLLT,
TO BOIL A CAULDRON OF INSPIRATION."

—LADY CHARLOTTE GUEST (TRANSLATOR), *THE MABINOGION* (1877),
"THE TALE OF TALIESIN"

Welsh enchantress Ceridwen (*keh-rid-wen*), despite appearing in a limited number of narratives compared to other deities, stands as an exceptionally impactful figure within Celtic mythology. As the goddess of creation and transformation, Ceridwen's mastery of *Awen* ("poetic inspiration") grants her abilities in shapeshifting and other magical feats. Modern pagans particularly venerate her as the Celtic goddess of enchantment, wisdom, and rebirth.

Her most significant mythological presence is within *The Tale of Taliesin*, a legendary account found in some modern editions of *The Mabinogion* (a collection of early pre-Christian British prose stories, sourced from manuscripts dated 1350–1410). This narrative primarily illustrates Ceridwen's connection to inspiration, wisdom, and profound transformation. The core of the tale involves Ceridwen brewing a potion of Awen in her cauldron for her son. Through an accident, a boy named Gwion inadvertently receives this inspiration, leading to a dynamic chase with multiple bouts of shapeshifting. This pursuit culminates in Gwion's metaphorical "death" (being swallowed by Ceridwen in animal form) and his subsequent rebirth through her as the legendary bard Taliesin.

This pivotal myth encapsulates Ceridwen's essence. Within Welsh literature, the process depicted highlights the belief that inspiration is intrinsically linked to cycles of death and rebirth. Taliesin's regeneration through Ceridwen represents inner change and metamorphosis, central tenets of Ceridwen's dominion over wisdom and transformation.

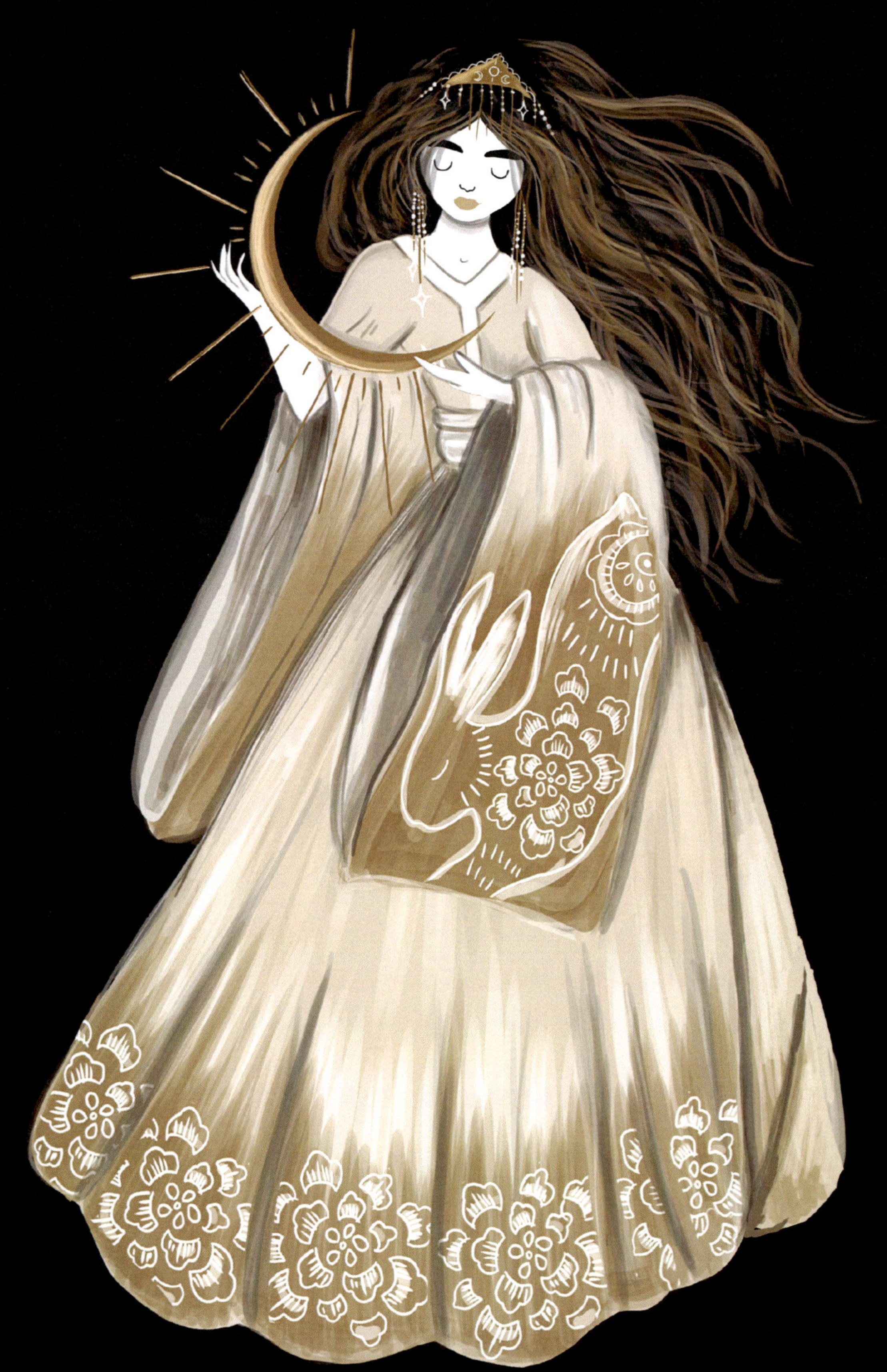

CHANG'E

"Yi shoots the ten Suns, and Chang'e ascends to the moon."

—*Guicang*, Zhou Dynasty (1046–256 BCE)

Moon goddess Chang'e (*chahng-uh*) is the supreme lunar deity within Chinese mythology, honored throughout China during the Mid-Autumn Festival. During this period, she is invoked for her blessings and to grant the most secret desires of her worshippers. Her tale has evolved over centuries, but the core narrative remains one of sacrifice, transformation, and eternal longing. She remains a recurring motif in Chinese art and literature, her image gracing countless paintings and inspiring poets throughout the ages.

The earliest fragments of Chang'e's story emerge during the Warring States period of 475–221 BCE. Initially, she appears as the wife of the celestial archer Hou Yi, who saves the earth from scorching heat by shooting down nine excess suns. As a reward, he receives an elixir of immortality, but Chang'e consumes it herself and ascends to the moon, becoming its solitary inhabitant. Later versions of the myth, particularly during the Han Dynasty (206 BCE–220 CE), add layers of complexity to Chang'e's motivations. Some portray her as nobly sacrificing herself to protect the elixir from a villainous apprentice. Others offer tales of regret and loneliness, with Chang'e forever separated from her beloved husband. A white rabbit or toad often appears as her lunar companion, representing the creation of the elixir.

Chang'e embodies a multitude of meanings within Chinese culture. She is intrinsically linked to the moon itself, representing its feminine yin energy, cycles of transformation, and a yearning for the unattainable. Her story evokes themes of sacrifice, beauty, and the bittersweet melancholy of separation. During the Mid-Autumn Festival, one of China's most important holidays, families gather under the full moon, sharing mooncakes and gazing upwards, their thoughts turning to the goddess as a symbol of unity and longing for distant loved ones.

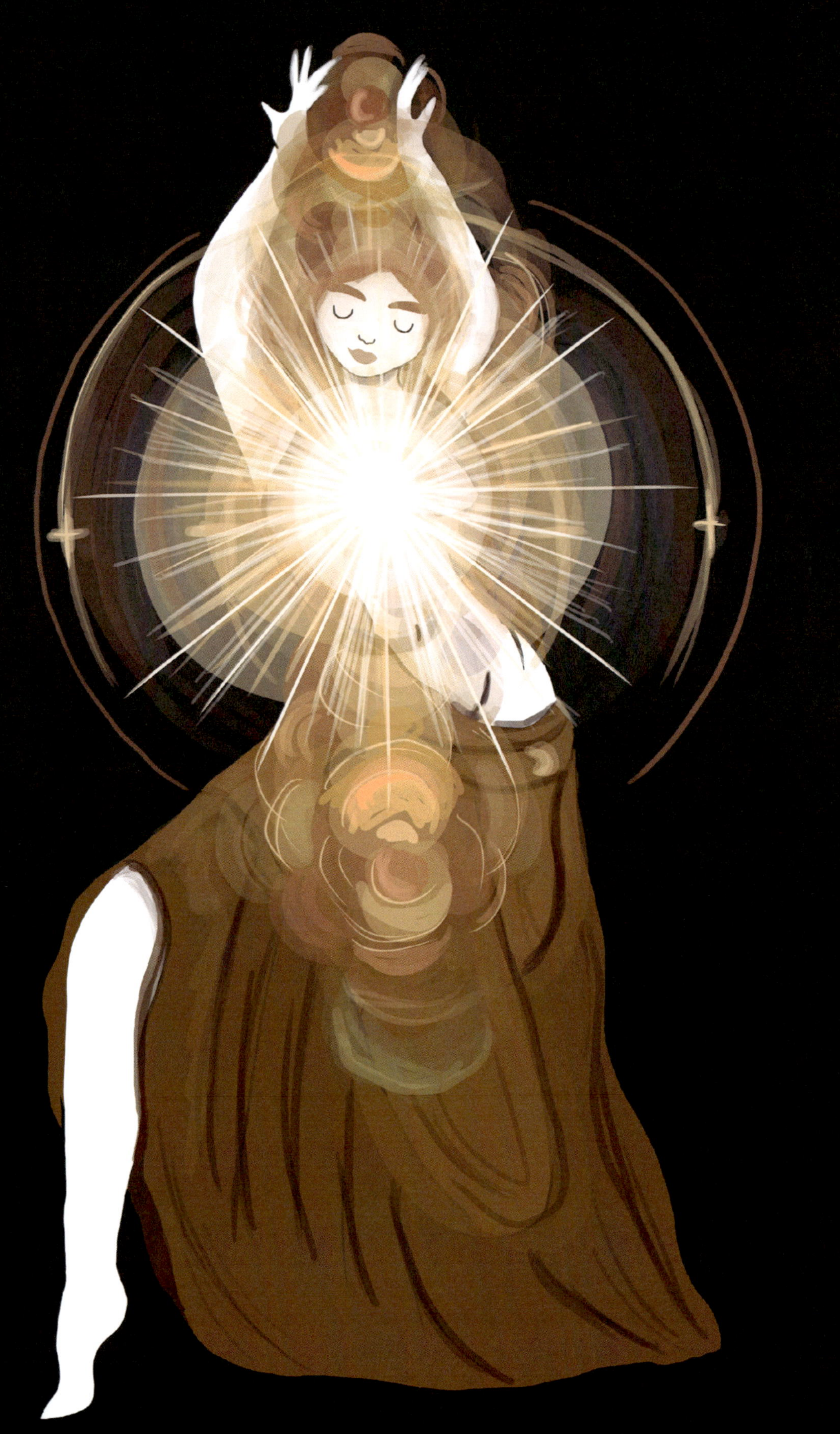

DAKINI

"WHEN YOU, GREAT DANCER, DANCE THE NINE DANCES OF LIFE, THE PURE PLEASURE
OF THE SACRED LOTUS IS EVERYWHERE DISCOVERED..."

—KEITH DOWMAN, *SKY DANCER: THE SECRET LIFE AND
SONGS OF THE LADY YESHE TSOGYAL* (1984)

The term "Dakini" (*dah-kee-nee*) is derived from the Sanskrit word *ḍākinī*, meaning "sky dancer" or "she who traverses the sky." This etymology reflects their association with the celestial realm and their ability to transcend ordinary limitations, emerging as powerful female figures representing wisdom, energy, and spiritual liberation. Dakinis are often depicted as beautiful, youthful women adorned with ornaments and sometimes possessing wings or other supernatural attributes. Their origins trace back to ancient India, where they were revered as both worldly and transcendent beings, often associated with the sacred feminine principle and the transformative power of spiritual practice.

In Buddhist tantra, Dakinis are considered to be avatars of enlightened female buddhas or bodhisattvas. They embody specific qualities or energies, such as wisdom, compassion, or fierce protectiveness. Serving as guides and teachers, Dakinis illuminate the path and present necessary obstacles for spiritual growth. In Hindu tantra, Dakinis are associated with the goddess Kali and other powerful female deities. They are revered for their fierce and transformative energy and are capable of both creation and destruction. Dakinis are often invoked in rituals and practices aimed at spiritual liberation and the attainment of supernatural powers.

The earliest depictions of Dakinis can be found in Indian art and literature dating back to the seventh century CE. They appear in various forms, from benevolent guides to wrathful protectors. Over time, the concept of the Dakini spread to other parts of Asia, including Tibet, Nepal, and China, where they were incorporated into local religious traditions. In Tibetan Buddhism, Dakini play a central role in tantric practices. They are believed to reside in sacred places such as mountains, caves, and charnel grounds. Practitioners seek to connect with Dakinis through meditation, visualization, and ritual offerings, believing that their blessings can lead to spiritual awakening.

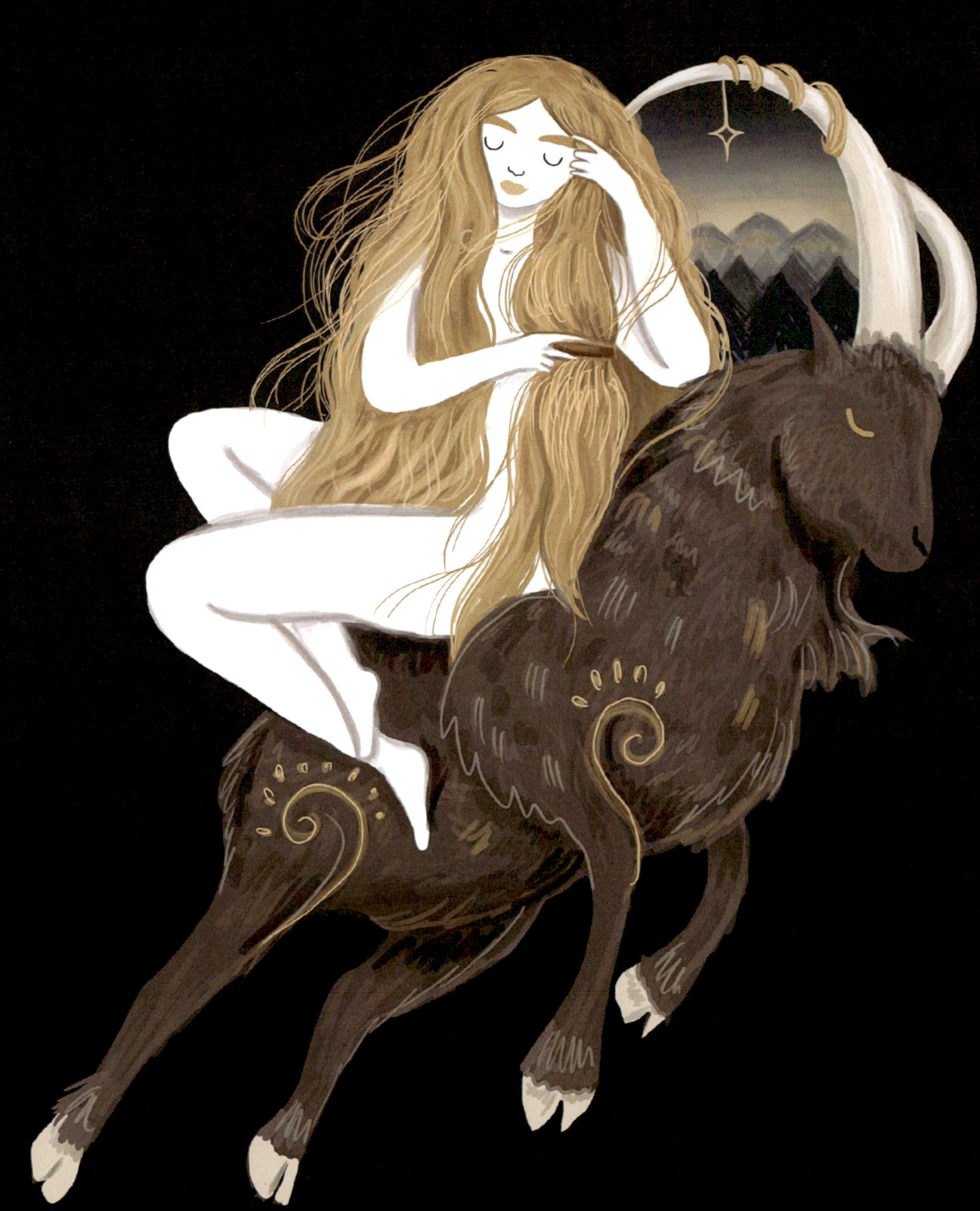

DALI

“ONLY WITH THE CONSENT OF THE MISTRESS OF THE BEASTS WOULD A HUNTER BE ALLOWED…”

—ELENE VIRSALADZE, *GEORGIAN HUNTING MYTHS AND POETRY* (1976)

Dali (*dah-lee*), goddess of Georgian mythology, represents the untamed spirit of nature and the power of the hunt. She is revered as the goddess of wild animals, particularly hoofed mountain creatures like ibex and deer. She is seen as their protector, ensuring their well-being and preventing overhunting. Hunters who respect her rules and offer sacrifices to her are believed to be rewarded with successful hunts and protection from danger. While historical evidence of her worship may be scarce, the legends of Dali have been passed down through generations of oral traditions, helping to shape our understanding of the natural world and relationship with the animal kingdom.

Dali is often depicted as a beautiful woman with long flowing hair, adorned with animal skins and carrying a bow and arrow. She is said to roam the mountains and forests, her presence both awe-inspiring and comforting to hunters who respect her domain. As the goddess of the hunt, Dali represents both the power and the responsibility associated with hunting. In Georgian mythology, she is sometimes portrayed as the daughter of the sky god, while other accounts associate her with the Underworld or the realm of the dead. In some versions of her story, she is a guide to the souls of the deceased, which adds another layer to her meaning in the lives of her followers.

While the traditional beliefs and practices surrounding Dali may have evolved over time, her legacy continues to resonate in Georgian culture. Her association with wild animals reflects the deep connection between the Georgian people and their environment. The mountains of Georgia, with their diverse flora and fauna, have long been a source of sustenance and inspiration for the inhabitants. Dali represents the raw power of the landscape itself, as well as the independent and resilient nature of the creatures that thrive within it.

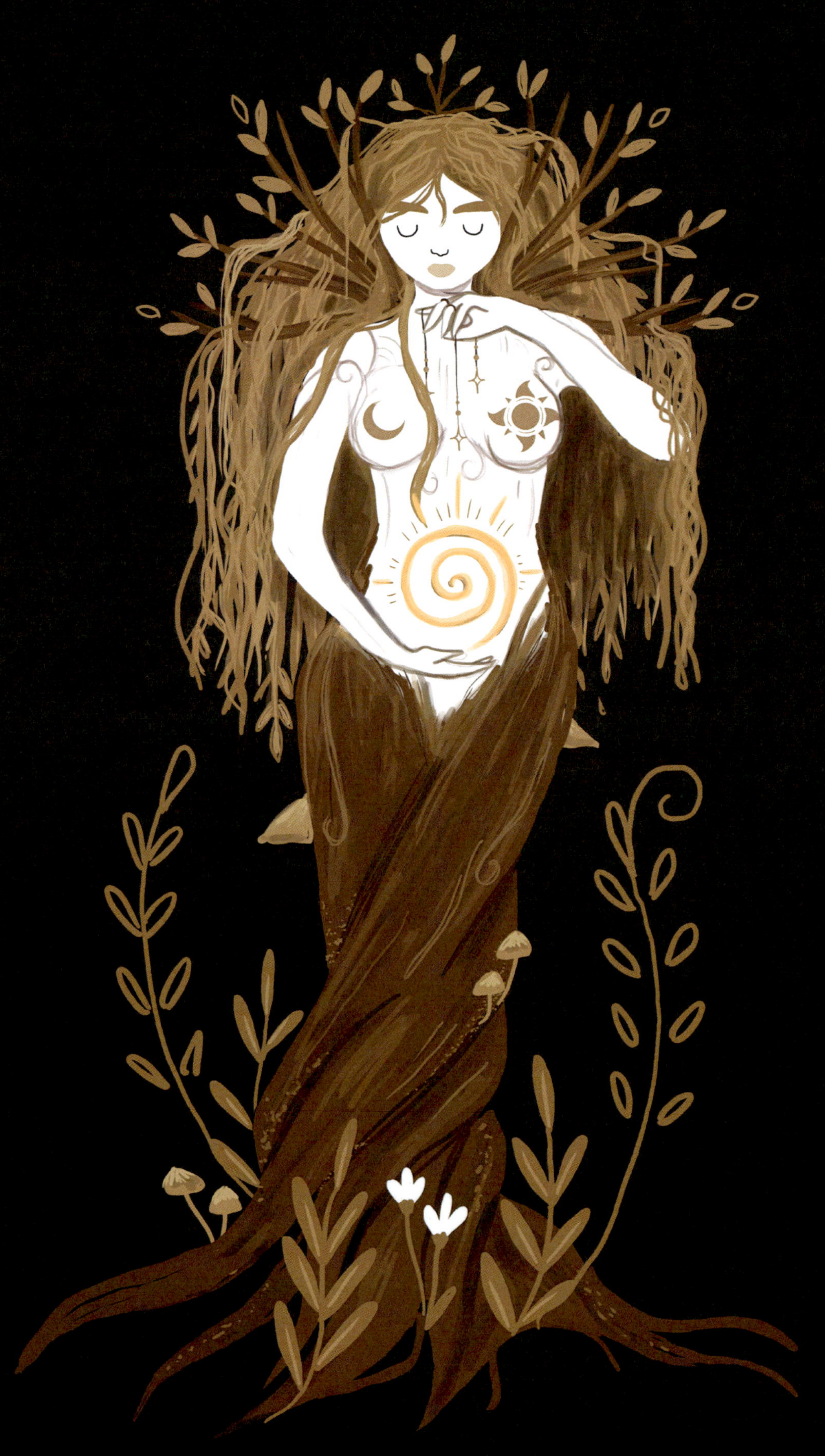

DANU

"...THEIR ORIGIN WAS OF THE *TUATHA DÉ* OF THE GODDESS WHOSE NAME WAS DANU."

—LEBOR GABÁLA ÉRENN

Danu (*dah-noo*) is the supreme mother goddess of the Celtic religion. Despite the fact that she is held in the utmost respect amongst those who worship her and is considered to be the ancestor of the Irish pantheon *Tuatha Dé Danann*, very little is actually known about this divine creator. She is absent from the most memorable of Celtic tales, yet thought to be the source of all creation, nobility, and power. Danu grants those of noble birth with sovereignty, so a great number of kings and chiefs claimed to draw their power from her blessings. Her affiliation with the earth means that she is also connected to fairies and the various standing stones that adorn Ireland.

The primary evidence for Danu's popularity lies within her name. It appears in the names of numerous Irish locations as well as the famous River Danube that crosses central and southeastern Europe. The word "Danu" likely has Indo-European roots, suggesting ties to ancient water deities and the concept of a divine, flowing force. The *Tuatha Dé Danann* themselves are often translated as "the people of the goddess Danu," making a strong case for her as their ancestral mother figure. However, no specific myths or stories exist detailing Danu's actions, relationships, or personality.

In spite of the lack of historical sources, Danu has become a particularly significant figure for modern Pagan and Wiccan traditions. She is often honored as a mother goddess, representing creation, abundance, and wisdom. Practitioners associate her with water, rivers, the land, and ancestral guidance. There are parallels between Danu and other possible Celtic mother goddesses, such as Anu in Irish mythology and Don in Welsh mythology. These figures are similarly associated with the land, fertility, and sovereignty, reinforcing the likelihood that Danu embodied similar concepts.

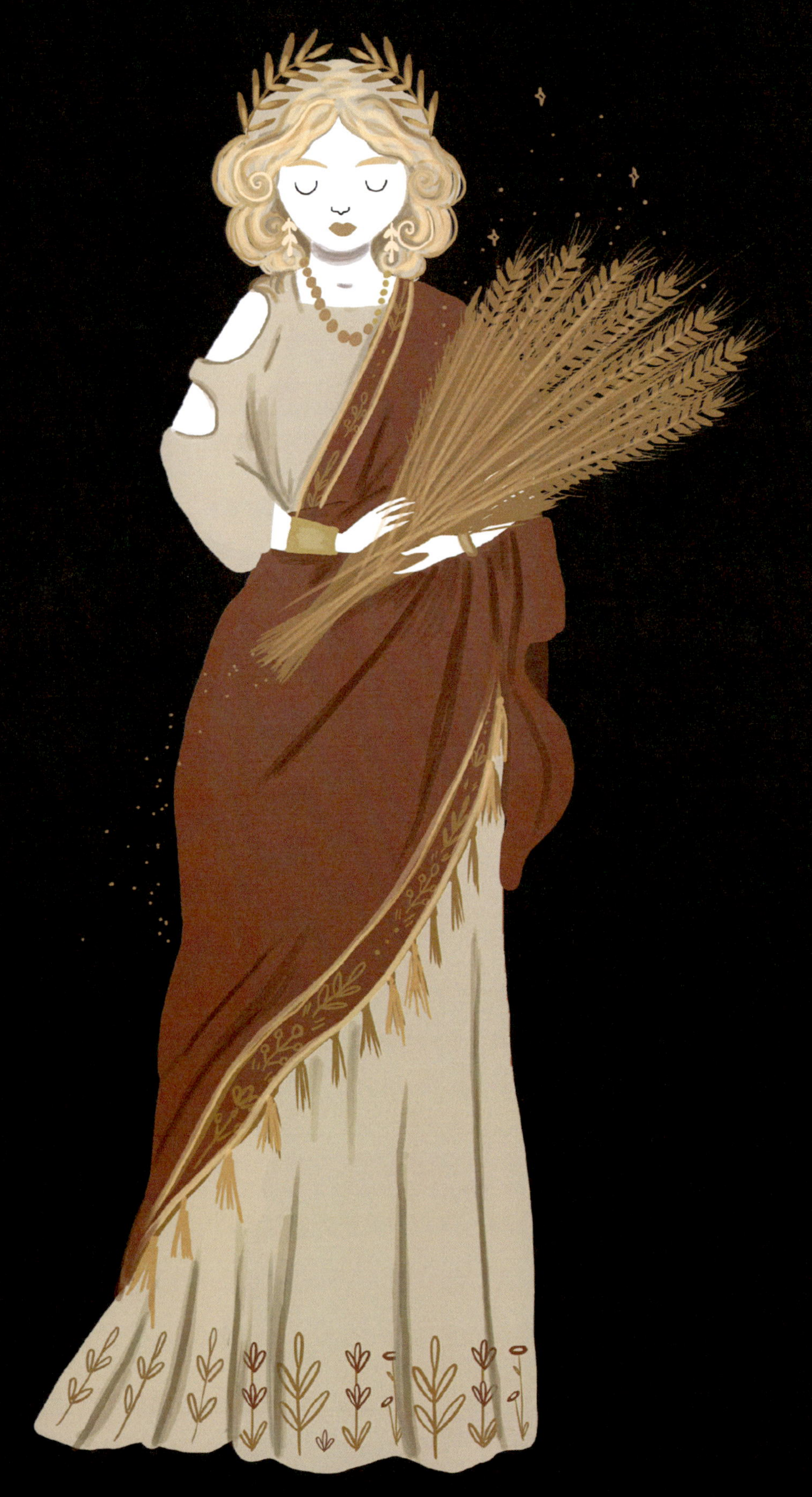

DEMETER

"...MUCH-PRODUCING QUEEN, ALL FLOWERS ARE THINE, AND FRUITS OF LOVELY GREEN."

—*ORPHIC HYMNS*, HYMN XXXIX ("TO CERES [DEMETER ELEUSINIA]")

As one of the oldest goddesses worshipped within the Greek pantheon, Demeter (*duh-mee-ter*) epitomized motherhood and divinity. Often referred to as "She of the Grain," Demeter presided over the flow of agriculture. She is commonly depicted as a regal and mature woman, bearing wheat in one hand and a torch in the other. As one of the original twelve deities who ruled over Mount Olympus, Demeter was highly revered by both gods and mortals alike.

Demeter's name translates to "Divine Mother," a designation that underscores her fundamental role as the nurturer of life, provider of sustenance, and maternal figure within the Greek pantheon. This is illustrated by her most famous myth, the abduction of her daughter, Persephone. According to the story, Persephone was abducted by Hades, god of the Underworld, with Zeus's consent. Demeter's profound grief over her daughter's disappearance resulted in a devastating withdrawal of her agricultural responsibilities, leading to a widespread famine that brought immense suffering to mankind. This severe impact on the mortal world compelled Zeus to intervene, and he ultimately orchestrated Persephone's return for a portion of the year to appease Demeter's sorrow and restore the earth's fertility.

This recurring cycle, intimately tied to Demeter's emotional state, is the mythological explanation for the changing seasons. When Persephone is required to join her husband Hades in the Underworld (typically represented by the barren months of autumn and winter), Demeter's profound grief causes vegetation and crops to wither and fail. Her daughter's subsequent return to the mortal realm, however, alleviates Demeter's sorrow, prompting the earth's renewal and abundant fertility during spring and summer. This foundational myth provides a powerful narrative framework for understanding the cycles of nature and the dependence of human civilization on divine benevolence.

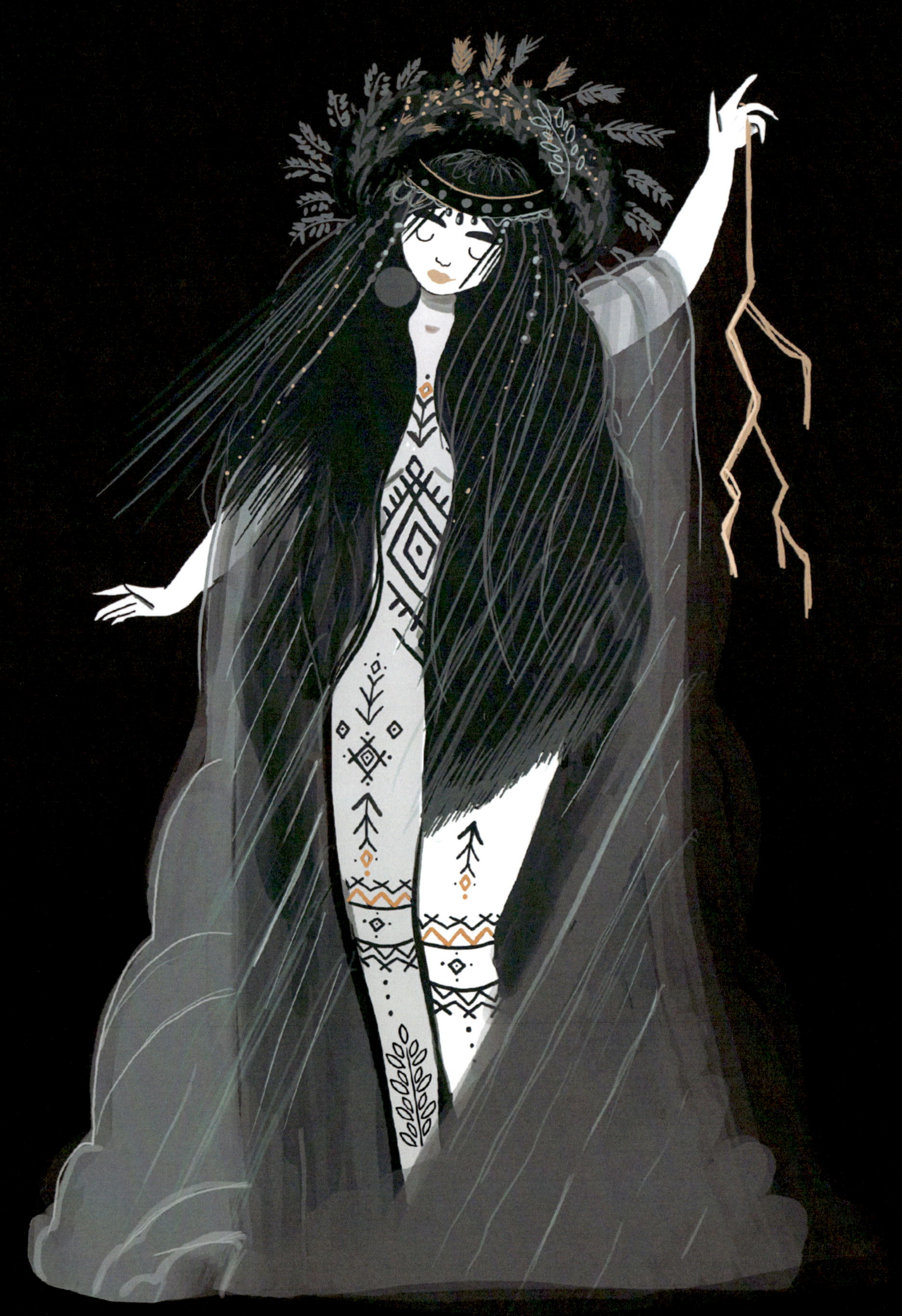

DODOLA

"OUR DODOLA IS WALKING TO PRAY TO GOD TO GIVE US RAIN."

—SIR JAMES FRAZER, THE GOLDEN BOUGH (1890)

While not as widely recognized within Slavic mythology as figures like Perun or Veles, the goddess Dodola (*doh-doh-lah*) served a powerful role in rainmaking rituals, and her association with fertility and vegetation point to a significant presence in the lives of ancient Slavic people. She was also known by a myriad of names, such as *Perperuna* or *Peperuda*, and she is theorized to be connected to the Lithuanian god of thunder, Dundulis. Beyond her specific association with rain, Dodola represented the overarching theme of nature's revitalization.

Dodola is primarily associated with the southern Slavic regions, particularly Serbia, Bulgaria, and Croatia. Her name likely derives from the word "doda," an affectionate term for a young girl or woman. Dodola is most often depicted as a young maiden, sometimes garbed in a dress made of leaves and vines, symbolizing her connection to vegetation and the natural world. In some traditions, she was likely portrayed as a joyous figure, representing the abundance brought by the rains, while in others, she might have taken on a more sorrowful aspect, perhaps reflecting the desperation felt during times of drought.

A key component of the religious practices associated with Dodola involved rituals designed to induce rainfall. When drought struck, these elaborate ceremonies were conducted as a way to call upon Dodola to bring the essential life-giving rains. During the rite, a young girl was chosen to embody the goddess and was transformed into "Dodola" through elaborate adornment with flowers, branches, and greenery. A procession would follow, with the villagers singing folk songs and imploring Dodola for rain. As they moved through the village, the participants would douse the Dodola with water, imitating the desired rainfall. This ritual, marked by both deep reverence and a touch of hopeful desperation, mirrored the absolute necessity of rain for a thriving agricultural cycle.

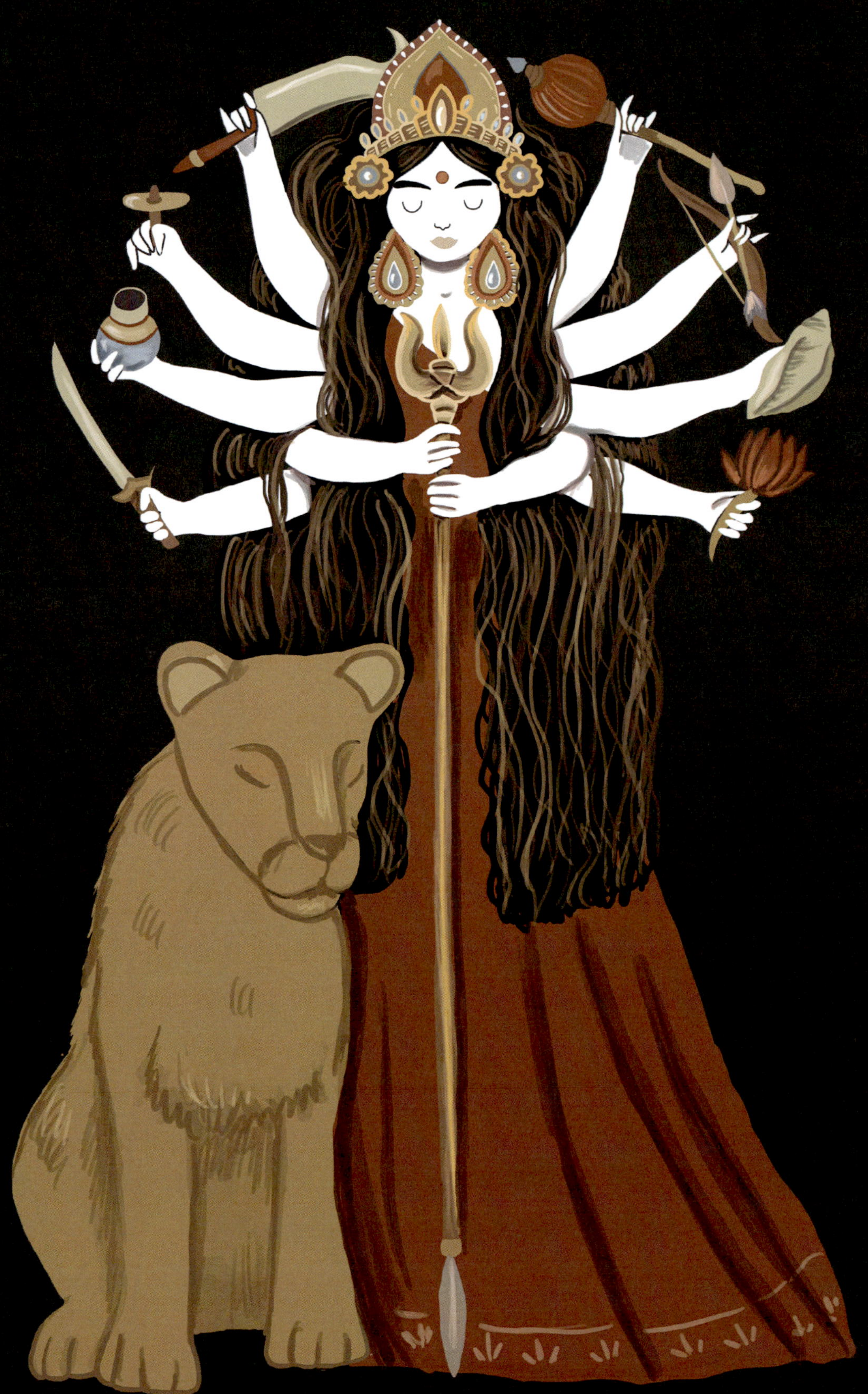

DURGA

"YOU WHO DESTROY THE GREAT FEAR OF THE TERRIFIED, O DURGA!"

—*DEVI MAHATMYA,* CHAPTER 4, VERSE 17

Durga *(door-gah),* the indomitable Hindu goddess, embodies the fierce energy of the feminine divine, known as *Shakti.* Her name, meaning "the inaccessible" or "the invincible," reflects her role as the protector of the righteous and the vanquisher of evil. She is often depicted as a beautiful woman, her multiple arms signifying both vast power and the ability to multitask, while her mount, a lion or tiger, emphasizes her fearlessness. Her weapons, gifted by the other gods, represent the various tools necessary to combat negativity in all its forms. Red, her characteristic color, symbolizes both energetic creation and destructive force, reminding us of her nurturing and wrathful aspects.

Durga's origins are complex and multifaceted. Some scholars suggest a connection to ancient deities associated with mountains and wild spaces. Her earliest references appear in Vedic hymns, connected to the warrior goddess Nirriti or as an epithet for the fierce goddess Kali. However, it is in a later period, particularly in the Mahabharata (400 BCE– 400 CE), that Durga begins to take on a more defined form as a powerful and independent goddess. Here, she is invoked by both Arjuna and Yudhisthira, seeking her blessings for victory in battle.

The early medieval period marked a key phase in the growing prominence of Durga's worship throughout India. She is central to the Shaktism sect of Hinduism, which emphasizes the "Divine Mother" as the supreme being. Durga Puja, her most significant festival, sees widespread celebrations, particularly in Eastern India. This multiday event includes elaborate rituals, feasting, and the creation of beautiful clay idols of the goddess, which are then immersed in water. Durga's worship extended beyond India, gaining widespread reverence within other Hindu populations. She remains a powerful aspect of the great Devi (alongside figures like Lakshmi and Saraswati) and sometimes acts as a consort of Shiva.

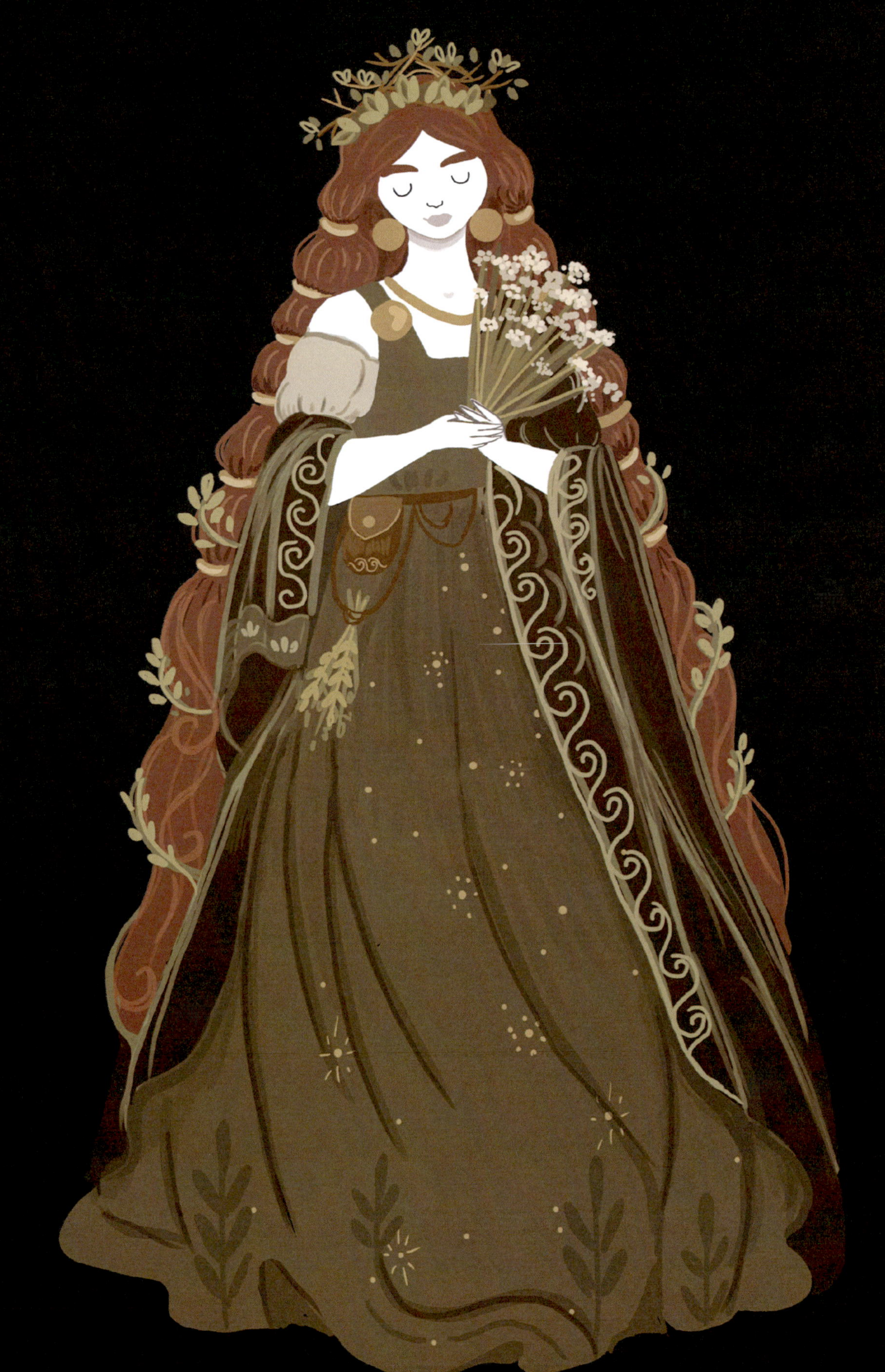

EIR

"THE WISE WOMEN GIVE PROTECTION, NO MATTER HOW DIRE THE PERIL THAT COMES
UPON MEN'S SONS THEY SAVE THEM FROM THEIR STRAITS."

—**SNORRI STURLUSON,** *POETIC EDDA* (THIRTEENTH CENTURY AD), "FJOLVINSMAL"

As one of the many handmaidens of Frigg, Norse goddess Eir (*ayr*) was known far and wide for her prowess as a healer and master physician. She was able to cure diseases and mend any wound, often overseeing childbirth, and was theorized to have possibly been a form of Frigg herself. Eir's role and origin were mentioned in several distinct ways throughout the Old Norse texts, which has added a layer of complexity to what role she might have held in Norse mythology. The *Prose Edda* states that Eir was a daughter of Odin and the giantess Gríðr, while other sources name her as wife to Njord and mother to Freyr.

The meaning of Eir's name, "help" or "mercy," was reflected in the precise way she administered these qualities when needed. Although listed as one of Frigg's attendants, she was also possibly enlisted by Odin as a Valkyrie: fierce female guardians that chose who lived and died in battle. If slain in battle with honor, the recently deceased would be escorted by the Valkyrie to Valhalla. However, it seems Eir's role amongst the Valkyries was determining who would return to health, given her propensity for healing.

In keeping with her position as the preeminent healing goddess, it was also noted that Eir would routinely instruct women on the subjects of science and medicine, guiding their excellence in the proto-Germanic medical field. When Norse and Germanic religions dominated northern Europe, the role of "doctor" was primarily held by women. Eir was often associated with various herbs and plants and was said to possess a deep knowledge of the medicinal properties of all living things. Her name appears in several runic inscriptions from the Viking Age, suggesting that she was specifically invoked during times of need. One such inscription, found in Sweden, reads "Eir help us."

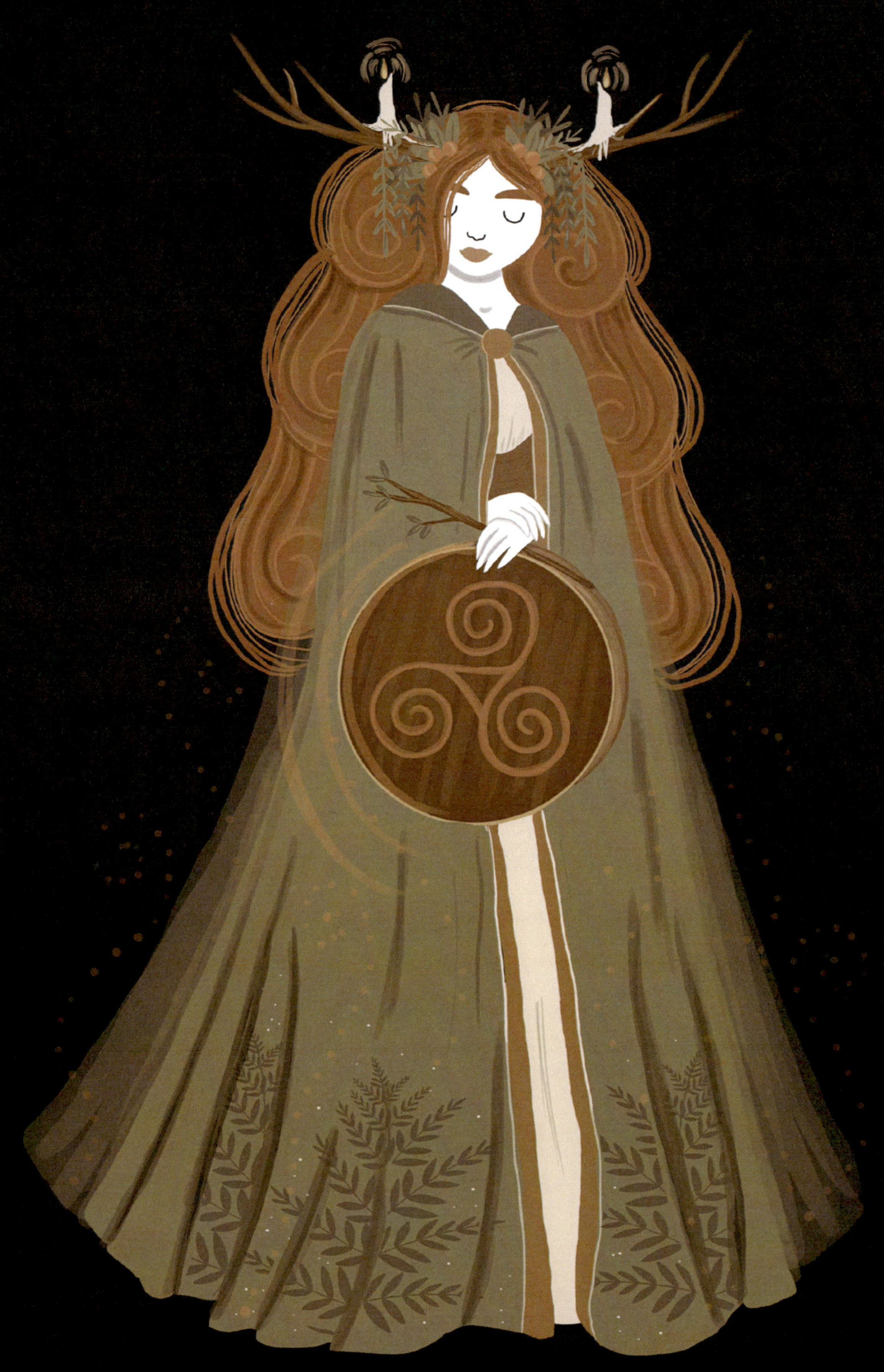

ELEN OF THE WAYS

"NOT MORE EASY THAN TO GAZE UPON THE SUN WHEN BRIGHTEST, WAS IT TO LOOK UPON HER BY REASON OF HER BEAUTY... SHE WAS THE FAIREST SIGHT THAT MAN EVER BEHELD."

—LADY CHARLOTTE GUEST (TRANSLATOR), *THE MABINOGION* (1877), "THE DREAM OF MACSEN WLEDIG"

Elen of the Ways is the Celtic protectress of pathways, both spiritual and physical. Unlike deities with established mythologies, her existence hinges on fragmented evidence and modern interpretations. She was known by varying names and attributes, such as Elen Luyddog (*eh-len loo-ith-og*), Elen of the Hosts, or sometimes Helen of Caernarfon. For those who revere her, she is the "antlered goddess," hidden amongst the forest shadows as the living embodiment of the balance of nature itself.

Elen of the Ways appears in *The Mabinogion*'s "Dream of Macsen Wledig," as a sovereign figure, not explicitly linked to nature or paths. Macsen, the Roman emperor, dreams of Elen and is immediately smitten. His search leads him to a magical castle, where he eventually discovers and marries her. As a result of his marriage to Elen, Macsen ascended to the kingship of Britain. This version stands apart from the popularized Elen of the Ways, which emerged in the late twentieth century, primarily through the work of scholar Caroline Wise. Drawing on scant historical references and intuitive interpretations, Wise depicts Elen as an ancient deer goddess who presides over crossroads, journeys, and the flow of life.

Advocates for Wise's theory point to place names containing variations of "Elen" near crossroads or ancient tracks in Britain. Additionally, depictions of antlered goddesses in European prehistory fuel speculation about a long-lost tradition. Elen of the Ways was also thought to be associated with ancient pilgrimage routes, such as the Avebury to Stonehenge Trail. At the Avebury Stone Circle, there is a standing stone known as the Longstone, which is said to be a marker for the entrance to the Otherworld, the Celtic realm of the dead. This would be a special spot for Elen of the Ways, ready to provide guidance for all who would journey beyond.

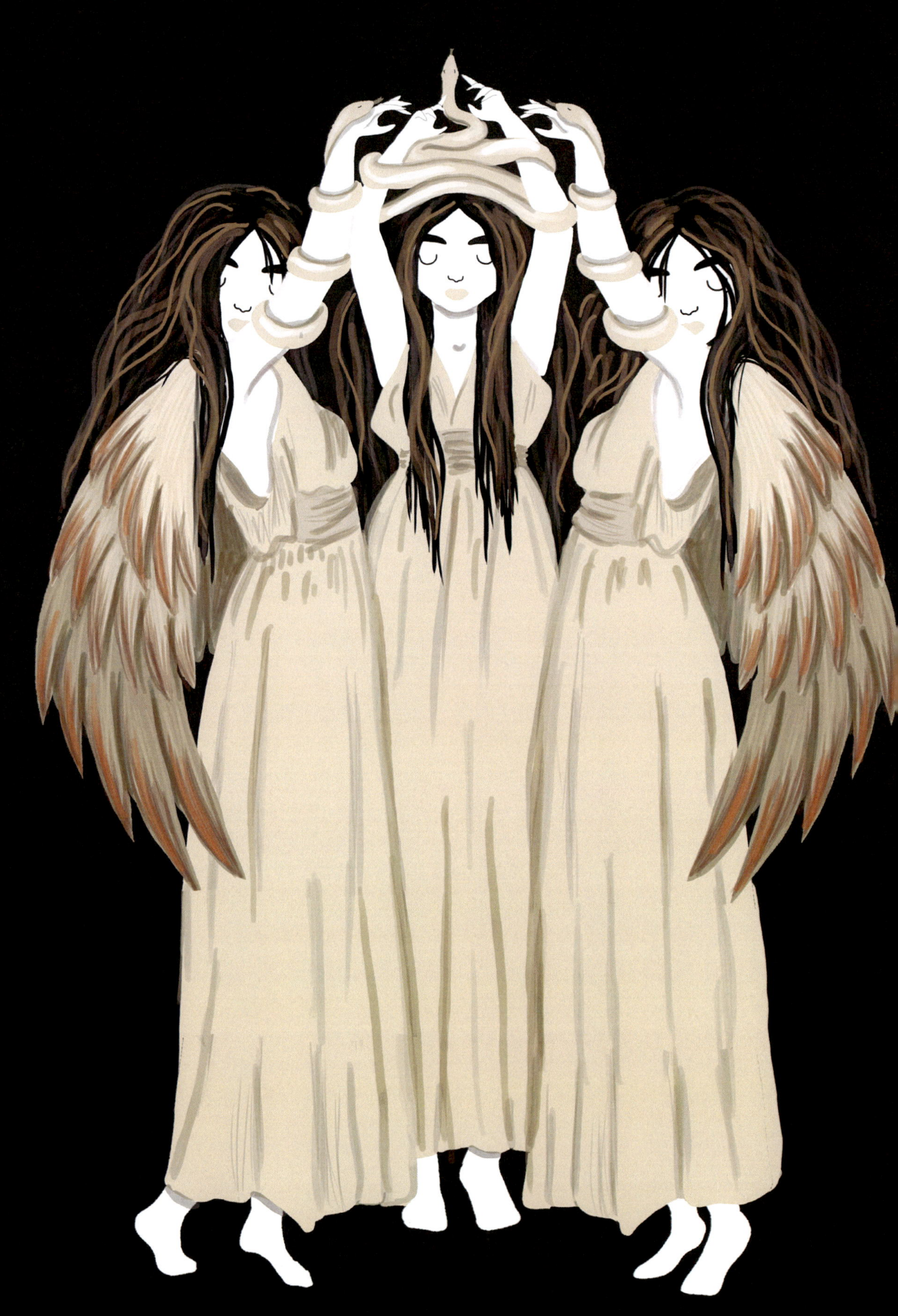

ERINYES

"THE YOUNG HOUNDS OF AN OLD HOUND'S BREED! I DREAM, BUT THEY—LIKE BACCHANALS IN DREAMS—HUNT DOWN THEIR QUARRY, PANTING BLOOD AND DRIPPING SLAUGHTER."

—AESCHYLUS, *EUMENIDES*, LINES 183–186

Within Greek mythology, the Erinyes (*ih-rin-ee-eez*), or Furies, occupy a shadowy realm as the embodiment of vengeance, retribution, and the inexorable consequences of violating the natural order of the cosmos. These ancient chthonic deities, feared by mortals, played a vital role in upholding cosmic justice and societal balance. Depictions of the Erinyes often emphasized their terrifying nature through vivid imagery: winged women with snakes entwined in their hair and eyes dripping blood. Sometimes they were shown carrying whips or torches, representing their relentless pursuit and the torment they inflicted.

Their monstrous visages served to visually externalize the terror and guilt felt by those who had committed crimes. Despite their formidable reputation, the Erinyes' motivations lay in upholding a higher justice, rather than in enacting personal vengeance. Transgressions against the natural order were their primary concern, with a particular emphasis on crimes involving blood kin, such as the murder of parents or siblings. They also punished perjury, offenses against the gods, and the violation of hospitality laws. As such, the Erinyes reflected the moral fabric of the Greek world, ensuring no violation went unanswered and that balance was ultimately maintained.

The Erinyes feature prominently in various Greek myths and literary works. Aeschylus's trilogy, the *Oresteia*, provides perhaps the most famous and nuanced portrayal of the Furies. The story recounts the relentless pursuit of Orestes by the Erinyes as retribution for the murder of his mother, Clytemnestra. However, through the intervention of Athena and Apollo, their wrath is transformed into a protective force, and they are renamed the Eumenides, or "kindly ones," signifying a shift toward a more benevolent and ordered justice system. The Erinyes also find a place in works like Homer's *Iliad* and *Odyssey* and the writings of poets like Sophocles and Euripides, who emphasize their role in maintaining order and punishing the wicked.

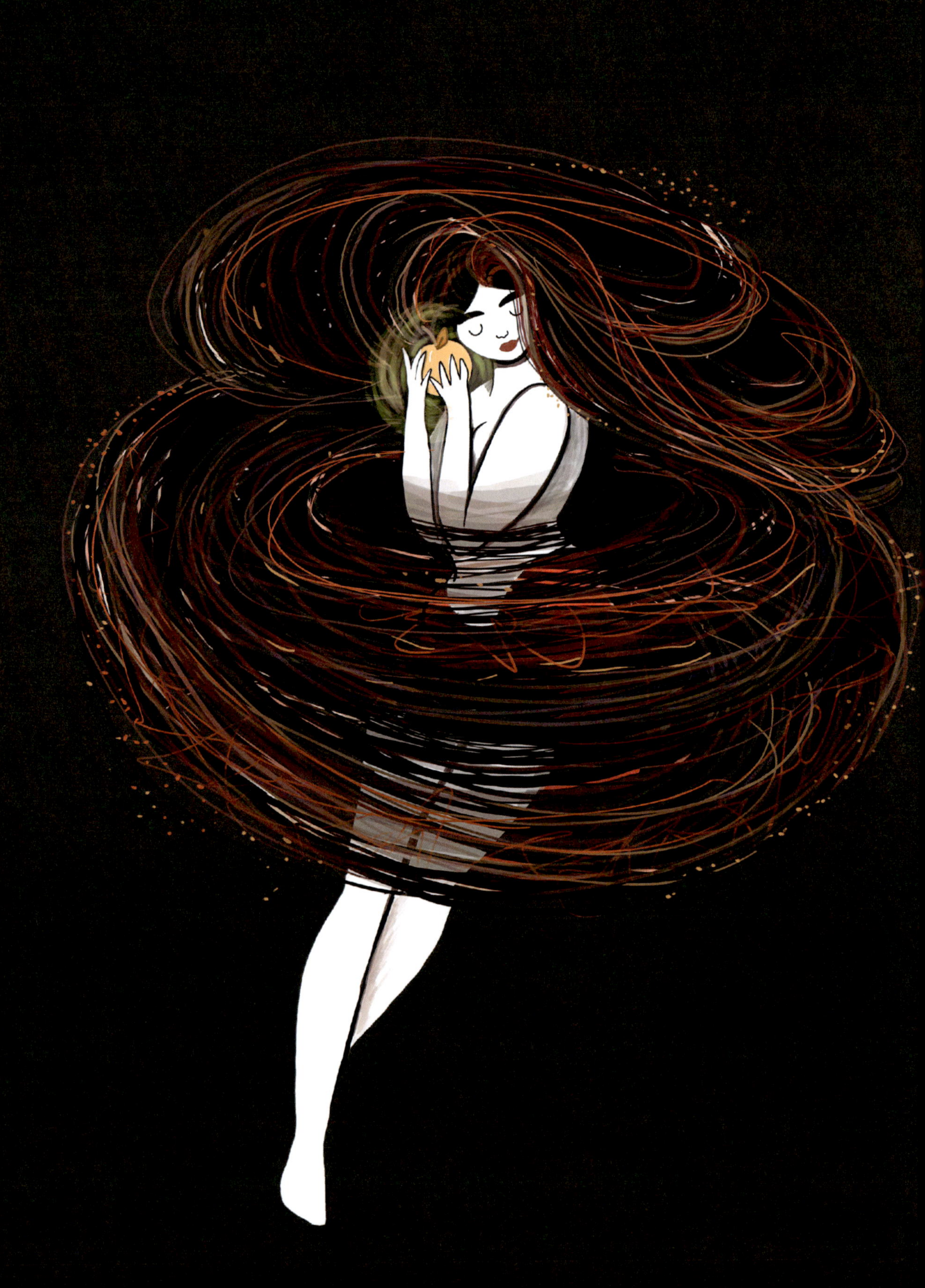

ERIS

"...SHE WHO NEVER TIRES OF HER FURY, AND CAST A SMALL THING AT THE FIRST,
THEN MADE IT GROW TILL ITS HEAD REACHED HEAVEN."

—*ILIAD,* BOOK IV, LINES 440–443

The Greek goddess Eris (*eh-riss*) embodies strife, discord, and rivalry, with her presence consistently serving as a harbinger of chaos. While not among the most widely celebrated Olympians, Eris holds a pivotal, often catalyzing, role in Greek mythology, her influence evident in several iconic legends. Hesiod, in his *Theogony*, identifies her as a daughter of Nyx, the primordial goddess of night, a lineage that underscores her inherent connection to the darker, tumultuous aspects of the cosmos. Other tellings alternatively propose Zeus and Hera as her parents.

Eris is often depicted as a winged female figure, her features contorted in fury, visually manifesting the turbulence she represents. Her iconography frequently includes a torch or a bloody dagger, symbolizing the destructive potential inherent in discord. A prime illustration of Eris's disruptive power is found in the myth of the Golden Apple, the event that famously led to the Trojan War. Angered by her exclusion from the wedding feast of Thetis and Peleus, Eris deliberately introduced an apple inscribed "To the fairest" into the celebration.

This act, seemingly minor, instigated a bitter feud between Hera, Athena, and Aphrodite, all claiming the title of "fairest." The Trojan prince Paris ruled in favor of Aphrodite in exchange for Helen's love, which was the direct catalyst for Helen's abduction and the subsequent devastating ten-year war between Greece and Troy. This narrative profoundly demonstrates Eris's capacity to initiate widespread conflict through seemingly small, but strategically placed, acts of disruption.

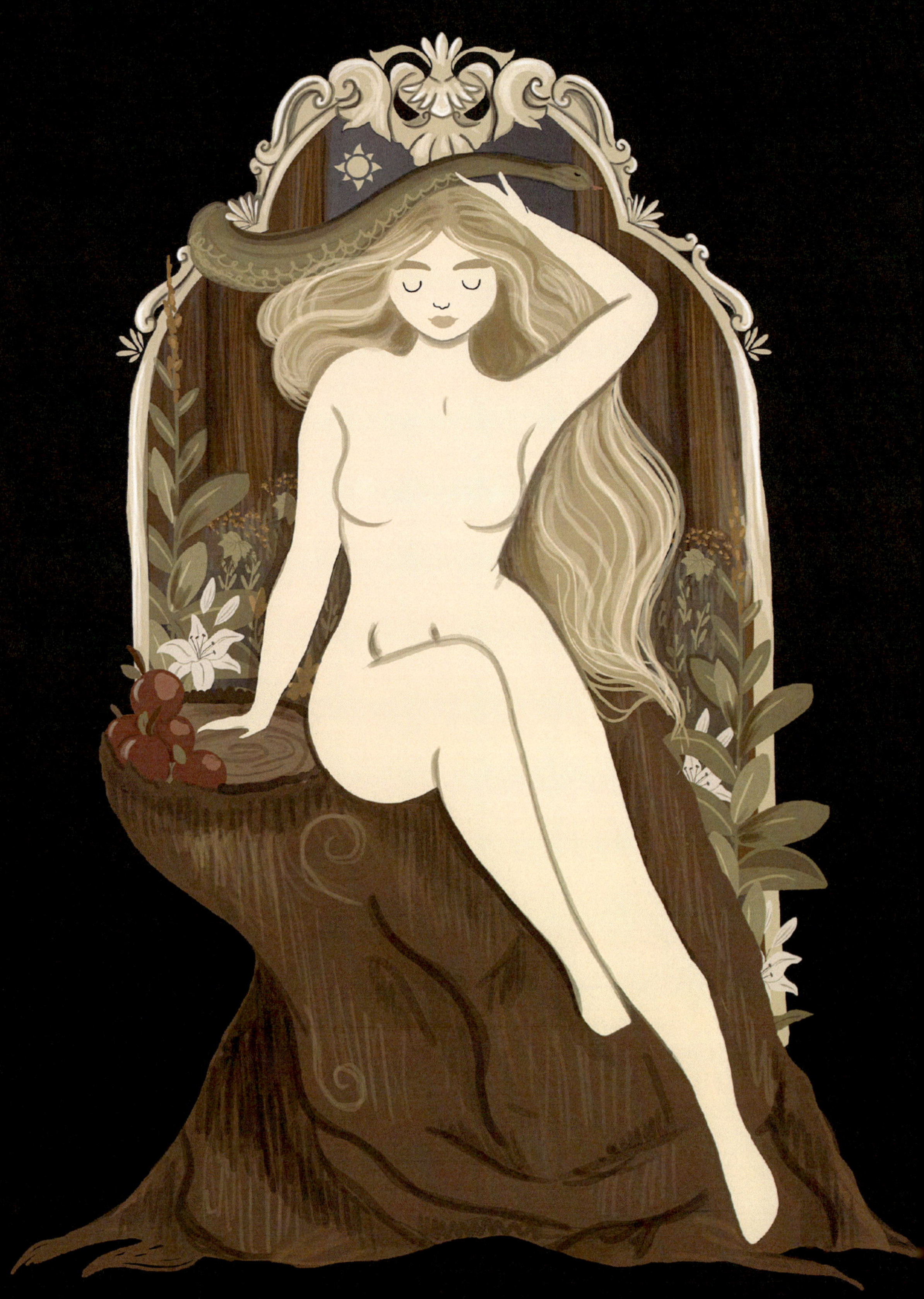

EVE

"AND THE MAN CALLED HIS WIFE'S NAME EVE, BECAUSE SHE WAS THE MOTHER OF ALL LIVING."

—GENESIS 3:20

Eve *(eev)*, the first woman in Abrahamic religions as told in the Book of Genesis, has been interpreted and reinterpreted throughout history, shaping religious beliefs, cultural norms, and gender roles. Positioned in the mythology of monotheistic traditions, she is not considered a goddess by the Christian, Jewish, or Islamic faiths, but her importance as humanity's mother is undeniable. While primarily known for her role in the fall of man, Eve's legacy extends far beyond the biblical narrative, as it has been reinterpreted by feminist and religious scholars in recent decades. Eve's origins are found in the second chapter of Genesis, where she is described as being created from Adam's rib. This act of creation establishes a fundamental connection between Adam and Eve, highlighting their shared responsibility for humanity's fate. Eve's name, derived from the Hebrew word *Havah*, meaning "life" or "living," underscores her role as the mother of all living beings.

The biblical narrative presents Eve as both a companion and a temptress. The depiction of Eve as Adam's equal stands in contrast to her succumbing to the serpent's enticement, leading to the consumption of the forbidden fruit and humanity's exile from paradise. This act of disobedience, known as "The Fall," is often interpreted as the origin of sin and human suffering. This act has been interpreted multiple ways: one side sees female curiosity and independence, while others vilify her as a symbol of temptation and weakness.

In Christian theology, Eve is often associated with the concept of original sin, with her actions being seen as the source of humanity's inherent wickedness. Scholars have offered alternative interpretations, challenging the traditional view of Eve as a mere temptress. They argue that the biblical narrative reflects patriarchal biases and that Eve's actions can be seen as a quest for knowledge and self-determination. Some readings posit Eve's act of eating the forbidden fruit as an essential stage in human evolution, one that facilitated greater awareness and understanding.

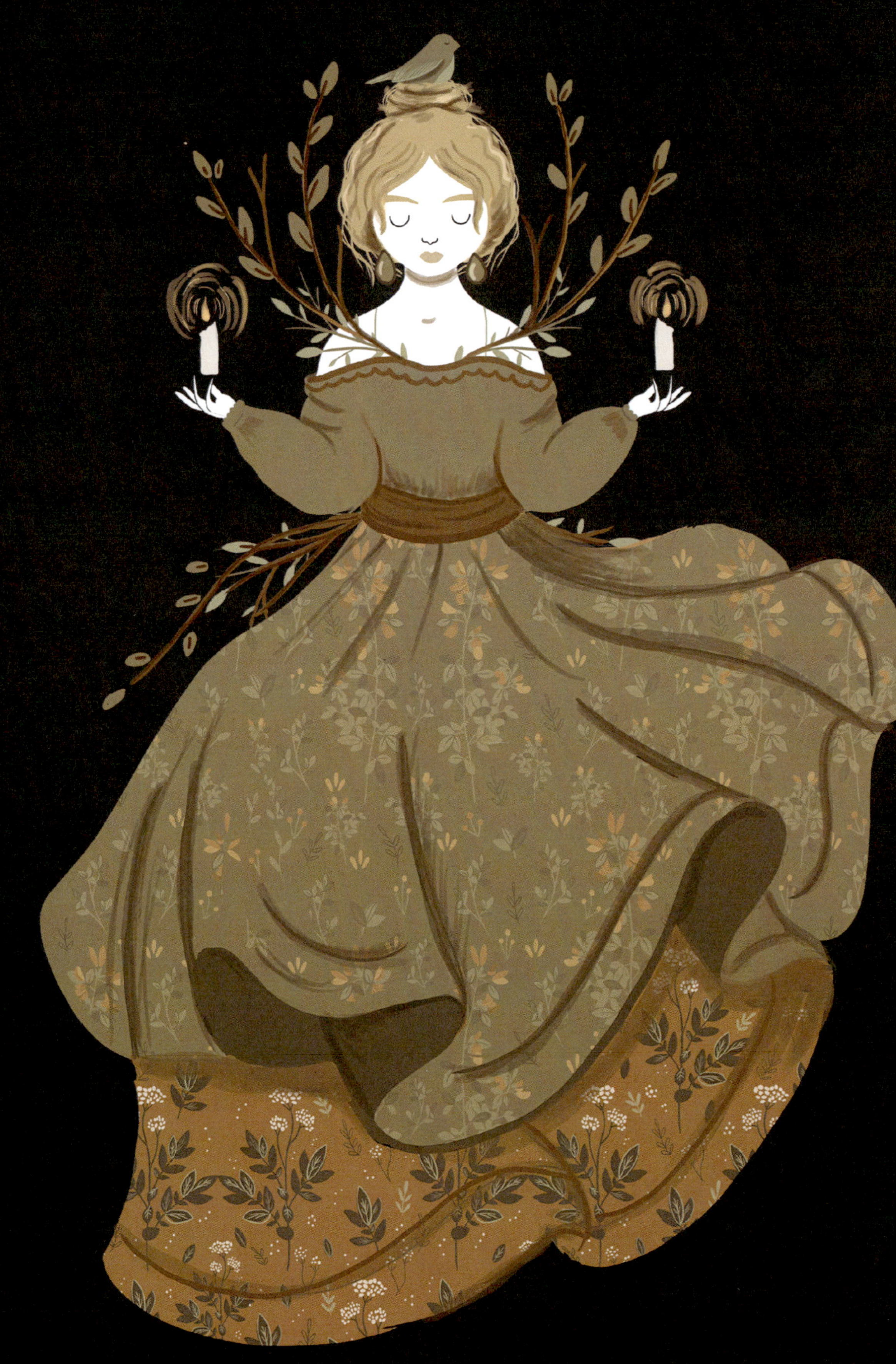

FERONIA

"...LET SLAVES SIT DOWN SO THAT THEY MAY STAND UP FREE."

—**PETER F. DORCEY,** *THE CULT OF SILVANUS* (1992)

Feronia *(feh-roh-nee-uh)* was a multifaceted goddess venerated in ancient Italy, particularly within the central regions of Etruria, Latium, and Sabina. Her name likely comes from an older Sabine word akin to "bearer" or "she who grants," hinting at her primary roles within the agricultural and natural spheres. Yet, Feronia's scope of influence was broad, evolving over time and encompassing aspects of fertility, the wild, commerce, and the liberation of slaves.

Foremost, Feronia was a goddess of nature and the untamed wilderness; her sacred groves were often located outside of urban centers. As a protector of wild spaces, she was also associated with wild and dangerous animals, particularly wolves. This connection affirmed the duality of her nature: both nurturing and potentially threatening. Her role as an agricultural deity included promoting crop and livestock fertility, and her connection to springs and water sources emphasized her role in providing bountiful harvests. Festivals held in her honor often involved agricultural offerings and prayers for the season ahead.

Another crucial aspect of Feronia was her role as a goddess of trade and commerce. This is most evident in her strong association with the town of Terracina (a vital trading hub in southern Latium) and the bustling trade fairs held near her sanctuaries. Feronia's role in establishing social cohesion and commercial exchange, especially among the close-knit Etruscan, Latin, and Sabine populations, cannot be understated. These sacred sites allowed for the flow of goods, ideas, and even cultures between these distinct groups. Importantly, Feronia was also viewed as a liberator, particularly for freed slaves. Her temples often became places of refuge for former slaves seeking integration into society. Rituals associated with achieving freedom from bondage have been linked to her worship.

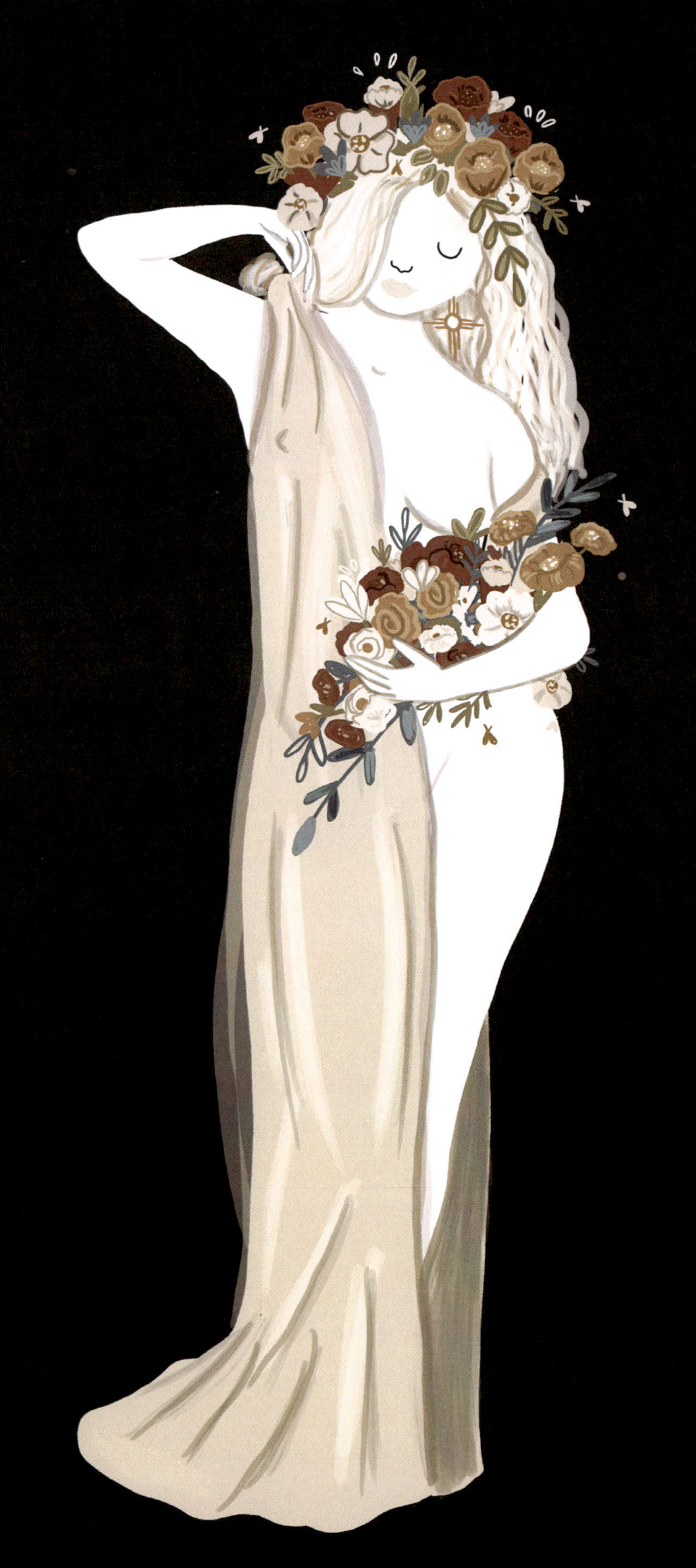

FLORA

"As my marriage-gift, he gave me to enjoy never-ending spring."

—**Ovid,** *Fasti*, Book V, Lines 195–200

Roman goddess Flora *(flohr-uh)* embodied the blossoming beauty of nature, with associations with flowers, springtime, and the renewal of life. She held a cherished place in Roman religion and inspired countless artistic representations. She likely originated as a Sabine deity, one of the Italic peoples who inhabited the region surrounding Rome. Her name, derived from the Latin *flos*, or "flower," clearly signifies her connection to the natural world.

As Roman influence expanded, Flora was integrated into their pantheon, infusing her with additional significance. While not a central figure in Roman mythology like Jupiter or Venus, Flora still held a specific and vital role and was associated with concepts of fertility and the cyclical nature of the seasons. She was the patroness of flowering plants, particularly those that held agricultural importance. Romans believed she oversaw the blossoming of grains, vineyards, and fruit trees, ensuring a bountiful harvest. The Floralia festival (held in her honor in late April or early May) was a time of joyous celebration, marked by feasting, games, and theatrical performances. The lascivious nature of some of these festivities hint at Flora's connection to fertility and pleasure.

Flora was also linked to youth and the fleetingness of beauty. Roman poet Ovid describes her as an eternally youthful nymph, perpetually adorned with flower garlands. The Roman philosopher Lucretius, in his work *De Rerum Natura*, or *On the Nature of Things*, depicts Flora as a figure who precedes Venus, spreading flowers across the earth in preparation for the goddess of love, suggesting her role as a harbinger of spring's vitality. Flora's artistic legacy extended far beyond the Roman era, as Renaissance and Baroque artists were captivated by her symbolism and she frequently appears in works by artists like Botticelli in his famous *Primavera*, as well as Titian and Rembrandt.

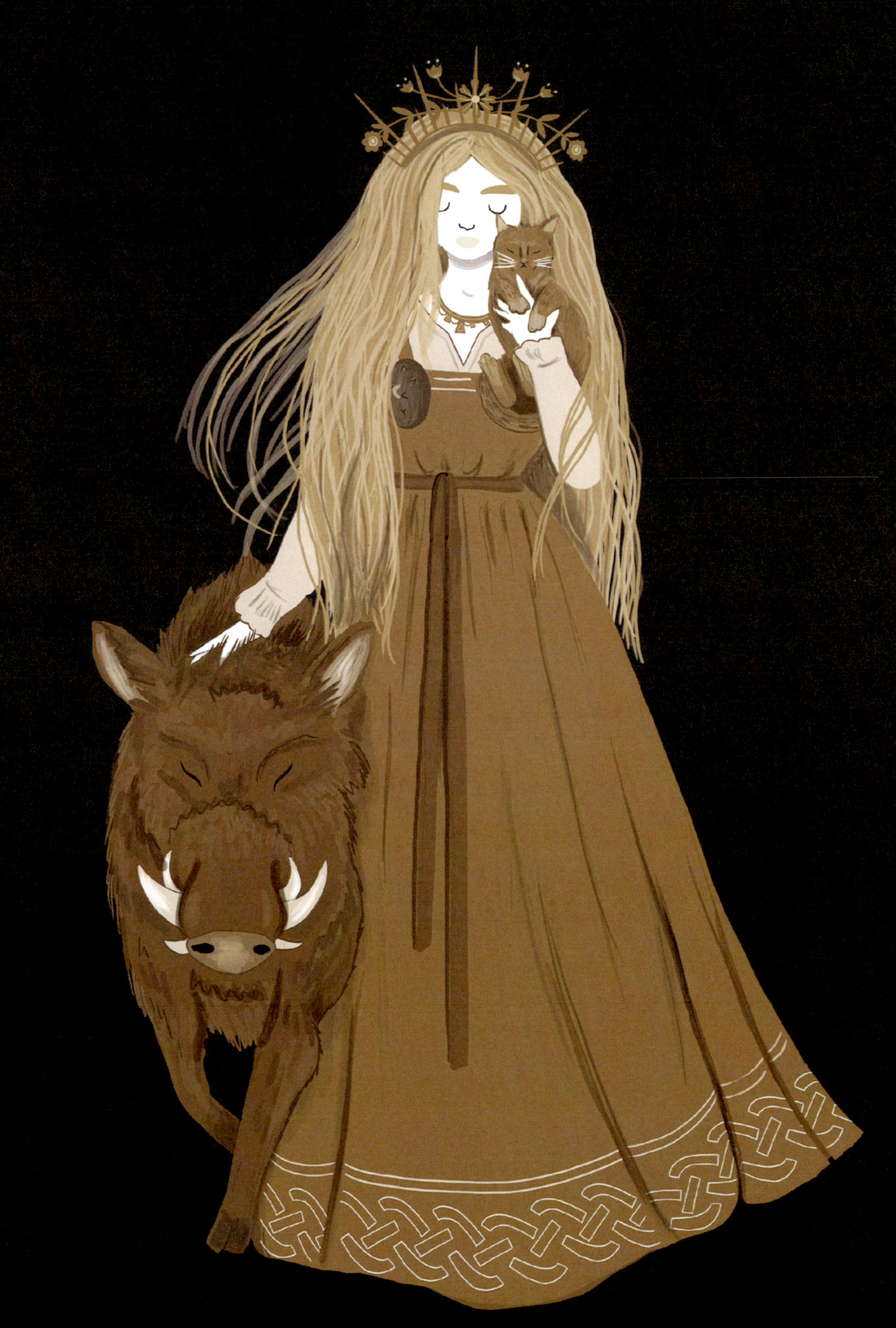

FREYJA

"THE NINTH IS FÓLKVANGR, WHERE FREYJA DECREES WHO SHALL HAVE SEATS IN THE HALL; THE HALF OF THE DEAD EACH DAY DOES SHE CHOOSE, AND HALF DOES ODIN HAVE."

—**SNORRI STURLUSON,** BENJAMIN THORPE (TRANSLATOR),
POETIC EDDA, "ÞRYMSKVIÐA"

As the most renowned goddess within Norse mythology, Freyja (*fray-yah*), or Freya, embodied the essence of passion, fire, and glory. Originally born amongst the Vanir, deities of earth and magic, Freyja and several others aligned themselves with the Aesir, deities of war and sky, in order to bring an end to conflict. In this conjoined celestial clan, she emerged amidst the newly enlisted Vanir as a truly prominent force through her own merits and abilities.

Various parallels seem to connect Freyja to the Norse goddess Frigg, whose dominion over fertility and childbirth mirror Freyja's power over sex and magic. Although the specifics of these deities remain debated, pre- and post-Germanic writings offer enough information to suggest that Freyja and Frigg were largely considered both the same and separate. It was said that Freyja's husband was the wandering Óðr, whose name can be traced to the same Old Norse sources as Odin, the Allfather, leader of the Aesir, and husband to Frigg.

Along with a mastery of charms and potions, Freyja was also a gifted shapeshifter and would occasionally lead the Valkyries into battle under the form *Valfreya.* In this battle-ready manifestation, she staked her claim on half of all dead warriors for her domain, Folkvang, while the other half made their way to Valhalla. Though she could fly whenever she wished using her feather cloak, Freyja also possessed a chariot drawn by two grey cats, as well as her golden-bristled boar *Hildisvini,* a name that directly translates to "battle swine."

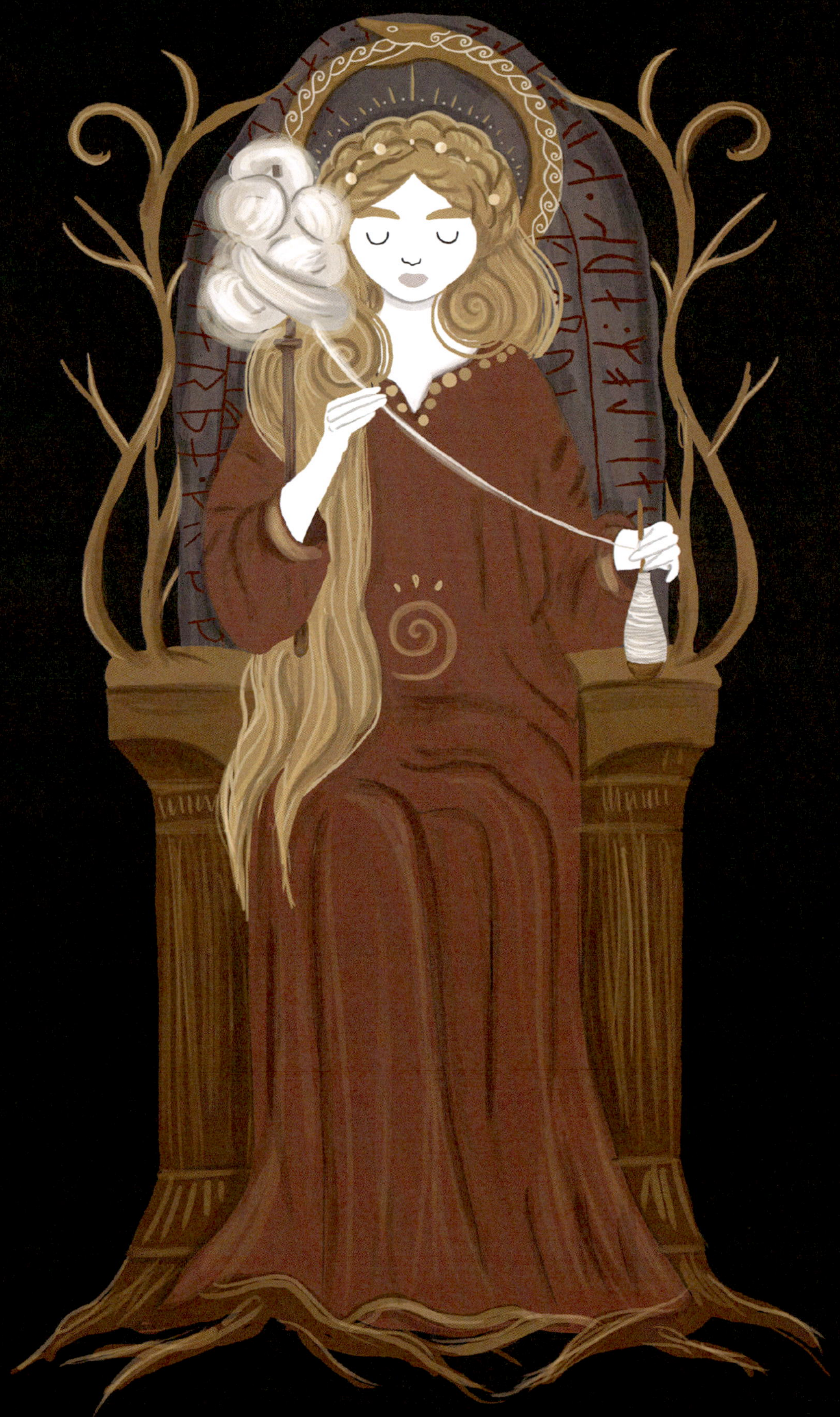

FRIGG

"...AND FRIGG TOOK OATHS TO THIS PURPORT, THAT FIRE AND WATER SHOULD
SPARE BALDR,
LIKEWISE IRON AND METAL OF ALL KINDS, STONES, EARTH, TREES, SICKNESSES, BEASTS,
BIRDS, VENOM, SERPENTS."

—**SNORRI STURLUSON,** *PROSE EDDA,* "GYLFAGINNING"

Frigg *(frih-g)*, the Norse goddess of divination, marriage, and motherhood, held the highest rank among the Aesir goddesses. Primarily known as the wife of Odin, the Allfather and leader of the Aesir, Frigg's significance within Norse mythology is considerable, despite a limited number of surviving sources specifically detailing her actions. She possessed the unique ability to perceive everyone's destiny, yet kept this knowledge secret. Frigg also maintained a close association with the Norns, the goddesses of fate, and is often depicted as assisting in the weaving of destinies.

Frigg, or Frigga, is commonly linked to the goddess Freyja, with many Norse texts simultaneously merging and distinguishing the two deities. However, Frigg's distinct focus on marriage, prophecy, and domesticity typically differentiates her from Freyja, the vibrant goddess of love, beauty, and war. Frigg's name itself, derived from the Old Norse word *frija* meaning "to love," encapsulates her core essence: she embodies marital love in its most enduring form. As queen, she presided over Asgard, the realm of the gods, as well as human marriages, with Frigg's Day (Friday) traditionally considered a favorable day for weddings.

Motherhood formed another cornerstone of Frigg's identity, profoundly exemplified by her relationship with her beloved son, Baldur, the god of light and wisdom. Her fierce maternal love is a central thematic element in Norse myths, particularly in accounts like the poem *"Baldrs Draumar"* (Baldur's Dreams). In this narrative, Frigg's clairvoyant knowledge of Baldur's impending death drives her to seek oaths from all entities in existence to protect him. However, a single oversight regarding the mistletoe plant ultimately allows the trickster Loki to orchestrate Baldur's death through the unwitting blind god Höðr. This tragic event not only highlights the unalterable nature of fate, despite divine efforts, but also serves as a pivotal point in the unfolding prophecies of Ragnarök.

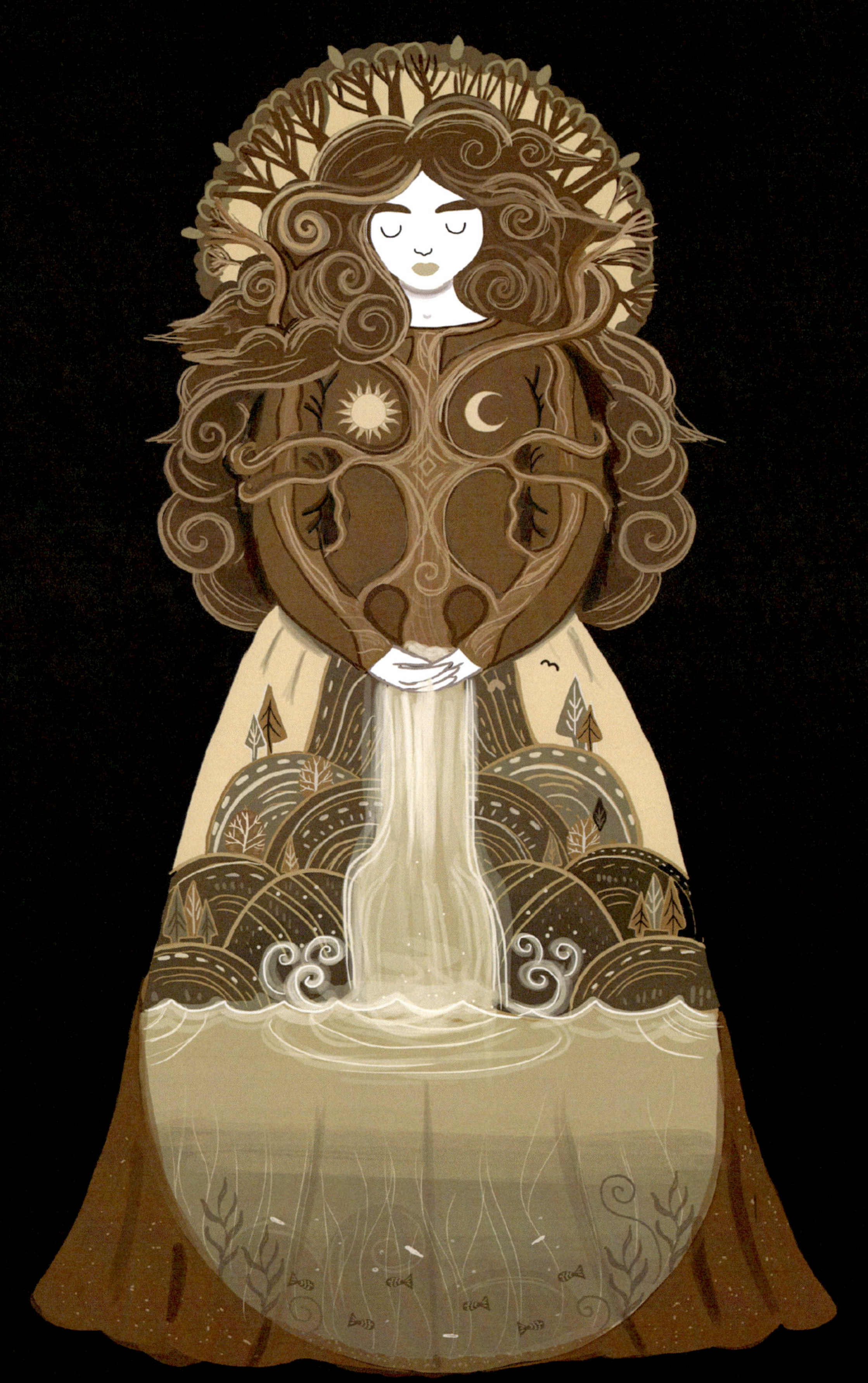

GAIA

"MOTHER GAIA, UNBEGOTTEN AND SELF-DELIVERED."

—NONNUS, *DIONYSIACA*, XXIX

Gaia (*guy-yuh*), the primordial personification of the earth in Greek mythology, emerged at the dawn of creation directly after Khaos, the void that filled the space between heaven and earth. Her foundational role in the cosmos is demonstrated by her creation of key entities, including Uranus (the sky), Pontus (the sea), and other celestial beings. Notably, she also gave birth to Kronos and Rhea, who would later become the parents of the Olympian pantheon. Gaia's interactions with other divine figures are frequently characterized by conflict, particularly with her son and consort, Uranus.

Their union, intended by Gaia to establish an equal counterpart over the sky as she ruled over the earth, led to the birth of powerful and often monstrous offspring, such as the Titans, the one-eyed Cyclops, Okeanos, Hyperion, and Kronos, who personified time and the harvest. A central dynamic of this period involves Uranus's disdain for his children, leading him to imprison them within Gaia herself. This act of oppression prompted Gaia to incite Kronos's rebellion against his father, a pattern of generational power struggles that continued when Kronos's own dominion was later usurped by his son, Zeus, the eventual ruler of Mount Olympus.

Despite these tumultuous mythological events, Gaia is consistently portrayed as being devoted to all her offspring. This unwavering maternal protectiveness, even amidst divine conflicts, forms a key aspect of Gaia's struggles within Greek mythology, offering insight into the concept of an all-encompassing "mother earth." In contemporary Paganism, she is revered as the spiritual embodiment of the earth and is often invoked in rituals and magical practices. Her enduring connection to the natural world resonates strongly with environmental activists and pagans alike, who view her as a potent symbol of the interconnectedness of all life.

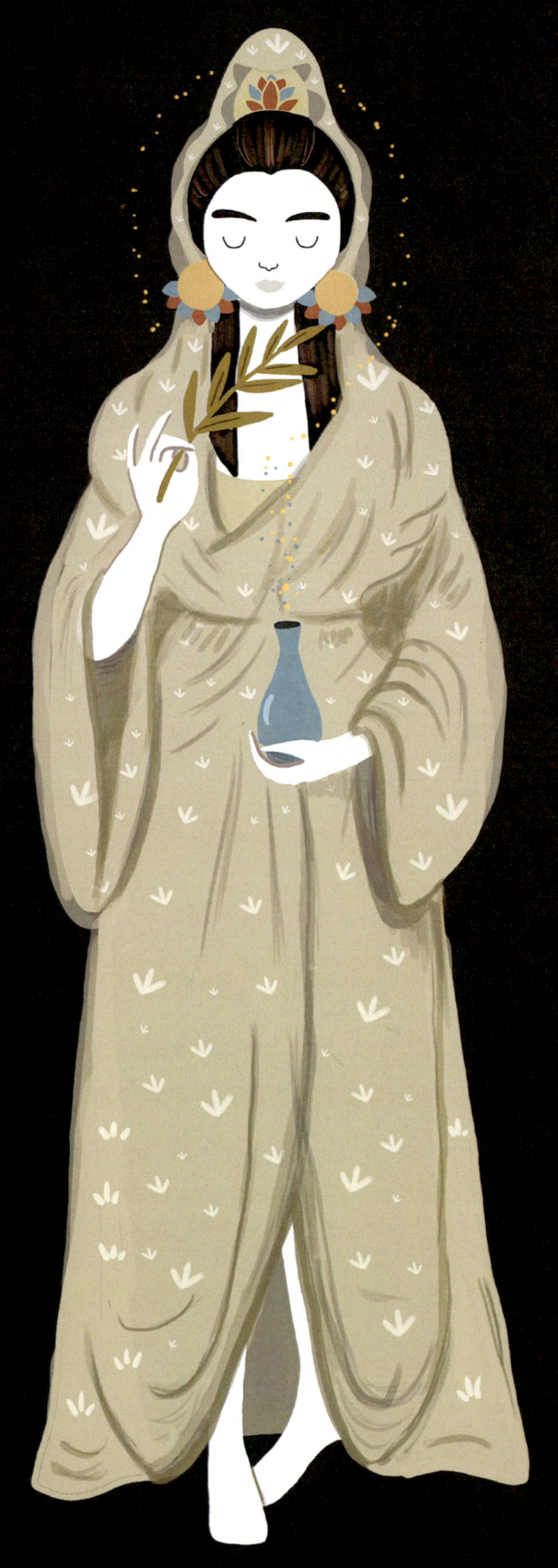

GUAN YIN

"IF A SENTIENT BEING, SEEKING TO BE DELIVERED, SHOULD CALL UPON THE NAME...
HE WILL IMMEDIATELY HEAR THEIR VOICE AND APPEAR IN THE FORM OF A WOMAN TO
DELIVER THEM."

—*LOTUS SUTRA,* CHAPTER 25

Guan Yin (*gwahn yi-hn*), also known as Guanyin, Kwan Yin, or Kuanyin, is the bodhisattva of compassion and is one of the most revered figures in East Asian Buddhism. Her name, a shortened form of *Guanshiyin*, translates to "The One Who Perceives the Sounds of the World." A bodhisattva in Buddhism represents a person dedicated to achieving enlightenment for the benefit of all sentient beings. With inexhaustible mercy, Guan Yin's receptiveness to the world's afflictions has established her as a beloved figure across centuries.

Guan Yin's origins can be traced to the Indian bodhisattva of compassion, Avalokiteśvara. The earliest known Chinese representation of Guan Yin as a male figure dates back to the fourth century CE. However, a profound transformation began during the Tang Dynasty (618–907 CE), and depictions of Guan Yin gradually shifted toward a more feminine form. This shift is attributed to various factors, including the growing influence of Daoist goddess figures and the increasing idealization of feminine virtues like compassion and nurturing within Chinese culture. By the Song Dynasty (960–1279 CE), Guan Yin's association with femininity was firmly established. This feminine form reflected the familiar figure of a merciful mother who extends compassion to those in distress.

This transformation of Guan Yin into a goddess reveals a fascinating convergence of Buddhist ideals and indigenous Chinese beliefs, highlighting the adaptability and cultural influence of Buddhism in China. She is a bodhisattva that varies depending on local and regional interpretations. In coastal regions of China, Guan Yin is revered as a protector of sailors and fishermen. In Japan, where she is called *Kannon*, there exists a popular pilgrimage route comprising thirty-three temples dedicated to her various manifestations. This vibrant tradition solidifies her place as a timeless symbol of hope in suffering and a source of profound solace for all who turn to her.

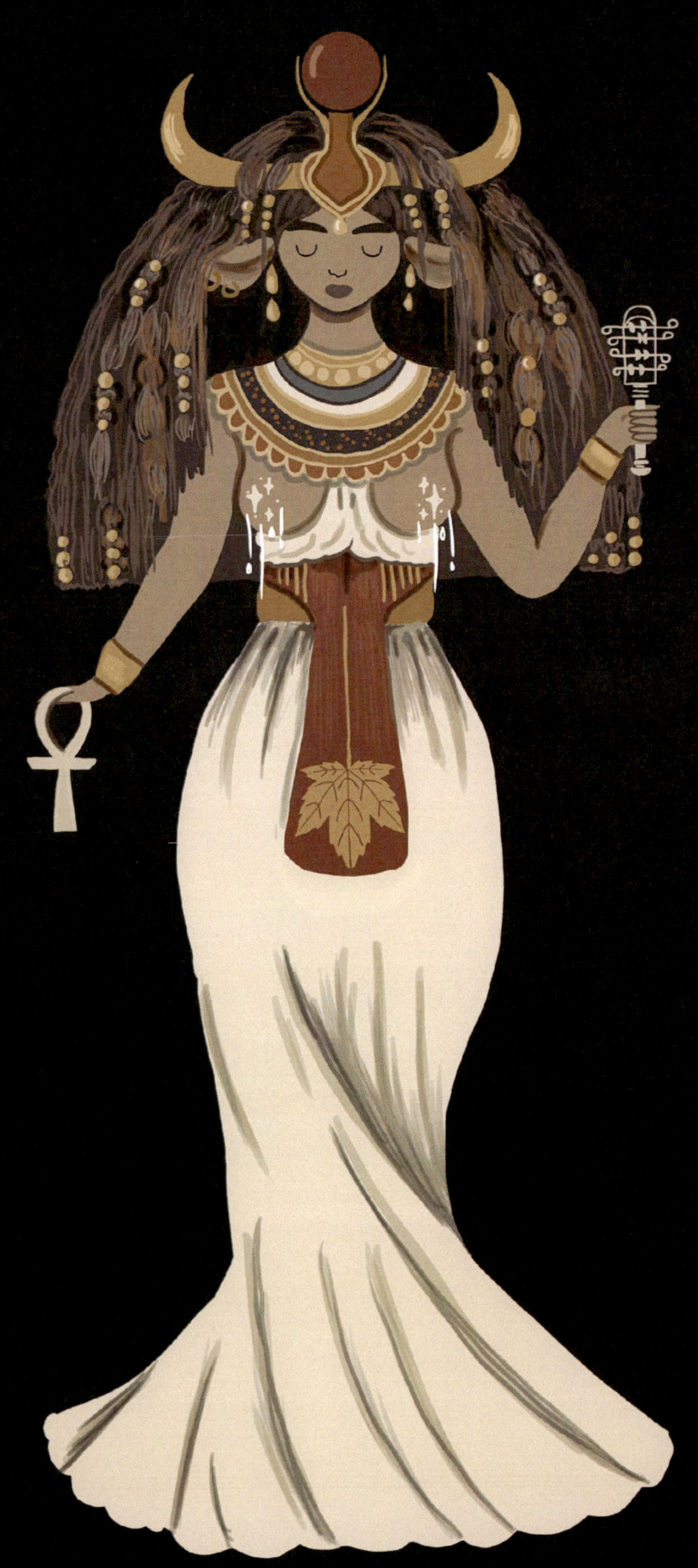

HATHOR

Hathor (*hah-thor*), known as "The Golden One" and "The Womb Above," stands as one of the most complex and beloved goddesses in the vast pantheon of ancient Egypt. Her spheres of influence were remarkably diverse, encompassing love, beauty, motherhood, fertility, music, dance, foreign lands, the sky, and even the afterlife. Hathor was known to be characterized as a woman with a cow's head, a warrior lioness under the guise of Sekhmet, a cobra, or a sycamore tree.

Hathor was tasked with providing food and care for the dead that would enter the Egyptian underworld. In contrast, she was also called upon during childbirth and linked to water, symbolizing the "beginnings of life," a connection that often draws comparisons to the Greek goddess Aphrodite. Another major aspect of Hathor was the "celestial cow," from whose breasts flowed the Milky Way, creating and nourishing all existence. She was commonly depicted as a humanoid cow with a pharaoh on her knee, symbolizing the divine sustenance and vitality bestowed upon the pharaoh, and by extension, humanity.

By the Old Kingdom (2686 BCE–2181 BCE), Hathor had emerged as a major deity. Her cult center was located at Dendera, where a magnificent temple complex was built as a testament to her power. Closely linked to the sky and the falcon-headed god Horus, whom she was sometimes considered mother or consort to, Hathor was also the patron of female royalty. Imagery resembling the goddess was found on the Narmer Palette, a ceremonial object dating back to the unification of Upper and Lower Egypt around 3100 BCE. This points to Hathor's prominence within the Egyptian belief system, even in antiquity.

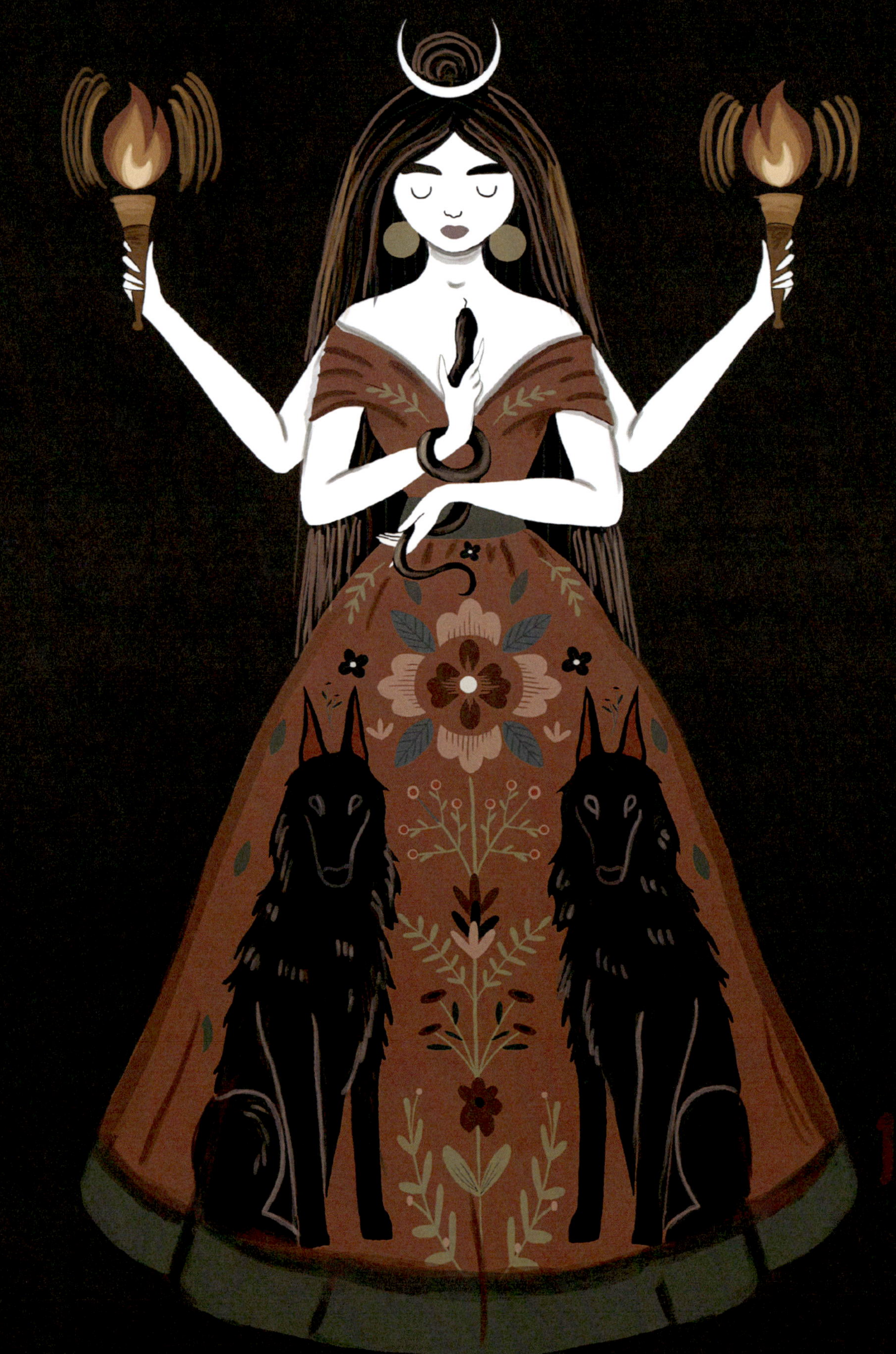

HECATE

"BY THE MISTRESS I WORSHIP…HECATE, DWELLING IN THE INMOST RECESSES OF
MY HEARTH,
NO ONE WILL BRUISE AND BATTER MY HEART AND GET AWAY WITH IT."

—EURIPIDES, *MEDEA*, LINES 394–397

Hecate (*hek-uh-tee*), both the "Light Bringer" (Hesiod, seventh century BCE) and the "Queen of the Night," (Valerius Flaccus, first century AD) is the goddess of crossroads, entranceways, witchcraft, and necromancy. Presiding over both life and death, she embodies their interconnectedness, reflecting the fundamental truth that one cannot exist without the other. She is usually depicted holding a torch in each hand, illuminating the dark and leading the less fortunate to safety. The actual origin of Hecate's mythos is widely unknown but predates several of her fellow deities. In the stories of Greek mythology, she was held in high regard by Zeus and assisted the goddess Demeter in the search for her missing daughter, Persephone.

Regardless of the location of her initial worship, most believe that the name Hecate, or Hekate, itself is born of Greek roots. Her name has various ties to the god Apollo and, in some texts, the goddess Artemis when translated as "the far reaching one" or the "worker from afar." Several theories exploring her origin also detail possible ties to Egypt based on a similar goddess named Heqet, or she could be from as far east as Turkey where citizens used variations of the name Hecate for their children.

In Greek mythology, she was said to have been born of Titans yet was the only one amongst them that retained her power after Zeus banished them to Tartarus. Such an act demonstrated the significant respect the Olympians held for Hecate, as Zeus even decreed her eternal safety from any harm. Under the guise of the "Crone," Hecate was worshipped alongside Demeter and Persephone in the form of the Triple Goddess: the embodiment of both female life through time and phases of the moon. Hecate was sometimes worshipped separately as the preeminent Triple Goddess in her own right, owing to her ancient depiction as being three physically separate, yet equal, deities.

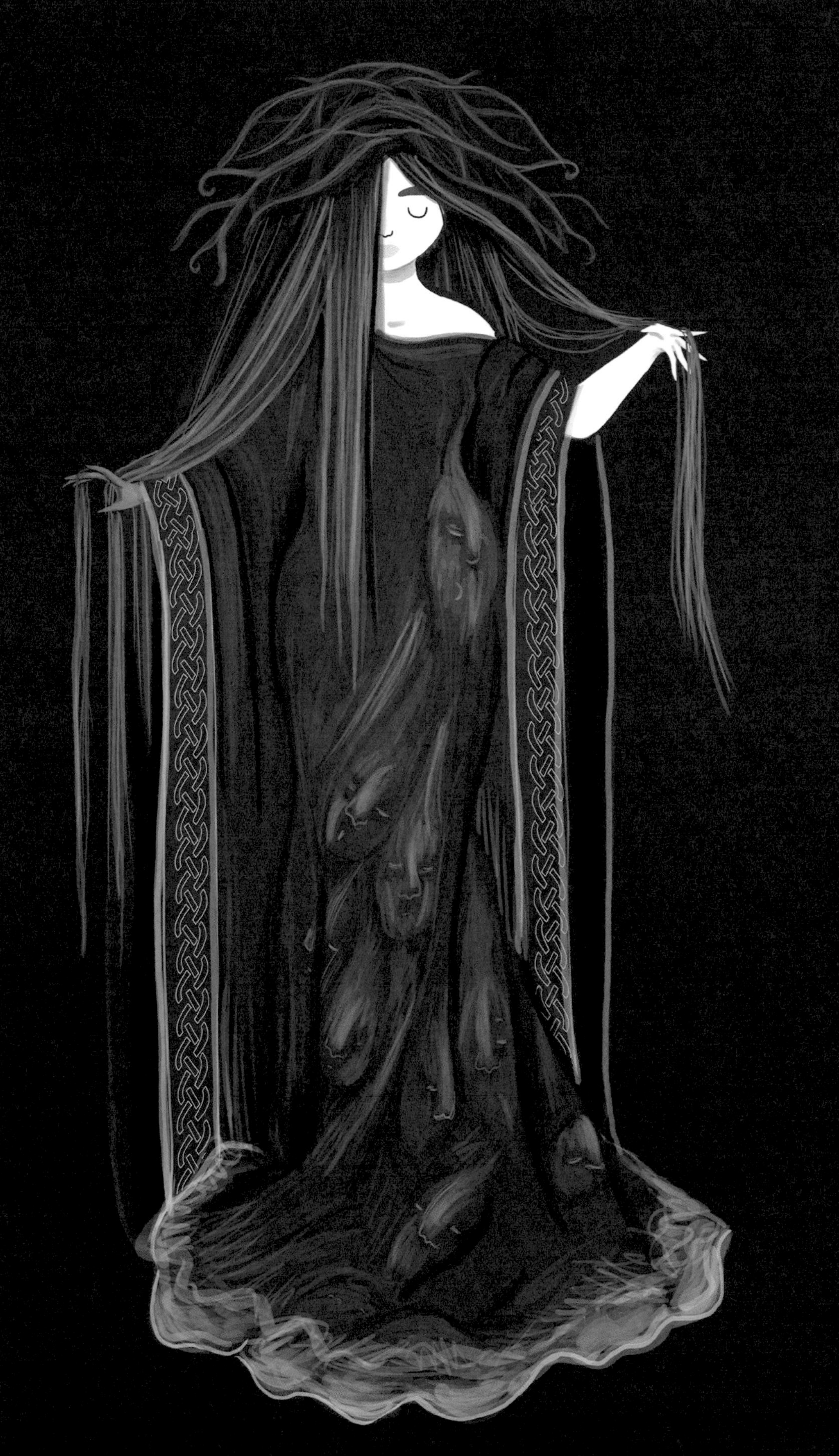

HEL

Hel (*hell*), daughter of the trickster demigod Loki and the giantess Angrboða, holds the title of queen of the dead within Norse mythology, ruling over Helheim, the "house of Hel." This realm serves as the destination for all who do not die in battle, contrasting with Valhalla, which is reserved for fallen warriors. Helheim is characterized not as a place of eternal torment nor as a paradise, but as a realm of passive existence and waiting, where the joys of the living world are absent.

Hel's own appearance visually reflects the nature of her domain. She is depicted as half-alive and half-dead, with decaying flesh on one side of her body and a healthy, youthful woman on the other. This striking duality serves to symbolize the transition from life to death, highlighting the beauty of the living in contrast with the inevitable decay of the dead. Her appointment to this role (as well as the fates of her monstrous siblings) was orchestrated by Odin. Upon learning of disastrous prophecies linked to Angrboða's children, Odin acted decisively, casting Jörmungandr into the sea, binding Fenrir, and consigning Hel to the depths of Helheim beneath the world tree Yggdrasil.

Despite her significant association with the realm of the dead, Hel occupies a surprisingly peripheral role in the majority of Norse myths, often appearing more as a custodian of the afterlife than an active participant in the sagas of gods and goddesses. A key distinction from underworld figures in other mythologies is that she does not sit in judgment or inflict punishments upon the deceased. However, Hel plays a significant role in the Norse apocalypse, Ragnarök, in which she is prophesied to emerge from her realm to lead an army of the dead in joining the forces of destruction.

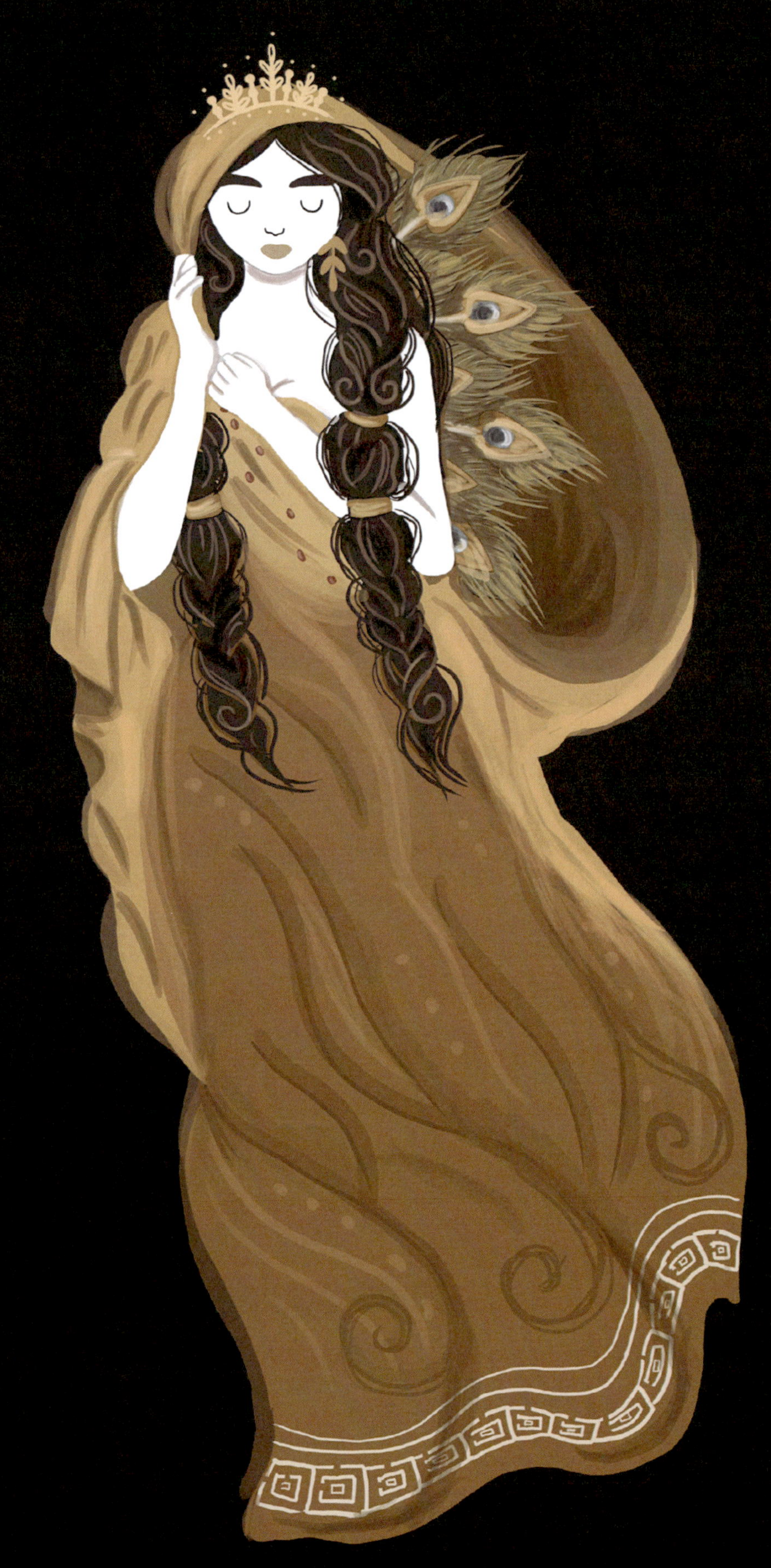

HERA

"Do as you will, great Zeus, high Lord of all. Yet I too am a god,
and of the same high lineage as yourself."

—*Iliad,* Book IV, lines 58–60

Hera (*hare-uh*), the majestic queen of the Olympian gods, is revered as the Greek goddess of marriage, women, and family. She presided over the sacred bonds of matrimony and the protection of women within its structure. Yet, Hera is equally renowned for her fiery jealousy, unshakeable wrath, and relentless pursuit of vengeance against those who crossed her, particularly the many seduced mortal women and illegitimate children that resulted from her husband Zeus's countless infidelities, creating a figure rife with enigmatic contradictions.

The turbulent power dynamics that sculpted the Olympian pantheon are intrinsic to Hera's lineage and rise to power. As the daughter of the Titans Kronos and Rhea, Hera and her siblings were swallowed at birth by their father, who was trying to avoid a prophecy that stated that he would be overthrown by his children. Hera's early mythology is largely defined by her emergence after Zeus's triumph over Kronos and her subsequent care by the sea deities Oceanus and Tethys. Her marriage to Zeus, often characterized by his relentless pursuit, served as a crucial act of consolidation for the burgeoning Olympian power, establishing a more stable hierarchy. As queen, Hera's presence not only legitimized Zeus's rule but also further solidified the dominance of the new generation of gods.

However, Hera's character is not solely defined by her marriage and jealousy. Representations of Hera frequently emphasize her regal beauty, grace, and dignity. She is often depicting wearing a diadem and holding a scepter. Furthermore, her sacred animals—the cow, peacock, and cuckoo—associated Hera with fertility, feminine power, and the natural world. While her primary domain was the protection of marriage and women (particularly wives and mothers), Hera's power also manifested as a fierce protectiveness against those who would violate these sacred bonds. The sanctity of marriage was paramount in ancient Greek society, and Hera staunchly upheld this institution.

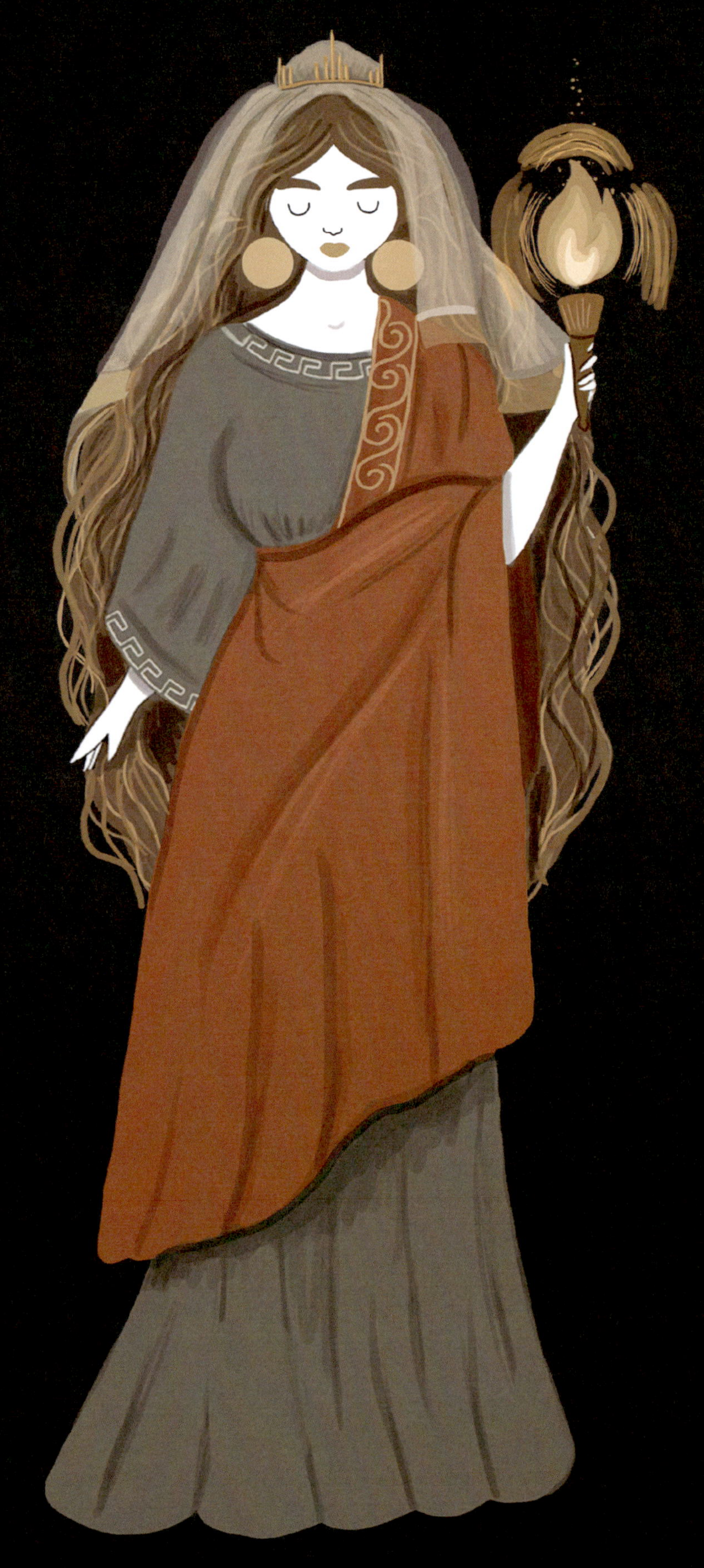

HESTIA

Goddess of the hearth, home, and family, Hestia (*hes-tee-uh*) represented the sacred center of ancient Greek life. While the narratives of her siblings, like Zeus and Poseidon, resonate with grand battles and heroic journeys, Hestia's influence, though less overtly dramatic, was undeniably profound in its own way. Her essence resided within the ever-burning hearth fire that symbolized domestic tranquility and the continuity of generations. The hearth was the heart of the Greek home, providing warmth, light, and the means to prepare food. By tending to the sacred fire, Hestia nurtured both the physical and spiritual well-being of the family.

The hearth served as the focal point of religious rituals, a gathering place for families, and a sanctuary for supplicants seeking protection. Hestia's presence imbued the hearth with an aura of sanctity. Every meal began and ended with offerings to her, ensuring unity and divine favor within the household. Hestia's role extended to the public realm as well. Each city maintained a central hearth dedicated to her; its initial flame would be brought from the new settlement's "mother city" to continue the connection to Hestia and each other, creating a symbolic link between the past and present.

Hestia was known for her gentle, unassuming nature and her commitment to chastity. While myths told of the Olympian gods' romantic exploits and rivalries, Hestia remained a virgin goddess. She famously resisted the advances of both Poseidon and Apollo, choosing instead to devote herself to the well-being of the divine and mortal realms. Consequently, she gained the respect of Olympus, a respect so profound they granted her the privilege of the initial offerings in every sacrificial rite.

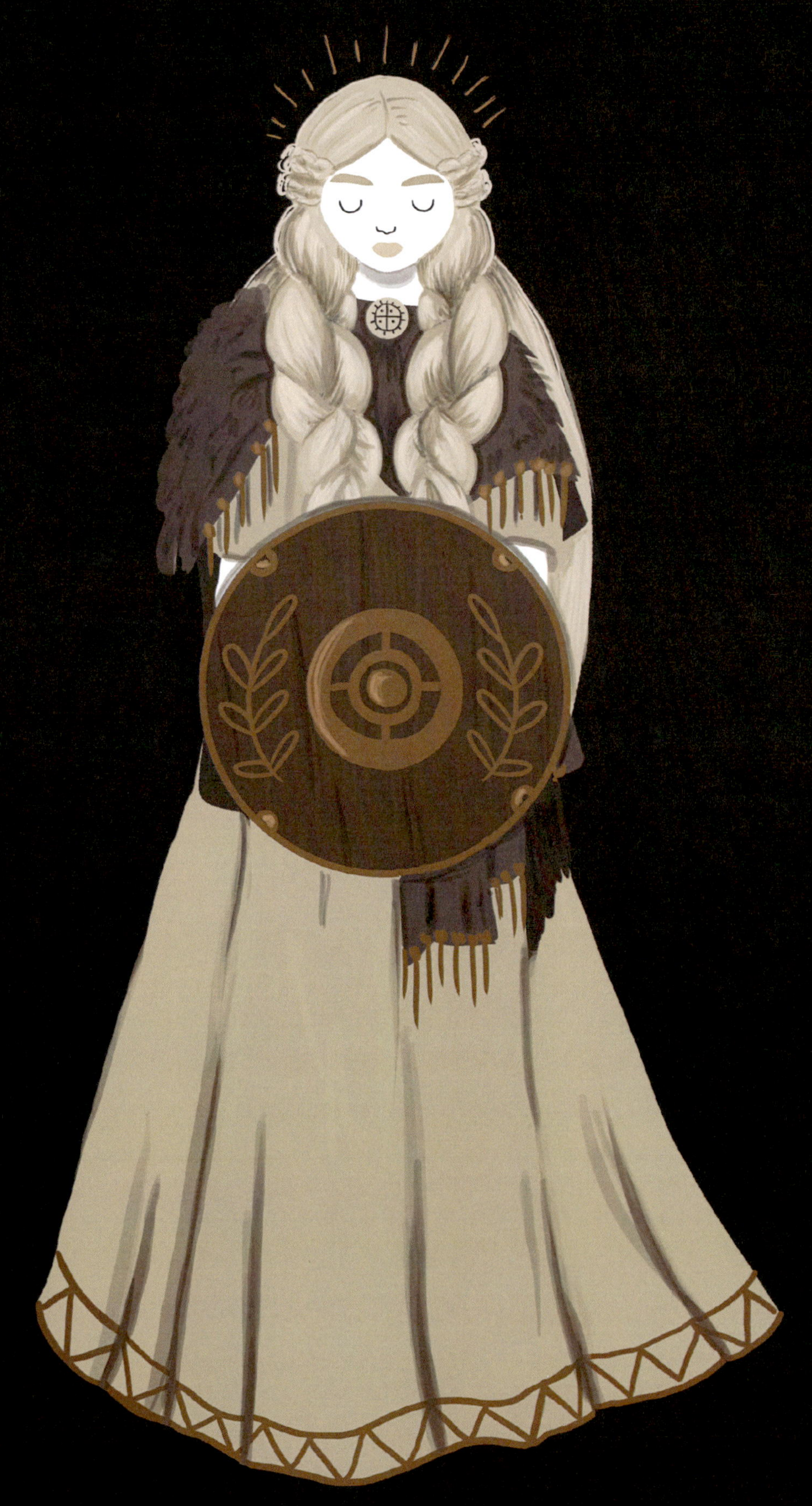

HLÍN

Norse goddess Frigg, wife to Aesir leader Odin the Allfather, was accompanied by a number of beautiful handmaidens who would attend to her needs in their own specific ways. Fulla carried her secrets, Gna delivered her messages, Lofn removed obstacles from the paths of lovers. Yet one maiden was mentioned within Norse literature more than the others: Hlín *(hl-inn)*, "the shield." She was the goddess of divine protection, tasked with hearing the lamentations of the world and providing solace to those Frigg wanted to save. With shield eternally in hand, Hlín was called upon to safeguard innocents from any harm that would befall them.

Hlín was especially protective over women in crisis. The name Hlín is likely derived from the Old Norse *hlína,* translating into "shelter" or "refuge," and even inspired the expression *hleinir,* meaning "peace and quiet." Hlín's protection extended to those who prayed to her. She would seek to soothe the misery of anyone mired in anguish, not to make them forget their troubles but to aid in healing through the stages of grief.

The Gylfaginning, a section within the *Prose Edda,* describes Hlín's duties: "Second is Hlín. She is given the task of protecting those people that Frigg wants to save from danger." This portrayal suggests a proactive form of guardianship, hinting that Hlín would intervene against threats. Moreover, Hlín is often interpreted as a goddess of consolation. She offers comfort to those in sorrow, wiping away tears and providing emotional refuge. This compassionate aspect further emphasizes her link to Frigg, who embodies nurturing and maternal qualities. Hlín guided the heavy-hearted through their distress, eventually encouraging a new hope for the future while respecting the mourning process as a necessary journey.

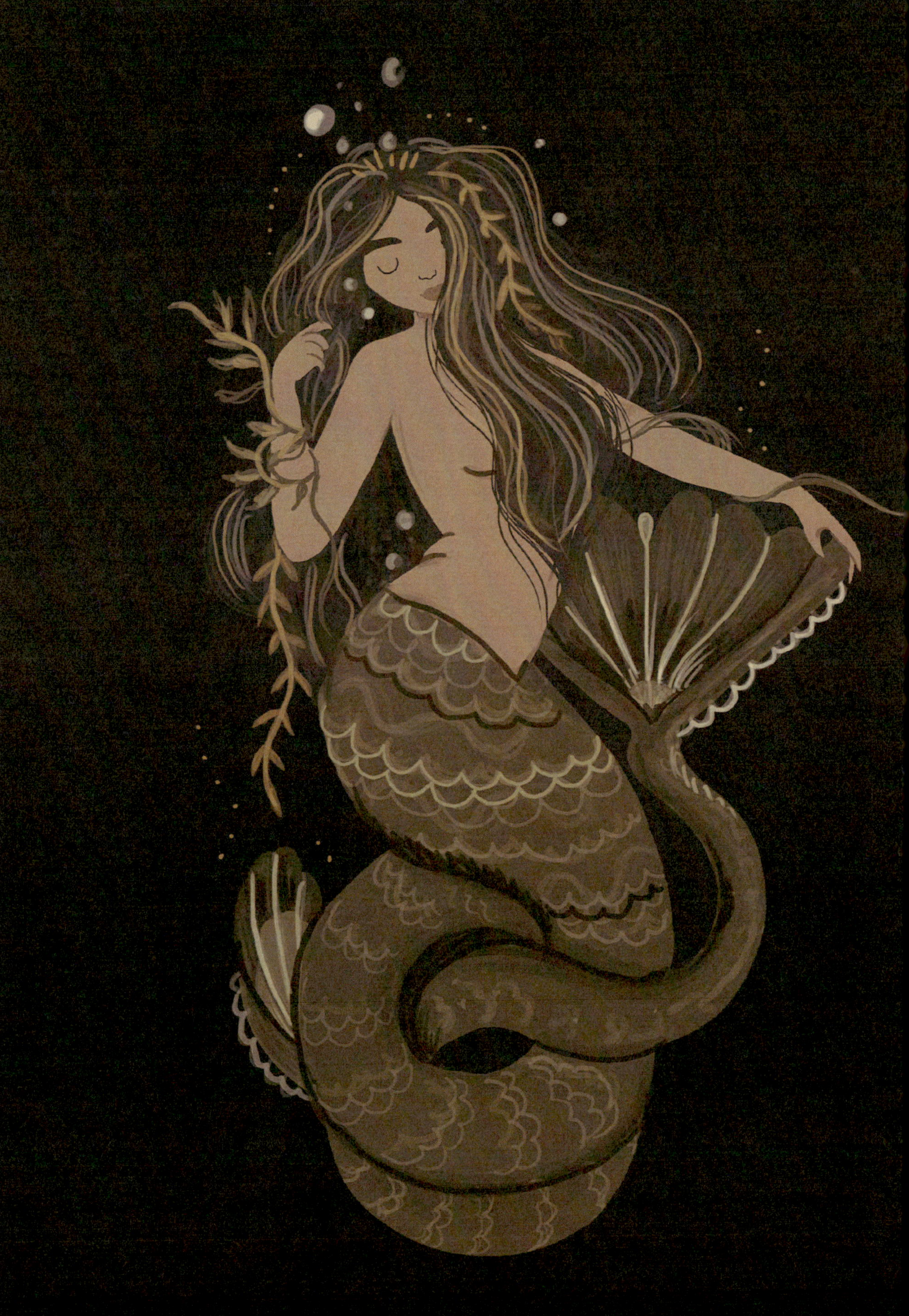

IARA

"The mother of God, lady of this village, you do not wish to be pressed..."

—**Eduardo de Almeida Navarro,** *Dicionário de Tupi Antigo* (2013)

Iara (*ee-ah-rah*), the "Lady of the Waters," is a significant figure whose legend is deeply woven into the cultural fabric of Brazil, embodying the blurring boundaries between the natural and supernatural. Her essence, evolving from indigenous roots, has become a potent symbol of feminine power, the allure of nature, and the perils of unchecked desire. Despite the historical influence of Christianity and the suppression of many indigenous beliefs, the figure of Iara has persisted, resonating deeply with the Brazilian people's intimate connection to the Amazonian rivers and their recognition of both the beauty and inherent dangers of the natural world.

Iara's origins are rooted in the rich cosmology of the Amazonian indigenous tribes. She is commonly envisioned as an alluring, long-haired, mermaid-like creature, sometimes described with green skin and eyes. Her name, likely derived from the Tupi words *y* ("water") and îara ("lady"), directly emphasizes her dominion over rivers and lakes. While earlier myths may have presented Iara in a more protective role associated with the life-giving power of water, her mythos progressively integrated themes of seduction and peril.

A central characteristic of Iara's legend is her irresistible beauty and mesmerizing voice, which she employs to draw individuals into the river's depths. This aspect of her myth symbolizes the dangers inherent in the alluring yet treacherous natural environment, often leading to the disappearance of those who succumb to her charms. Furthermore, Iara's legend encompasses various transformative origin stories. Some narratives present her as a tragic figure, detailing a past as a mortal woman who was either betrayed by her brothers or cursed by a powerful deity, leading to her metamorphosis into a water spirit. These variations add significant complexity to her portrayal, hinting at underlying themes of pain and longing beneath her seductive persona.

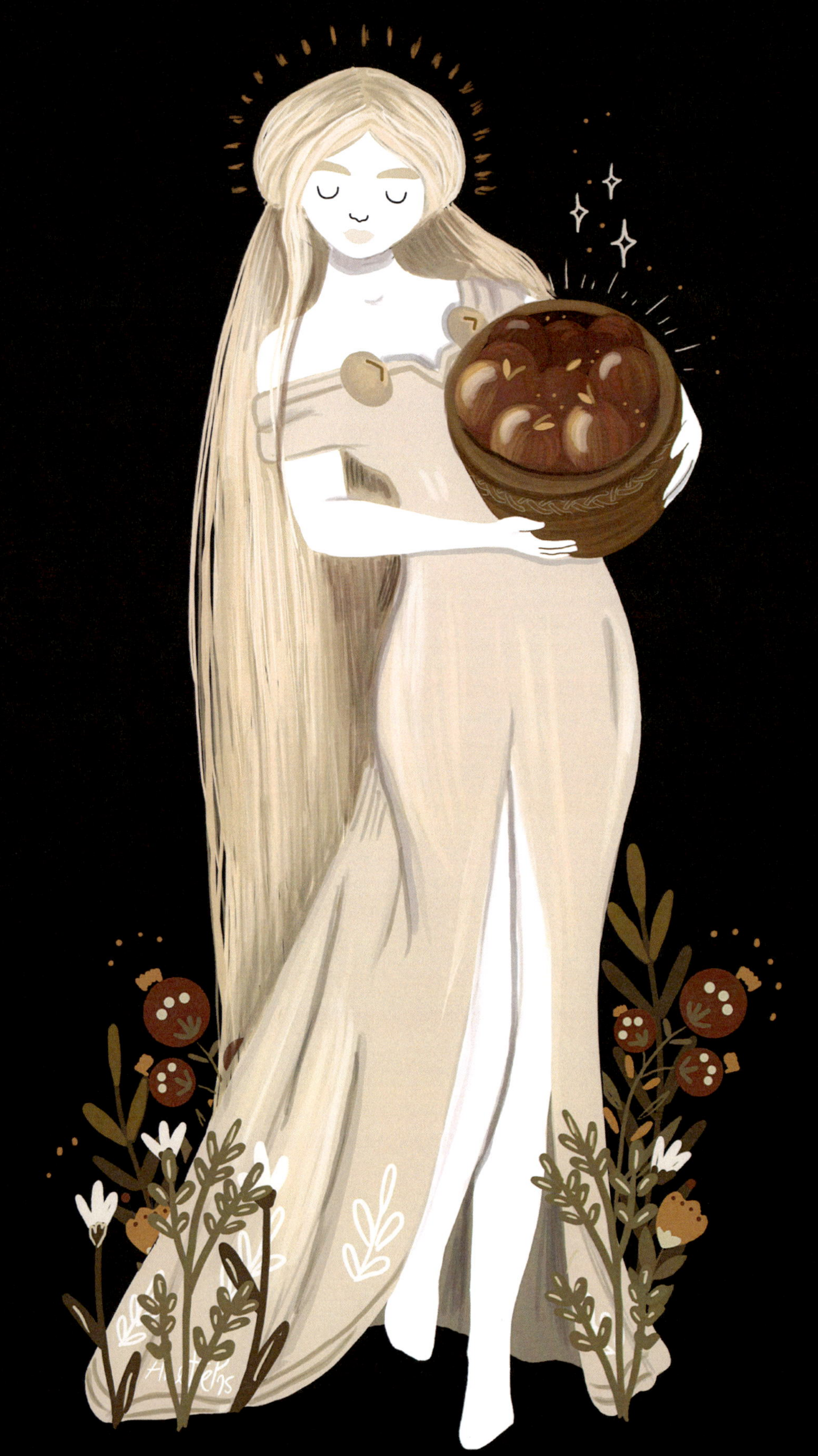

IÐUNN

As the Norse goddess of spring and rejuvenation, Iðunn (*ee-thun*) was specifically tasked with the guardianship of the magic apples of immortality, which were essential for the deities to preserve their eternal youth. Iðunn possessed exclusive access to these vital apples, which were typically depicted as being carried in a box made of ash and connected to Yggdrasil, the world tree encompassing all realms of existence. Highly respected amongst the Aesir, she was considered one of the Ásynjur, or "higher goddesses," and was frequently described as radiant and embodying vitality.

Her name's etymology remains uncertain, though some scholars propose a link to the Old Norse word *iðja*, meaning "to rejuvenate," directly reflecting her core function. Notably, Iðunn's mythological presence is largely confined to her role as the apples' guardian. This singular focus on the golden apples, with their power to defy aging and mortality, anchors her in the perpetual cycle of life, death, and renewal.

The critical importance of Iðunn's role is particularly highlighted by a notable myth, recounted in the poem *Haustlöng*, concerning her abduction by the giant Thjazi. This event directly resulted in the gods' rapid aging and weakening, demonstrating their fundamental reliance on her and her apples for their vitality. Her temporary absence can be understood as a metaphor for the harshness of winter, where nature appears barren and the forces of life diminish. Conversely, her subsequent rescue by the gods signifies spring's return and the ultimate triumph of vitality over decay. Moreover, Iðunn's association with apples resonates with broader cross-cultural symbolism, where apples often signify knowledge, temptation, and immortality. The Norse gods' dependence on her apples broadly reflects the universal theme of youth's fleeting nature and the anxieties surrounding aging and mortality, experienced by both divine and mortal beings.

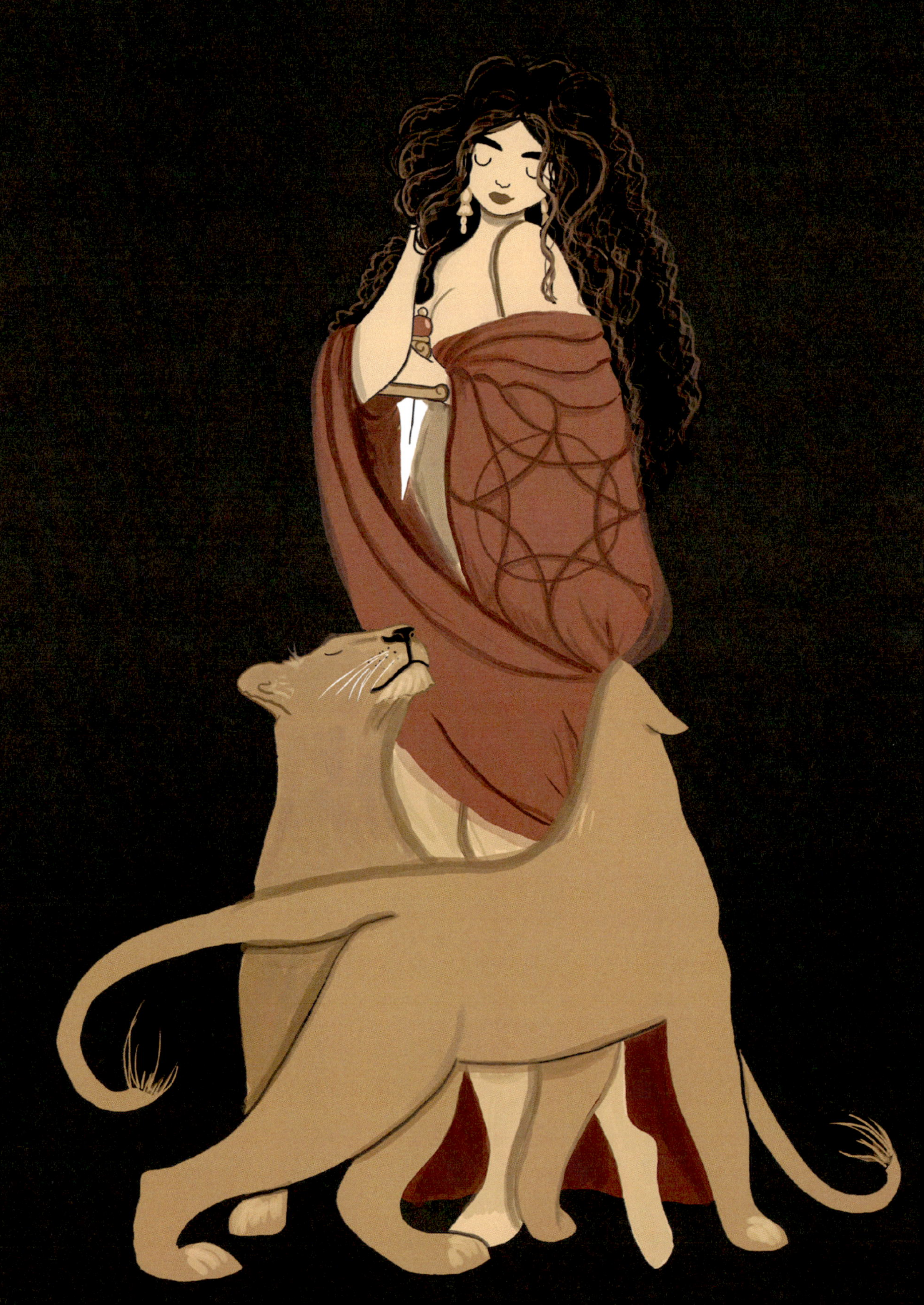

INANNA

"...THE LIGHT OF THE WORLD, INANNA, QUEEN OF THE HEAVENS AND OF ALL THE LANDS."

—SUMERIAN HYMN, "THE EXALTATION OF INANNA"

War and fertility goddess Inanna (*ih-nah-nuh*) is one of the oldest recorded deities from ancient Sumer, notable for her embodiment of autonomy and self-liberation. To the Akkadians, Babylonians, and Assyrians, she was known as Ishtar, a deity of a similar essence, and was often considered interchangeable with her counterpart. Inanna is usually accompanied by a lion, a symbol of great ferocity and courage, and is associated with the planet Venus. Despite her powerful and self-determined nature, the increasingly patriarchal and religious societal shifts of the time eventually led to her being deemed unfit as a primary deity in some religious practices.

Inanna's origins lie in the ancient Sumerian city-states, particularly Uruk, where she was worshipped as early as the fourth millennium BCE. Her symbols, the eight-pointed star and the ringed gatepost, adorned temples and artifacts, serving as a testament to her widespread worship. She consistently presented a paradox: functioning as a patroness of love and sensuality, while simultaneously being revered as a ferocious warrior. She represented a potent blend of sexuality, political power, untamed energy, and the transformative cycles of life and death.

A pivotal myth illustrating Inanna's command over transformation and the cycles of life and death is the *Descent of Inanna*, detailing her journey into the Underworld ruled by her dark sister Ereshkigal. This narrative, a prominent feature of ancient Mesopotamian literature, depicts Inanna shedding her worldly symbols of power as she traverses seven gates, ultimately confronting the forces of death. The story is widely interpreted as a metaphor for personal transformation, emphasizing the necessity of shedding old identities and confronting challenging aspects of existence to achieve rebirth. Beyond the divine realm, Inanna held immense political significance. Sumerian kings derived their legitimacy through association with her, often participating in sacred marriage rituals where they symbolically wed the goddess to secure her favor.

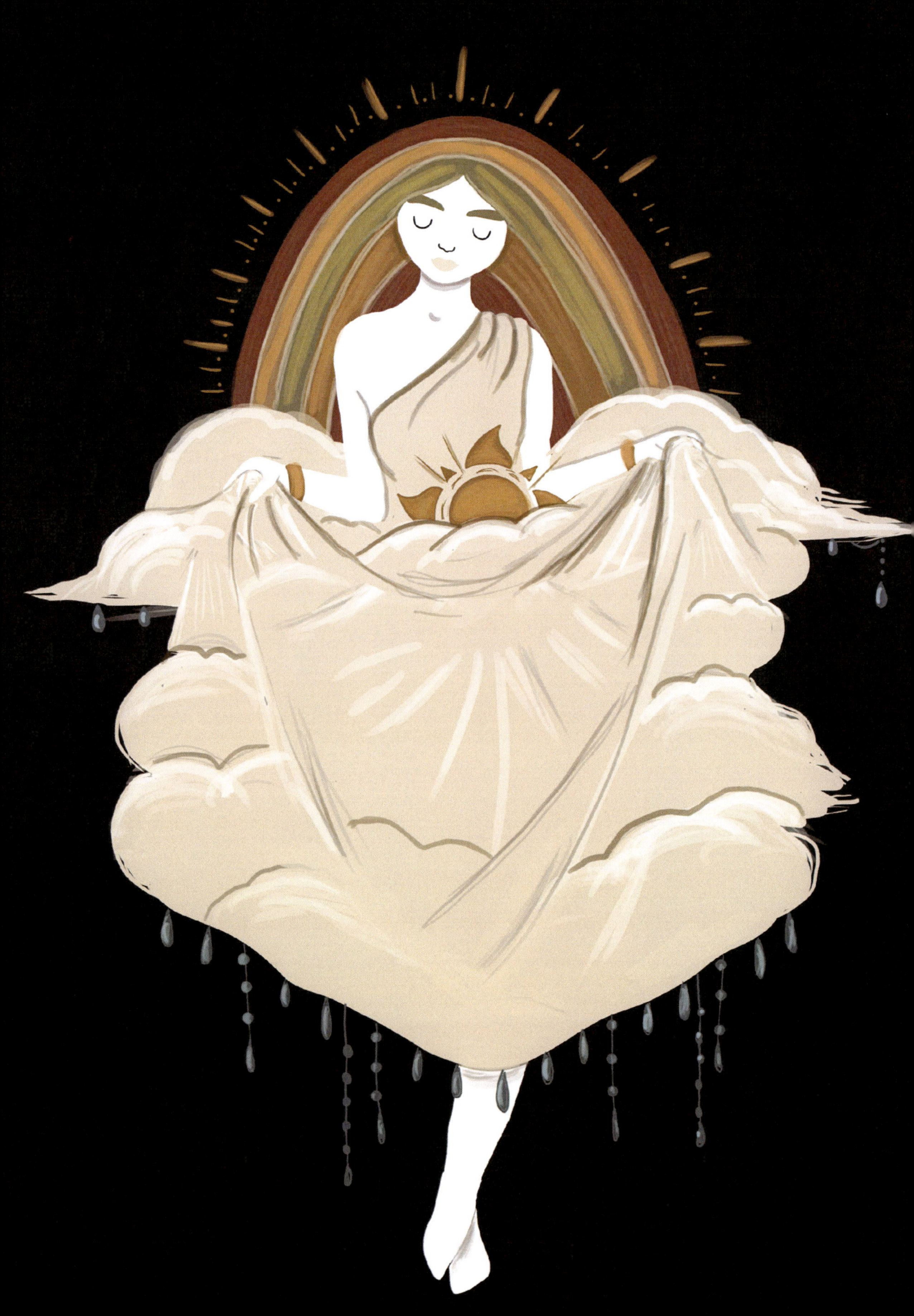

IRIS

"UP SPRANG FLEET-FOOTED IRIS AT HERA'S WORD, AND SPED UPON HER WAY."

—*ILIAD,* BOOK XV, LINE 144

Iris (*eye-riss*), the Greek goddess of the rainbow, primarily served as a symbol of hope and divine communication. Her role extended beyond the colorful atmospheric phenomenon, establishing her as a swift and trusted messenger of the gods, a vital link between the divine realm of Mount Olympus and the mortal world. As the herald of the Olympians, particularly Queen Hera, Iris moved with unparalleled speed and grace, her golden wings enabling rapid transit across the cosmos to deliver messages. Her celestial path was sometimes identified with the vibrant arc of a rainbow, serving as a visual testament to her ethereal journeys.

Unlike Hermes, her fellow messenger god, Iris is characterized not as a trickster or manipulator, but as a loyal conduit who conveyed the commands of the Olympians without distortion or personal agenda. Her parentage, being the daughter of Thaumas, a sea god known for wonder, and Electra, an Oceanid, places her at the intersection of sea and sky. This lineage serves as a fitting origin for a goddess whose function was to bridge these elemental domains.

While Iris is not the subject of many myths herself, her established functions are highlighted through her significant appearances in major Greek stories. During the *Titanomachy*, the war between the Titans and the Olympians, Iris's unwavering loyalty to the Olympians contrasted with her sister Arke's alignment with the Titans, with Iris's communication role for the victorious side often interpreted as symbolic of the triumph of order over chaos. Her divine speed proved an invaluable asset during the dynamic events of the Trojan War, to which she was frequently dispatched by Hera. In this context, her role was to ensure the swift and accurate relay of vital commands and strategic communications among the Olympian gods, who were actively intervening in the human conflict.

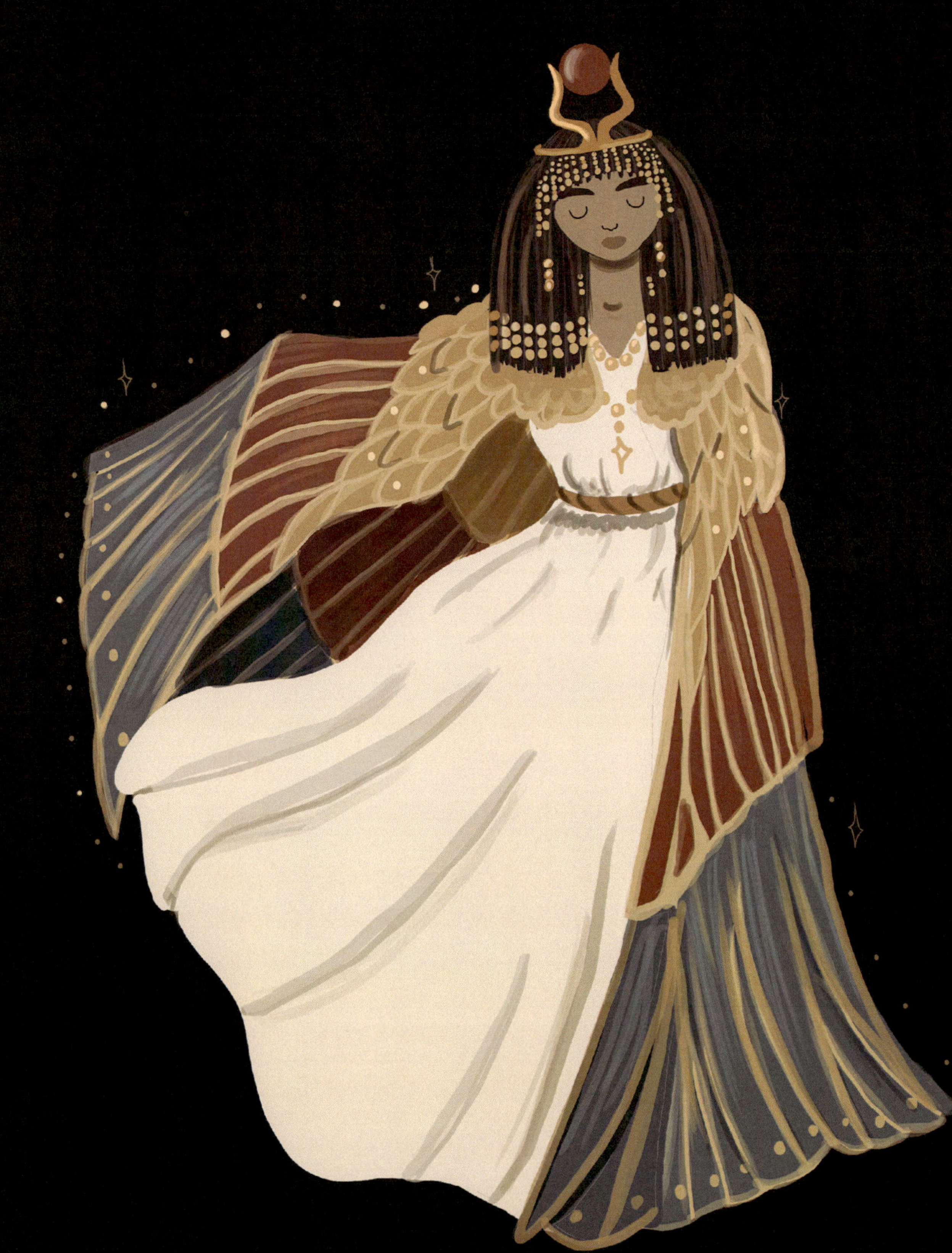

ISIS

"THE NOBLE IMAGE ISSUED FROM YOU, NOURISHES GODS AND MEN...
YOU FLOW FROM YOUR CAVERN FOR US IN YOUR TIME..."

—*THE LAMENTATIONS OF ISIS AND NEPHTHYS* (323 BCE)

The goddess Isis (*eye-siss*) is widely considered one of the most revered deities within Egyptian mythology. Her early prominence is evident from her mention around 2686 BCE in the foundational myth of Osiris, where her central role in her husband's resurrection, followed by the birth of their son Horus, established her as a powerful figure. Horus later became the falcon-headed god of kings and skies, securing a crucial lineage. Over time, the worship of Isis surpassed many others, and she became associated with supreme magical powers. Unlike deities with singular domains, Isis uniquely embodied a multitude of roles.

Isis's magical command extended to healing, protection, clairvoyance, and bestowing fertility upon those seeking her divine intervention. Her connection to the resurrection of Osiris significantly linked her to the ability to restore life and to safely shepherd the deceased into the afterlife. Through her divine maternity to Horus (who oversaw kings and pharaohs) and her partnership with Osiris (who watched over ancestors), Isis was distinguished as the embodiment of "mother and wife" of sovereignty.

The name "Isis" itself, incorporating the hieroglyphic symbol of the throne, directly linked her mythos to the personification of royal divinity and rule. Her origins can be traced back to the Old Kingdom period (circa 2686–2181 BCE) as part of the Heliopolitan Ennead, a pantheon of nine deities. Initially associated with the throne and possibly the Nile River, her prominence grew steadily throughout Egyptian history. With the subsequent fall of Egypt to Greek rule in 323 BCE, Isis became associated with goddesses such as Persephone, Artemis, and Demeter. Her cult later thrived and spread throughout the Mediterranean world during the Roman Empire, often merging with local deities. This remarkable adaptability and resonance with universal themes like love, motherhood, and the afterlife ensured her continued worship for centuries.

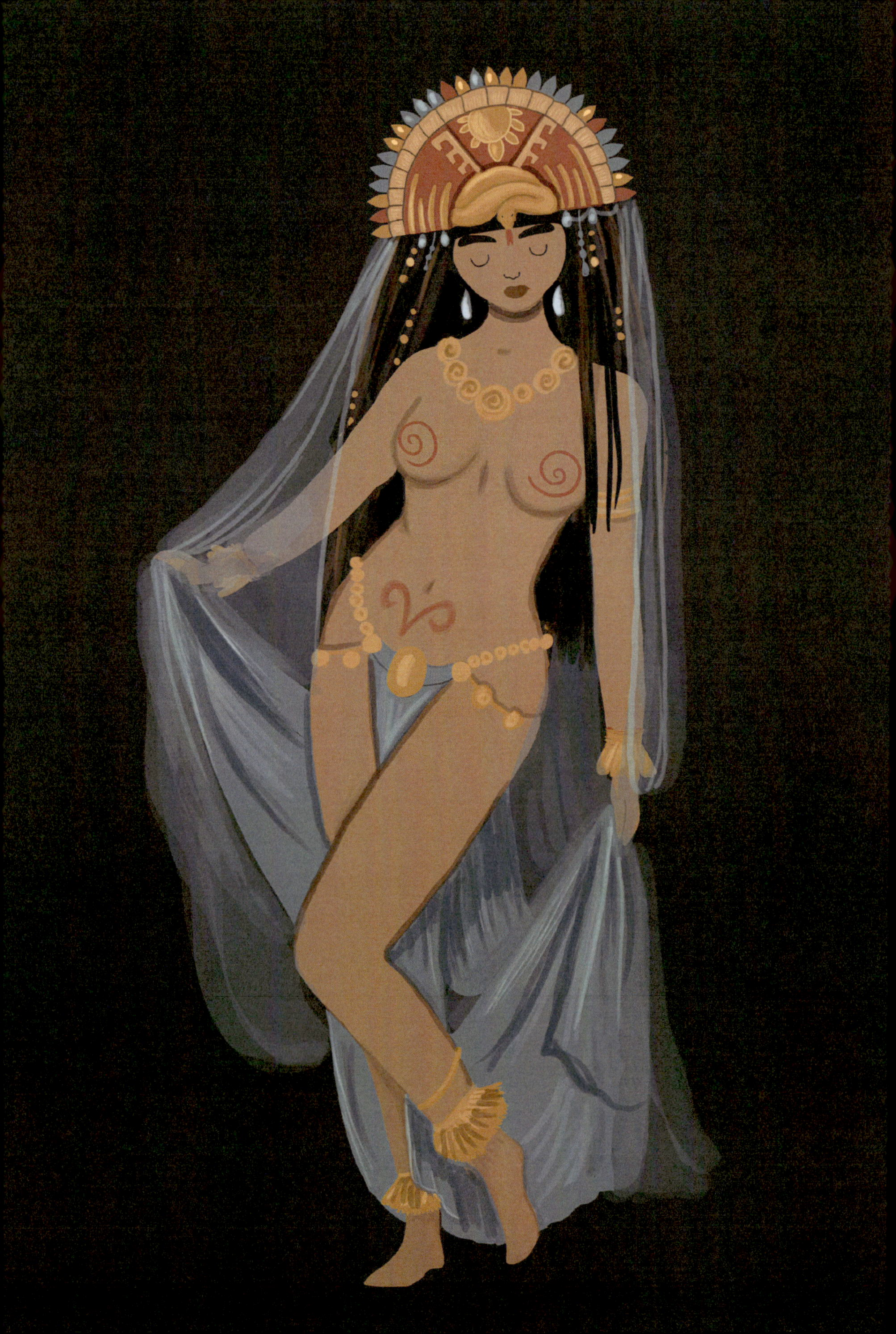

IX CHEL

"…FOR SHE APPEARS TO BE A GODDESS OF THE FLOOD AND WORLD DESTRUCTION."

—KARL ANDREAS TAUBE, *THE MAJOR GODS OF ANCIENT YUCATAN* (1992)

Ix Chel (*eesh shell*), the Mayan goddess of sex, healing, and creativity, directly represents the waters of life, encompassing both the sea and the creative potential within the womb. Her waters can also manifest as a destructive force, bringing torrential rains, hurricanes, and floods. Often associated with the moon, Ix Chel was revered as a multifaceted goddess in the Mayan pantheon, holding a significant role in the spiritual and cultural lives of the Maya people. Her mythology includes narratives in which, after a relationship with the sun god, she emerges as a fierce advocate for women in crisis, symbolizing courage and solace.

The origins of Ix Chel's worship trace back to the Preclassic period of Mayan civilization, with evidence of her veneration found in archaeological sites across the Maya region. Her name, meaning "Lady Rainbow," evokes a profound connection to the celestial realm and the natural world. One of Ix Chel's primary roles was as a goddess of fertility and childbirth, with women seeking her blessings for conception, safe delivery, and the well-being of their children. She was also prominently associated with weaving, a skill highly valued in Mayan society, where the intricate patterns woven into textiles represented the interconnectedness of life and the cosmic order.

Ix Chel's connection to water was another essential aspect of her worship. As a life-giving force, water was critical for the sustenance of crops and the well-being of communities. She was believed to control the rains and was frequently depicted with a water jug or vessel. Despite the Spanish conquest and the suppression of indigenous religions, the veneration of Ix Chel persisted in various forms, demonstrating her enduring power within Mayan culture.

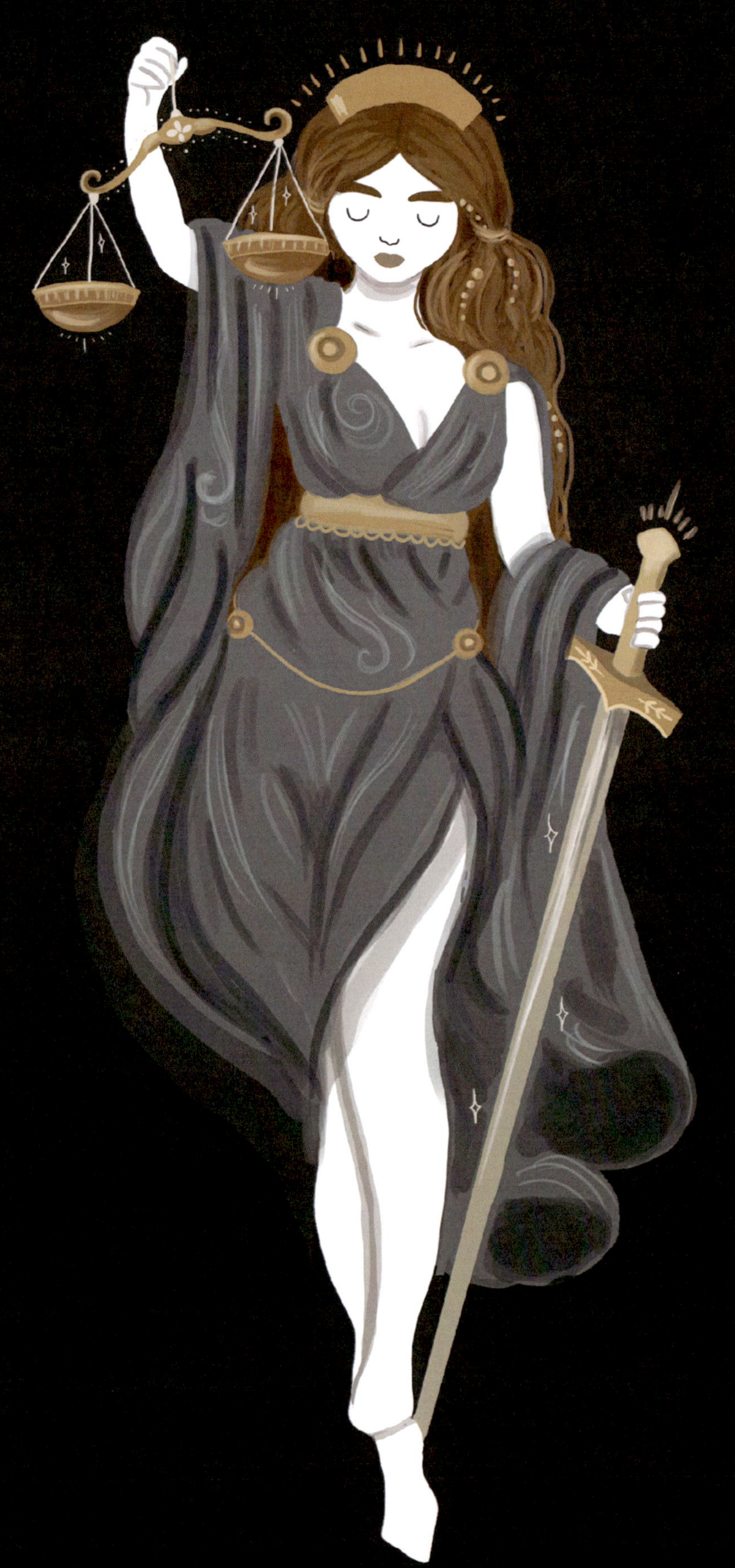

JUSTITIA

"BLINDFOLDED, SHE WEIGHS THE EVIDENCE WITH IMPARTIAL SCALES,
AND WITH THE SWORD OF AUTHORITY, SHE ENFORCES WHAT IS RIGHT."

—MARCUS TULLIUS CICERO, *DE OFFICIIS*, BOOK III, CHAPTER 6

As the Roman goddess of justice, Justitia (*jus-tish-ee-uh*) holds a significant place in both ancient mythology and modern legal systems. While not as prominent as many other Roman deities, she has transcended time and continues to be emblematic of justice and fairness in legal contexts around the world. In Roman mythology, Justitia was the personification of justice itself. She was often depicted as a blindfolded woman carrying scales and a sword. The blindfold represented impartiality, the scales symbolized the weighing of evidence, and the sword signified the power to enforce the law. This depiction, which originated in Roman art and sculpture, has become so deeply ingrained in our understanding of justice that she can still be spotted in courthouses and legal imagery today.

The origins of Justitia can be traced back to earlier Greek goddesses, such as Themis and Dike, who also embodied justice and lawfulness. However, Justitia emerged as a distinct figure in Roman culture, particularly during the reign of Emperor Augustus. Augustus promoted the values of justice and fairness, and Justitia became a symbol of his commitment to these principles. She was depicted on coins and other official objects, solidifying her role as a patron of the legal system. During the Renaissance, Justitia experienced a resurgence in popularity. Artists and philosophers rediscovered classical mythology and began to incorporate its figures and themes into their works. Justitia, with her timeless symbolism, became a popular subject for sculptures and paintings.

The worship of Justitia likely involved rituals and offerings aimed at seeking her favor and ensuring just outcomes in legal disputes. However, the specifics of her cult are not well-documented. Nevertheless, her essence resonated with the Roman people, and her image persists to this day.

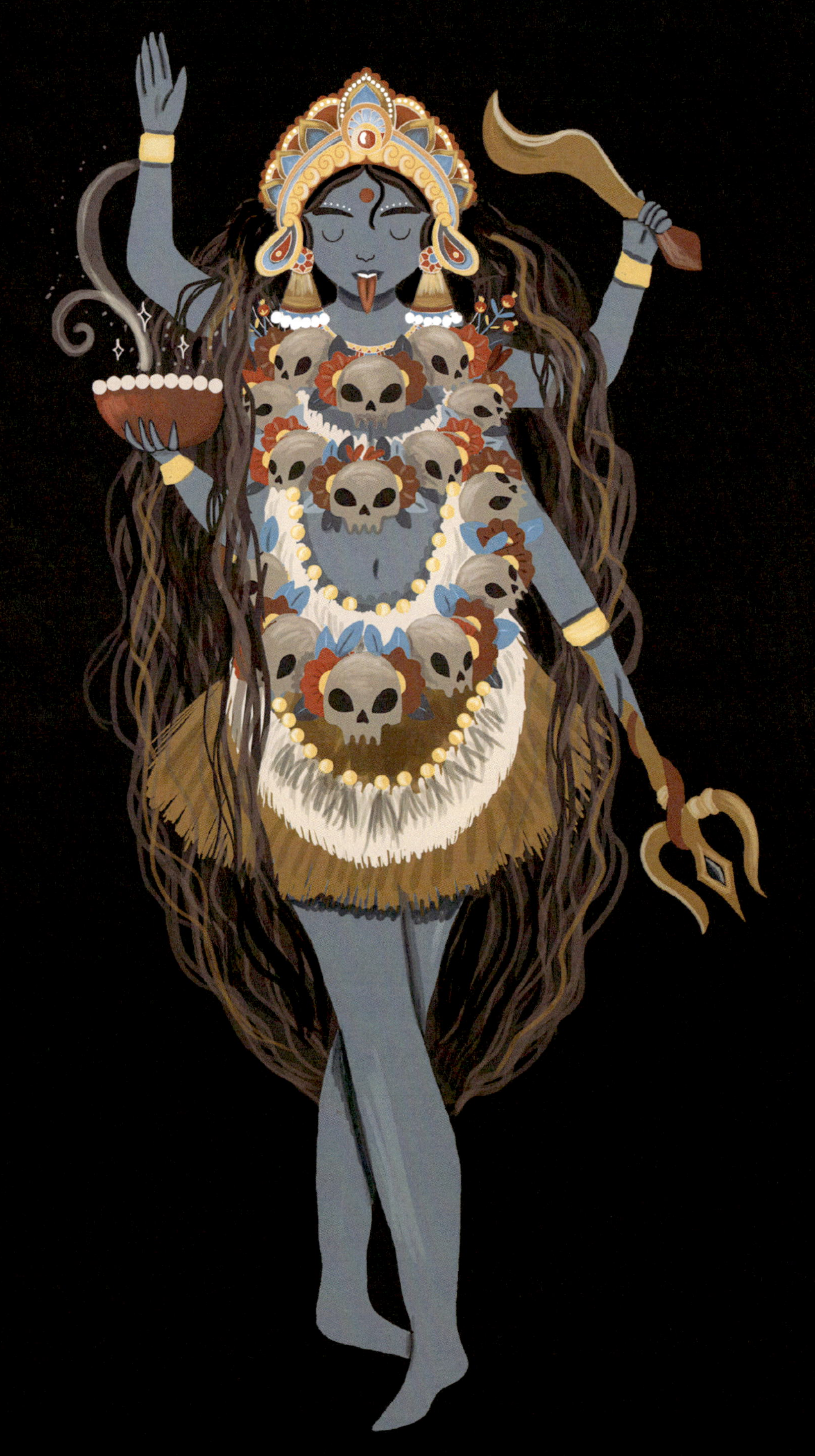

KALI

"WITH A DREADFUL ROAR, KALI, HER FACE DISTORTED WITH FURY,
SPRANG UPON THOSE GREAT DEMONS AND DEVOURED THEM."

—*DEVI MAHATMYA,* CHAPTER 8, VERSE 63

During the Gupta period (fourth to sixth centuries CE), the worship of Shakti, the divine feminine power, gained prominence in Hinduism. As a result, Kali (*kah-lee*) as a manifestation of Shakti became an important deity in Shaktism. Her role expanded beyond destruction and death to also encompass creation and transformation. Often depicted with a fierce expression, black or blue skin, a necklace of skulls, and a protruding tongue, Kali's fearsome appearance underscores her role as a protector and mother goddess. Kali's origins can be traced back to ancient Vedic texts, where she is associated with the goddess Ratri, the personification of night, and Nirriti, the goddess of destruction.

The *Devi Mahatmya,* a sixth-century Sanskrit text, is a pivotal work in the development of Kali's mythology. In this text, Kali emerges as a fierce warrior goddess, vanquishing demons and protecting the righteous. Her association with the battlefield and violence solidified her reputation as a powerful and awe-inspiring deity. In the medieval period, Kali's worship continued to evolve. The tantric tradition, with its emphasis on ritual practices and esoteric knowledge, further shaped Kali's iconography and mythology. The *Kalika Purana,* a ninth-century Sanskrit text, provides detailed descriptions of rituals and practices in honor of Kali, as well as her various forms and manifestations.

Kali's powerful ties to cremation grounds, places of ultimate transformation and the release of the physical form, alongside her significant role as the devourer of time, which relentlessly drives all toward change and eventual end, further emphasized her complex connection to both death as a transition and the destructive forces that pave the way for renewal. Kali's popularity has also spread beyond India. In the West, she has been adopted by New Age spiritualists and pagans, who see her as a symbol of transformation and personal growth, as well as a representation of female empowerment and strength.

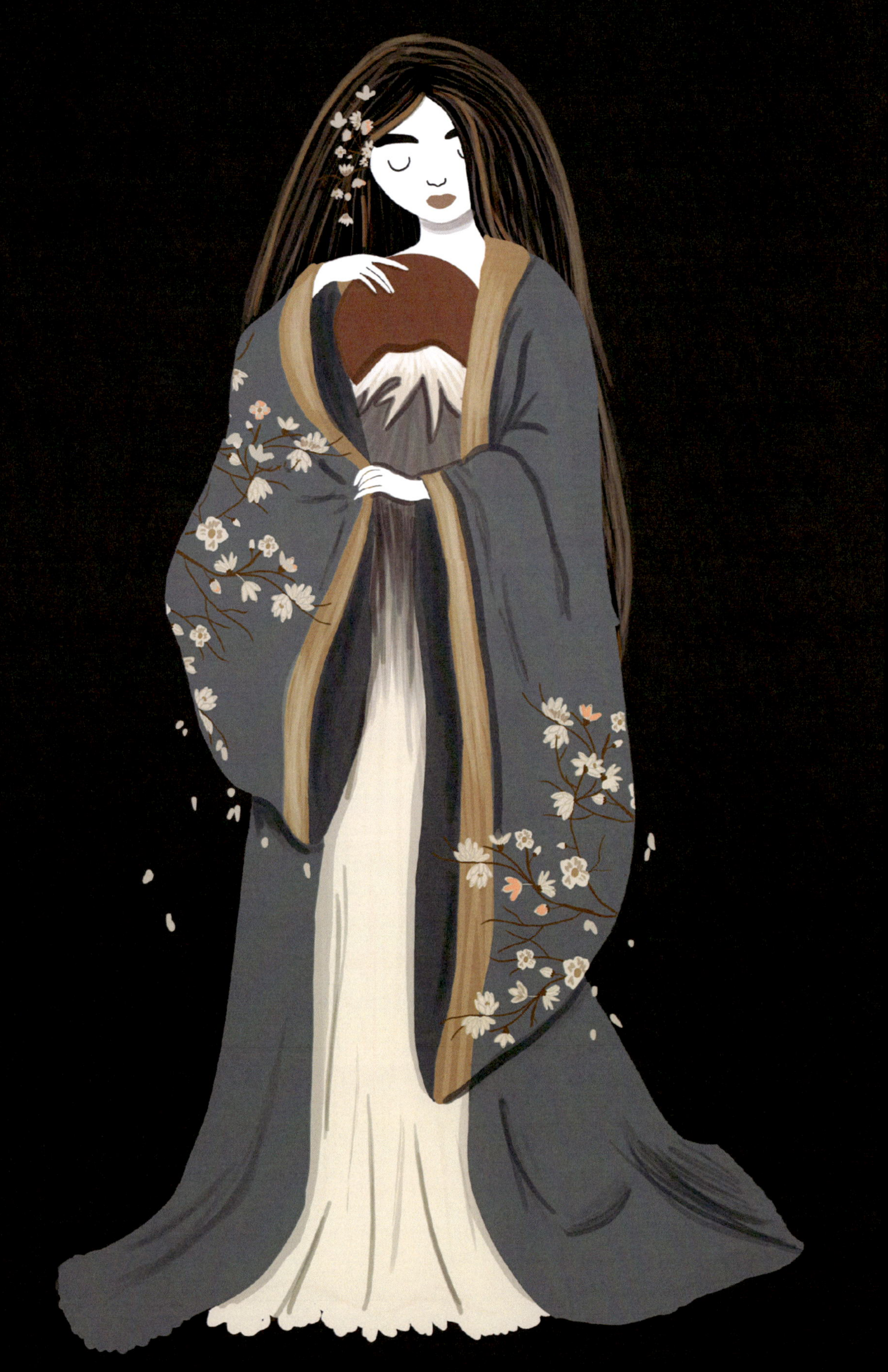

KONOHANASAKUYA-HIME

"...THEREUPON HE MET A VERY BEAUTIFUL MAIDEN."

—*KOJIKI,* BOOK 1

Within Japanese mythology, Konohanasakuya-hime (*koh-noh-hah-nah-sah-koo-yah hee-meh*) is the living embodiment of Mount Fuji, as well as the goddess of all volcanoes. Her name translates to "the cherry-tree blooming princess," a symbol of delicate mortal existence upon the earth. Her presence permeates various aspects of Japanese life, from religious practices to artistic representations and seasonal celebrations. Konohanasakuya-hime's mythological origins are deeply intertwined with the narratives of the *Kojiki* and *Nihon Shoki*, the two oldest chronicles of Japanese history. According to these texts, she is the daughter of the mountain god, Ohoyamatsumi, and is often associated with delicate beauty, feminine grace, and the ephemeral nature of life.

As the goddess of volcanoes, Konohanasakuya-hime embodies both the destructive and creative forces of nature. While volcanic eruptions are a manifestation of her immense power, the fertile volcanic soil nourishes the land and gives rise to new life. One of the most prominent associations with Konohanasakuya-hime is her connection to her namesake cherry blossom, or sakura. The annual blooming of cherry blossoms is a highly anticipated event in Japan, indicating the arrival of spring. These delicate blossoms, however, last only for a brief period, serving as a poignant reminder of the impermanence of all things.

Konohanasakuya-hime guards Mount Fuji to keep it from erupting, and it is said that anyone who approaches Mount Fuji is also approaching the goddess; therefore their approach must be undertaken with the utmost respect. Her association with Mount Fuji has also made her a popular figure in Shinto shrines located around the mountain. These shrines, collectively known as Asama or Sengen shrines, serve as important pilgrimage sites for worshippers seeking blessings for fertility, safe childbirth, and protection from natural disasters. To celebrate their goddess, the followers of Konohanasakuya-hime undertake the long journey to the summit of the mountain to greet her.

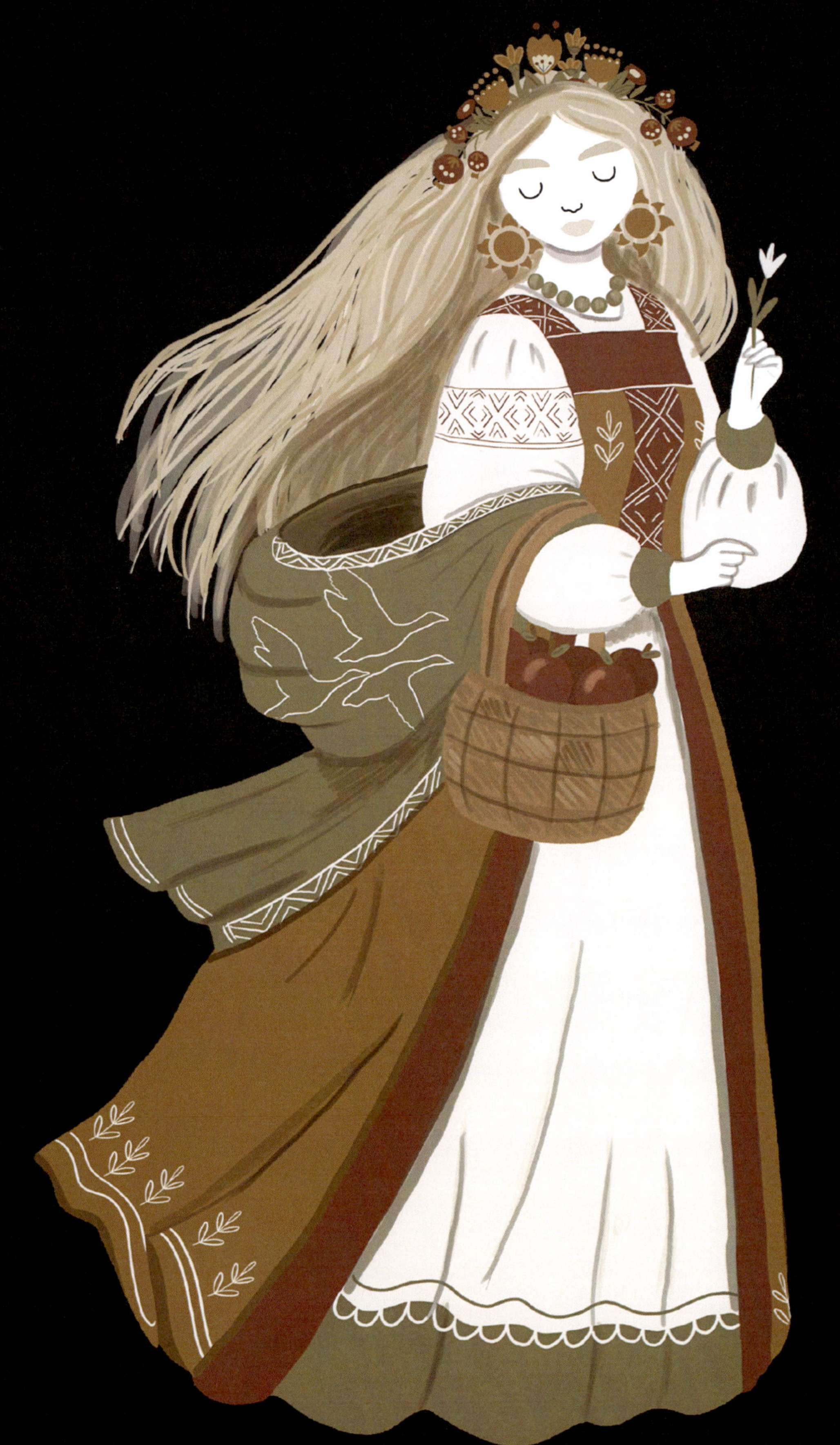

LADA

"The torch is burning, the wheat is growing, amen, amen..."

—**Radmila Petrović**, "Some Aspects of Formal Expression
in Serbian Folk Songs" (1970)

The Slavic goddess of love, beauty, and spring, Lada (*lah-dah*) lives deep within the earth and only emerges during the vernal equinox to signal the end of winter. She is said to travel across Europe and the Baltics to inspire happiness and harmony amongst her followers, blessing marriages and households with peace and bliss. The earliest documented mentions of Lada date back to the fifteenth century, primarily in Polish church records condemning pagan practices. These records associate Lada with spring rituals and festivities, suggesting she might have been a deity of fertility and renewal. In later centuries, references to Lada appear in various texts, including folk songs, chronicles, and ethnographic accounts.

Some scholars argue that her name might derive from the Slavic word *lad*, meaning "harmony" or "agreement," and that she might be a personification of love and marital concord rather than an actual goddess. Others suggest that Lada could be a later creation, potentially influenced by classical mythology or a misinterpretation of folk traditions. That said, her name appears in various Slavic languages, suggesting widespread recognition and veneration. In Russia, when a couple has found themselves happily married, it is said that they "live in Lada." In some texts, she has a masculine counterpart known as Lado, and they are seen as the divine twins. Her association with spring rituals and fertility aligns with the broader patterns of pre-Christian Slavic beliefs, which often centered on agricultural cycles and the natural world. It has been proposed that the absence of earlier written sources about Lada could be attributed to the lack of literacy and the predominantly oral transmission of knowledge in early Slavic societies.

The various interpretations and debates surrounding Lada highlight the challenges of reconstructing ancient mythologies based on fragmented and often contradictory sources. She represents a complex interplay between pre-Christian Slavic beliefs, Christian influences, and folk traditions.

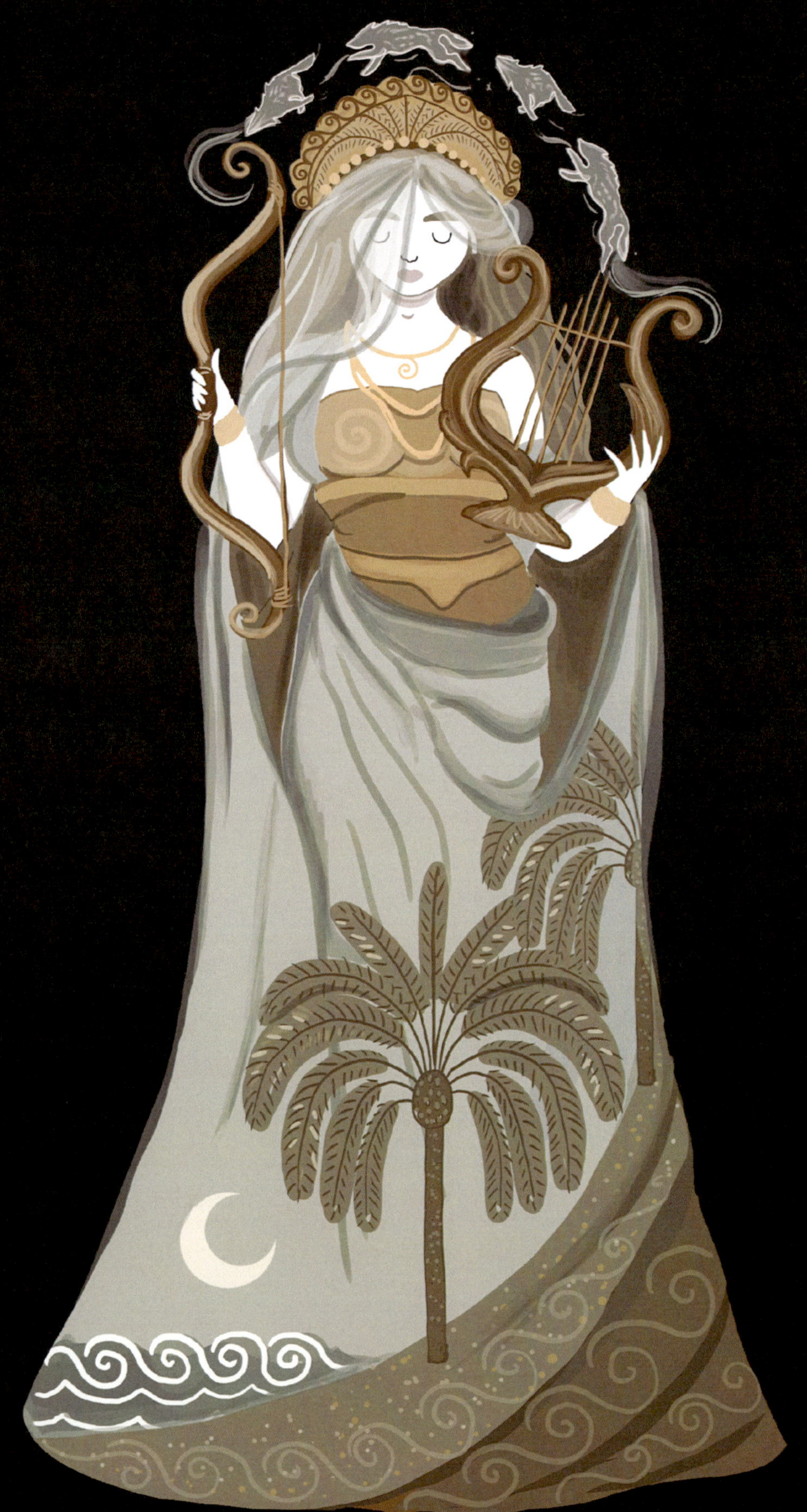

LETO

"FOR ALL LANDS SHRINK IN FEAR, AND NONE IS WILLING TO RECEIVE MY SON,
GREAT THOUGH HE BE, UNTIL I COME TO YOU."

—*HOMERIC HYMNS,* HYMN III ("TO DELIAN APOLLO"), LINES 50–57

The Greek goddess of maternity, modesty, and kindness, Leto (*lee-toh*) is the revered mother of the powerful twin deities, Apollo and Artemis. While the specific origins of her name remain somewhat obscure, many historians theorize it derives from the word *lethô*, meaning "to move unseen." Her mythological experiences primarily underscore themes of persecution, perseverance, and ultimately, triumph as a mother and protector of her children.

Leto's parents are the Titans Coeus and Phoebe, establishing her as a powerful figure within the primordial generation of deities. Her affair with Zeus often brought her into direct conflict with his wife, Hera, whose wrath was notoriously invoked against Zeus's many partners. This divine antagonism resulted in Hera's decree that Leto would be denied childbirth on any land. Consequently, Leto desperately searched for a refuge, eventually finding sanctuary on the island of Delos, which was said to be floating on top of the sea and so didn't count as "land." There she successfully gave birth to Apollo and Artemis. This pivotal narrative highlights the extreme challenges Leto faced in her children's births.

In Greek mythology, Leto's identity is profoundly shaped by her role as a mother. This central characteristic provides crucial insight into her position within the Olympian hierarchy. Her fierce and unwavering protection of her twin children, Apollo and Artemis, stands as a testament to a maternal love that overrode the often self-serving nature of the gods. Depicted as a serene and nurturing figure, Leto was frequently shown offering guidance, comfort, and unwavering support to her offspring as they navigated their burgeoning divine powers and faced various trials. The lengths to which she went to shield Apollo and Artemis, enduring hardship and seeking refuge across the ancient world, powerfully illustrate a mother's enduring love and determination.

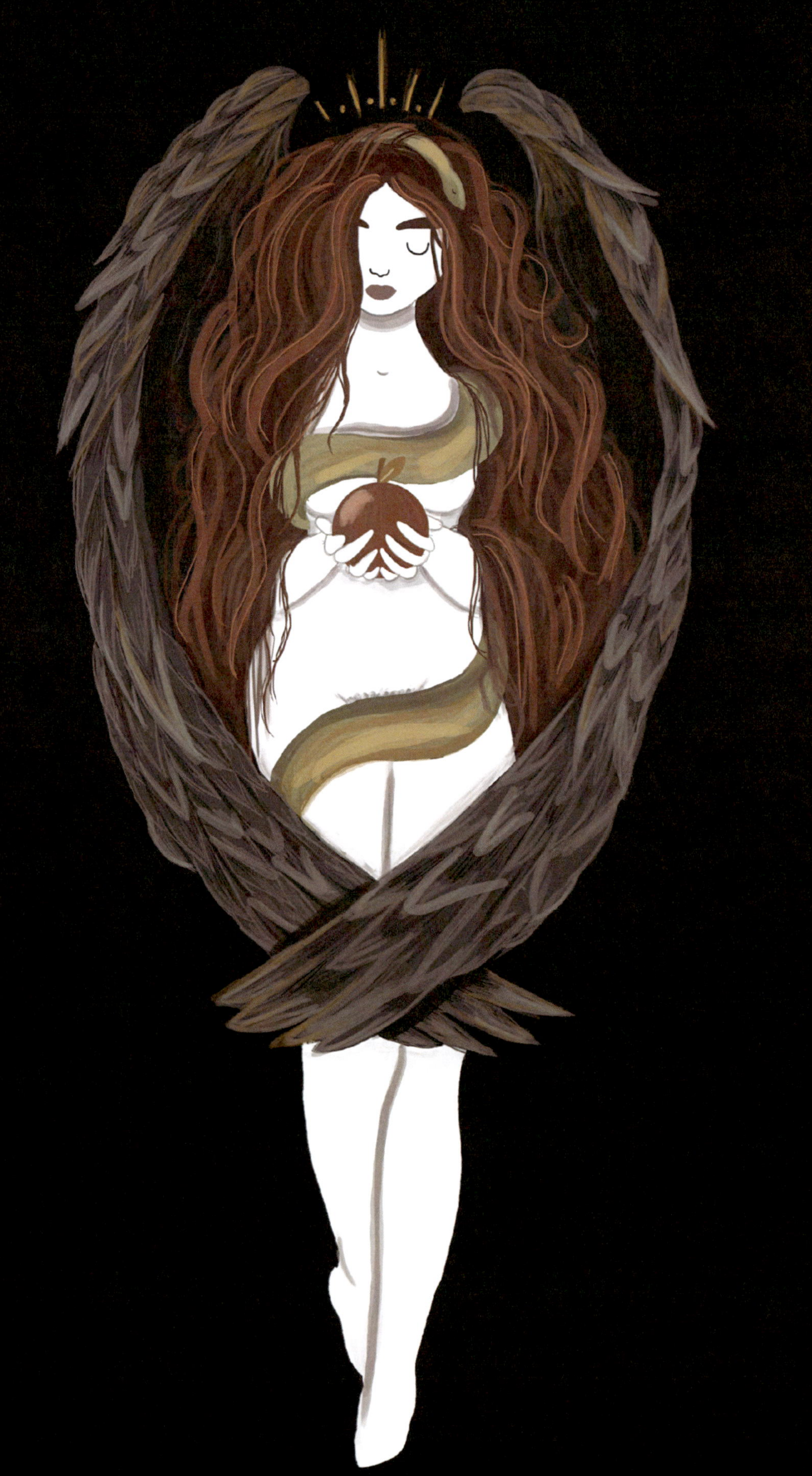

LILITH

The origins of Lilith (*lih-lith*) trace back to ancient Mesopotamia where she appeared in texts as a demon associated with the night, storms, and wilderness. Over time, her character evolved and spread across different cultures, taking on various roles and interpretations. The earliest references to Lilith can be found in Sumerian texts, where she is described as a *Lilitu,* a class of female demon associated with stormy weather. These Lilitu were believed to be responsible for causing harm to pregnant women and infants, reflecting a widespread fear of female power and the dangers of childbirth in ancient societies.

In Mesopotamian mythology, Lilith is often depicted as a winged creature with talons and sometimes with the lower body of a serpent. She is associated with the god Pazuzu, a protective deity who was believed to ward off the harmful influence of Lilitu. Lilith's presence extended beyond Mesopotamia, finding its way into Jewish tradition and folklore. In the *Alphabet of Ben Sira,* a medieval text, Lilith is portrayed as Adam's first wife who was created from the same earth as him. However, she rebels against his authority, refusing to submit to his will. This act of defiance leads to her expulsion from the Garden of Eden, where she is replaced by Eve, who is created from Adam's rib.

The story of Lilith and Adam serves as a commentary on gender roles and power dynamics in ancient societies. In some interpretations, she is also seen as a symbol of female sexuality and the dangers it posed to patriarchal structures. Lilith's association with demonic forces continues in Jewish folklore, where she is often depicted as a succubus, a female demon who seduces men in their sleep. Her refusal to conform to traditional expectations of female subservience establishes her as a powerful symbol of female empowerment and independence.

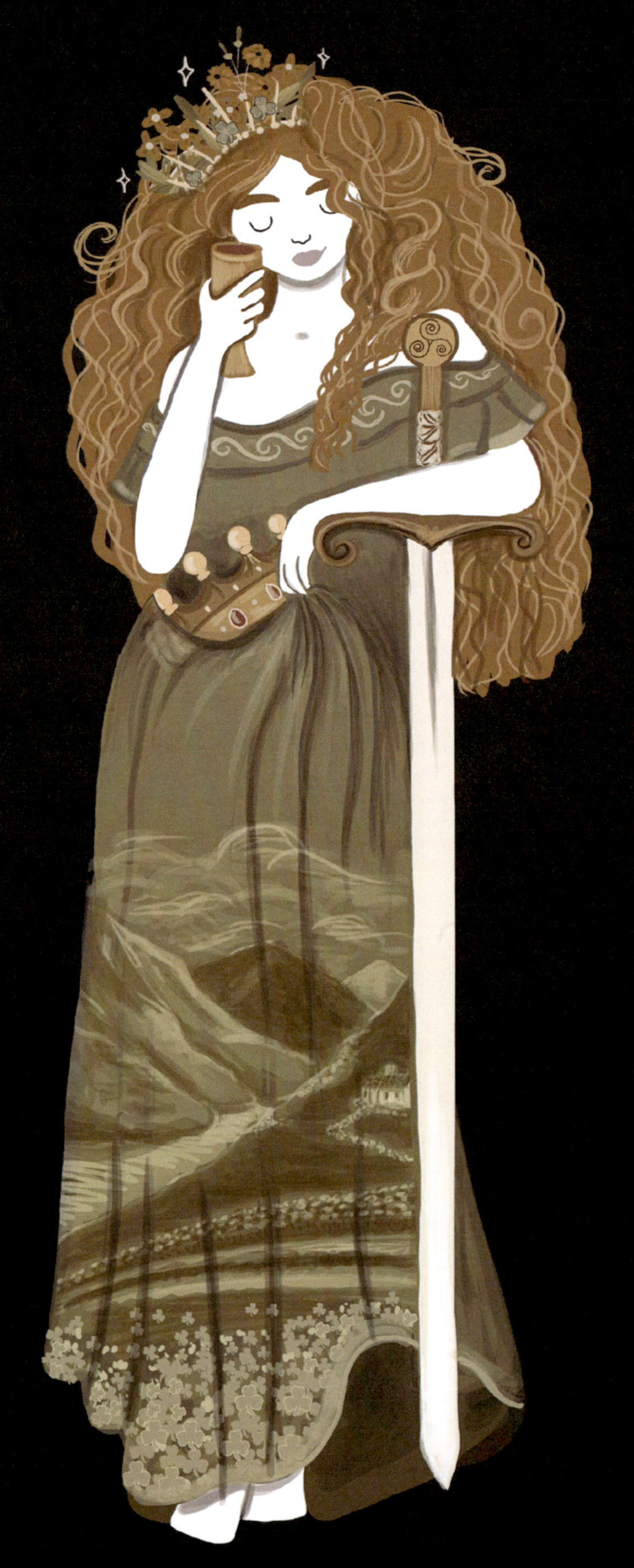

MAEVE

"BE NOT DISHEARTENED NOW. FIGHT ON BRAVELY, AND VICTORY WILL BE OURS."

—*TÁIN BÓ CÚAILNGE*

Maeve (*may-vv*) stands as a fiercely ambitious warrior-queen of Irish mythology and the goddess of supreme sovereignty. She is a prominent figure throughout the *Ulster Cycle*, a collection of ancient Irish tales, which describes her reign as the formidable queen of Connacht and her role in instigating epic conflicts. Mythological tradition holds that true rule over Ireland required a sacred, satisfying ritual with Maeve, signifying her critical link to royal legitimacy. While concrete historical evidence for her existence remains elusive, her mythological portrayal offers valuable insights into the cultural and societal values of ancient Ireland.

Maeve's guidelines for sovereignty dictated that a king must exhibit courage, generosity, and an absence of jealousy. Any ruler blessed by the goddess who demonstrated fear or disloyalty was deemed unworthy of their crown. Her ambition and determination are famously showcased in "The Cattle Raid of Cooley" (*Táin Bó Cúailnge*), a central narrative in the *Ulster Cycle*. This conflict was initiated by Maeve's desire for the prized bull of the neighboring kingdom of Ulster, Donn Cúailnge, leading to a massive military campaign. This pursuit of wealth and power culminated in a devastating and bloody war that profoundly tested the strength and resilience of both kingdoms.

The mythological portrayal of Maeve has been subject to various interpretations. Some scholars view her as a representation of female empowerment and agency, asserting her authority and ability to challenge traditional gender roles within a patriarchal societal context. Others interpret her as representing the destructive nature of ambition and greed and serving as a cautionary figure against unchecked power. While there are no definitive historical records of Maeve's existence, the abundance of oral and written traditions surrounding her attests to her enduring and significant place in the collective imagination of the Irish people.

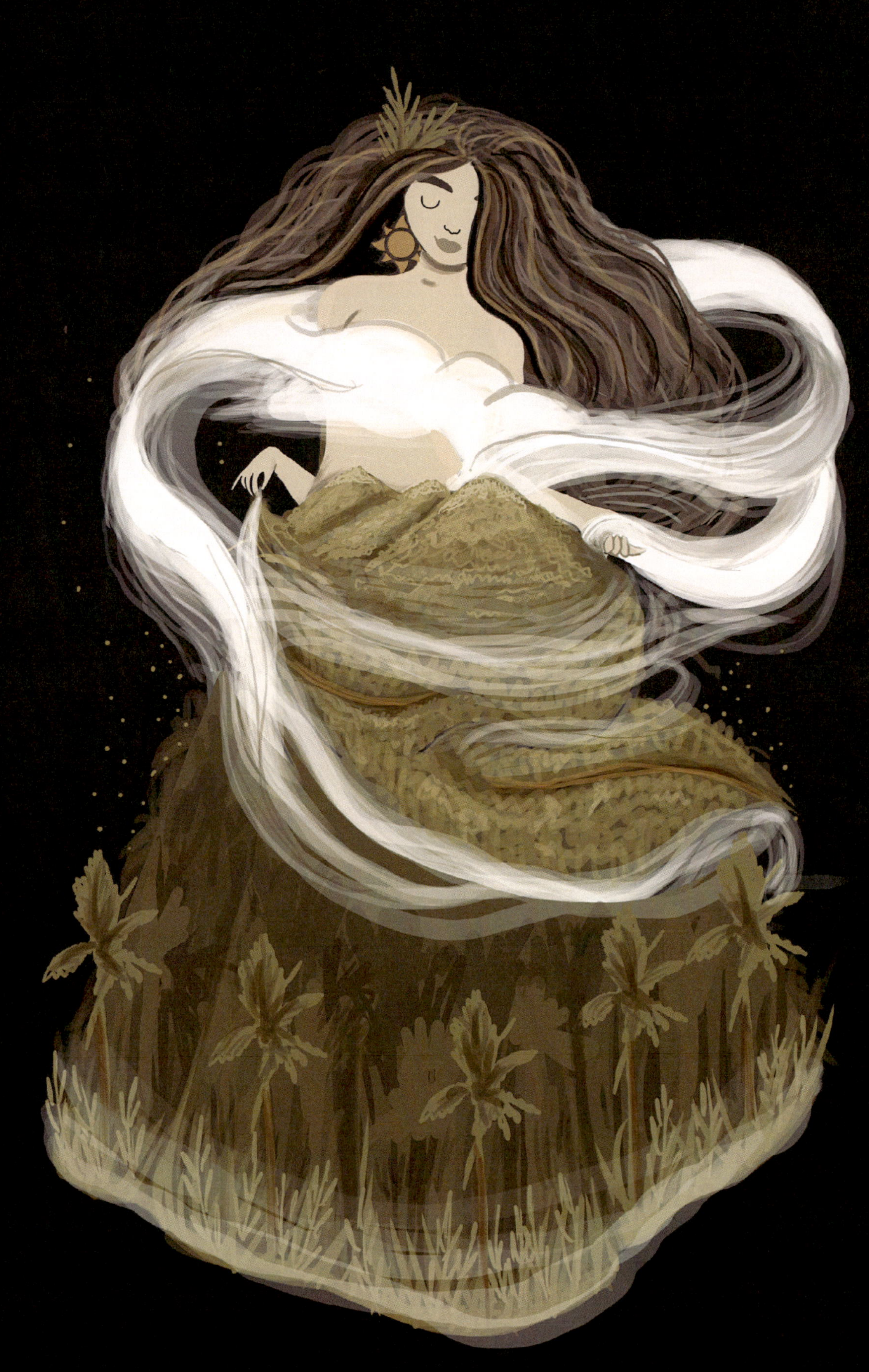

MARIANG MAKILING

"…SO NIMBLE AND AIRY THAT NOT EVEN THE FLEXIBLE BLADES OF GRASS WERE BENT."

—**JOSÉ RIZAL** (1890)

Often referred to as the "Muse of Mount Makiling," Mariang Makiling (*mah-ree-ahng mah-kee-ling*) is a mountain goddess prominent in Philippine mythology and folklore. Deeply rooted in the precolonial animistic beliefs of the Tagalog people, she is revered as the guardian spirit or "diwata" of Mount Makiling, a dormant volcano located in the Laguna province. Within Philippine mythology, diwatas are supernatural beings associated with specific locations like mountains, forests, or rivers. Mariang Makiling is considered one of the most powerful and beloved of the diwatas, known for her beauty, kindness, and generosity. She is often depicted as a young woman with long flowing hair, dressed in white, and surrounded by the lush flora and fauna of Mount Makiling.

Mariang Makiling's interactions with mortals are depicted in various legends. She is known for providing sustenance, healing, and other gifts to those who respectfully enter her domain. Conversely, she also demonstrates a fierce protectiveness of her mountain and its resources, punishing individuals who exploit or harm the environment. A prominent theme in her enduring legends is her relationships with mortals that often end tragically due to betrayal or greed. In one final example, Mariang Makiling experienced a profound heartbreak due to the disloyalty of a mortal, leading her to withdraw from direct interactions with humanity.

Mount Makiling is not merely a geographical feature but a sacred space imbued with spiritual significance. Mariang Makiling, as its guardian, represents the importance of preserving and protecting natural resources for the well-being of both humans and the environment. She is seen as a source of abundance, fertility, and healing and symbolizes the interconnectedness of all living beings. Furthermore, Mariang Makiling's stories and legends serve as powerful cautionary tales, reinforcing the possible consequences of disrespecting nature and exploiting its resources.

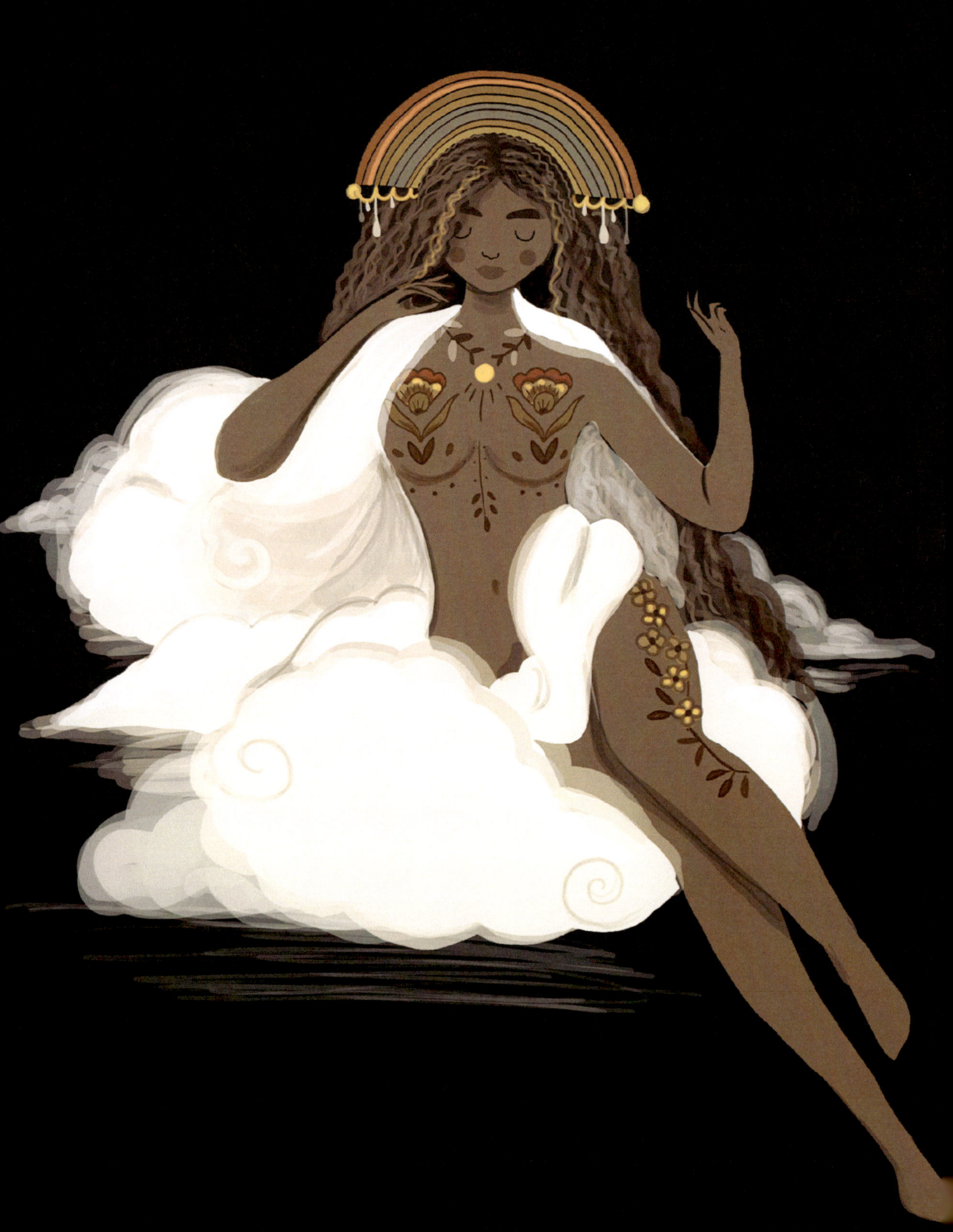

MBABA MWANA WARESA

"THE GODDESS NEVER MARRIED AND NEVER WILL...
BUT SHE CONSIDERS ALL *IZINTOMBI* HER DAUGHTERS."

—**KENDALL,** "THE ROLE OF IZANGOMA IN BRINGING THE
ZULU GODDESS BACK TO HER PEOPLE" (1988)

Mbaba Mwana Waresa (*mm-bah-bah mwah-nah wah-reh-sah*), the revered Zulu goddess of rain, fertility, and abundance, holds a prominent place in the pantheon of Zulu deities. She is often associated with rainbows, symbolizing her connection to the heavens and her ability to bring life-giving rain to the earth. Her story began with the Zulu people of southern Africa, where she remains an important cultural and spiritual symbol. Through her trademark rainbow, she bridges the gap between the earthly and divine realms and directly interacts with humans.

In Zulu mythology, Mbaba Mwana Waresa is believed to be the daughter of the sky god Umvelinqangi. She possessed the power to shapeshift into various animal forms, a trait reflected in her alternate name, *Nomkhubulwane,* meaning "she who chooses the state of an animal." Her primary role as the bringer of rain is essential for nourishing crops and ensuring successful harvests; during droughts, her followers pray and leave offerings to ensure more favorable weather. Revered as the bringer of bountiful harvests, Mbaba Mwana Waresa's association with fertility extends to human reproduction as well, with followers often invoking her protection for safe and speedy childbirth.

One legend concerning Mbaba Mwana Waresa illustrates her engagement with the mortal realm, notably through her quest for a mortal husband. This narrative highlights her discerning nature, as she is depicted as descending from the heavens to test various suitors, ultimately choosing one who could perceive her true essence despite her divine transformations. The historical origins of Mbaba Mwana Waresa are rooted in Zulu oral traditions, which have transmitted her stories and legends across generations, shaping the Zulu understanding of the natural world and their relationship with the divine.

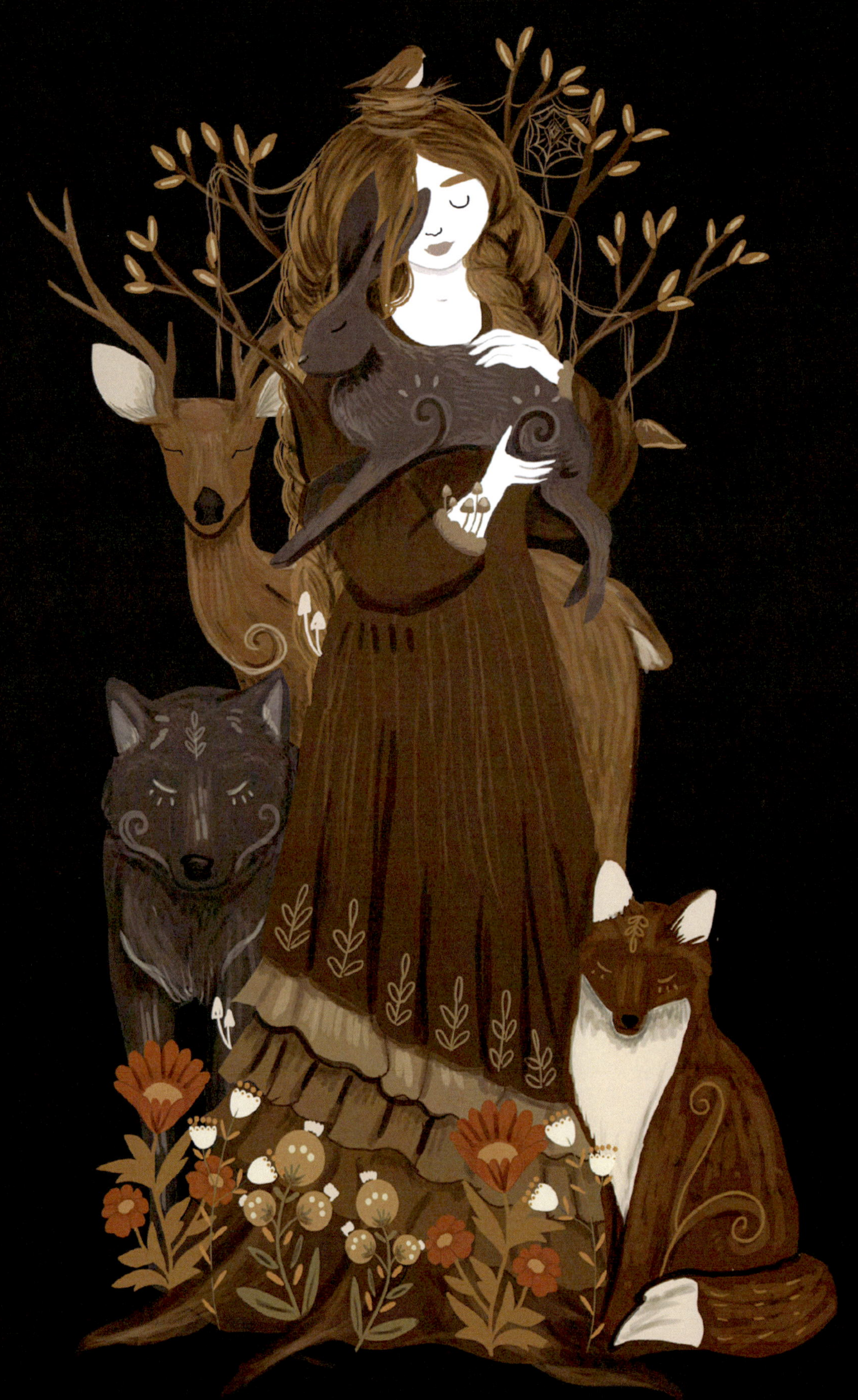

MEDEINĖ

"...MEDEINE TOLD OF THE WARNING THAT ONCE THE FORESTS WERE DESTROYED,
SO TOO WOULD THE LITHUANIAN NATION FALL."

—THE KNIGHTS OF LITHUANIA, *VYTIS* (1973)

Lithuanian goddess Medeinė (*meh-deh-ee-neh*) is the preeminent protector of the forests, standing guard over all wild animals that reside within the Baltic states. Her origins trace back to pre-Christian Baltic traditions, and she is particularly prominent in Lithuanian and Latvian folklore. Her most famous symbol is the hare, used by the goddess to lure hunters away from animal trails. King Mindaugas, the thirteenth-century ruler of Lithuania, held Medeinė in such high regard that, despite his Christian beliefs, he would avoid hunting altogether if he ever spotted a hare along the path. She is often compared to the Roman goddess Diana or to the Greek goddess Artemis.

Medeinė is often depicted as a young woman with flowing hair and adorned with leaves and flowers. As the guardian of the natural world, she is believed to possess the power to nurture and protect wildlife. Animals were considered sacred to Medeinė, and hunting rituals were often conducted to appease her and ensure the abundance of game. Medeinė's association with the forest also linked her to the cycle of life, death, and rebirth. The shedding of leaves in autumn and the regrowth in spring were seen as manifestations of her power over the natural world. This connection led to Medeinė being invoked during times of transition, such as births, marriages, and funerals.

With the arrival of Christianity in the Baltic region, Medeinė, like many other pagan deities, underwent a process of syncretism. Her attributes and functions were merged with those of Christian saints, particularly St. Mary. This blending of traditions allowed Medeinė to persist in folk beliefs and practices, albeit in a modified form. Pagan movements have also rekindled interest in Medeinė, with some seeking to revive her worship and claim her as a symbol of nature's power and resilience.

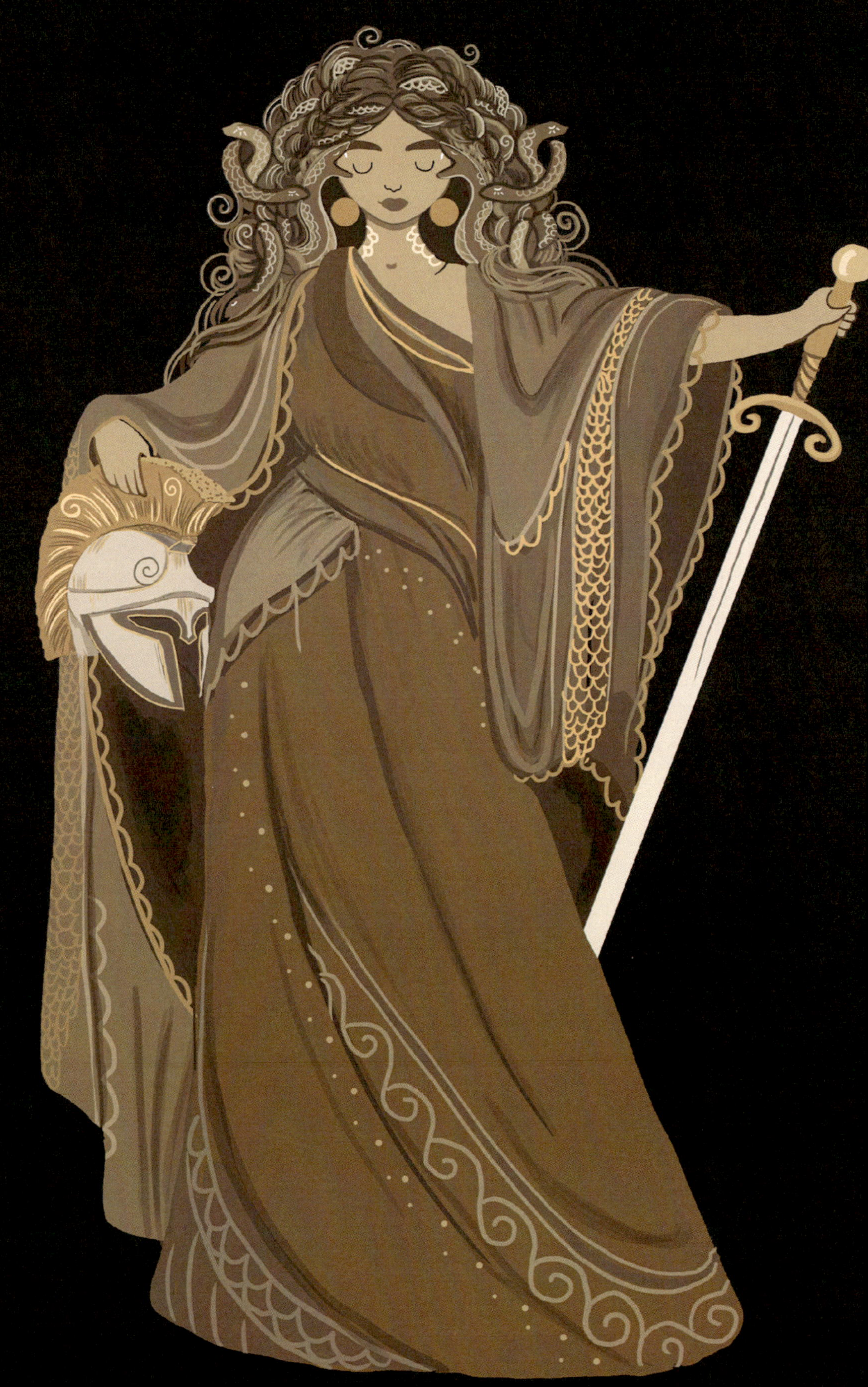

MEDUSA

"WORDS WOULD FAIL TO TELL THE GLORY OF HER HAIR, MOST WONDERFUL OF ALL HER CHARMS."

—**OVID,** *METAMORPHOSES,* BOOK IV, LINE 706

Greek mythology is littered with tales of adventure and ill-fated journeys, yet Medusa's is definitely a most unfortunate one. Some versions of her story portray Medusa as a temple priestess who was seduced by the sea god Poseidon, then transformed into a gorgon by Athena. However, most of the myths depict Medusa as a vengeful monster, hell-bent on death and destruction.

In more typical portrayals, Medusa was a monstrous entity, one of three Gorgon sisters. Usually described as having snakes for hair and a gaze that turned men to stone, Medusa represented the dangers of the uncivilized world. Her association with the sea due to her parents (the primordial sea gods Phorcys and Ceto) further cemented her as a creature of untamed chaos. A later version of the myth, recounted by the Roman poet Ovid, offered a more nuanced perspective. Ovid's Medusa was originally a beautiful priestess who was violated by Poseidon in Athena's temple. As punishment, Athena transformed Medusa into the horrifying gorgon. This characterization introduces themes of victimhood and a resentment of divine power, sparking reinterpretations of Medusa as a tragic figure.

Medusa was a captivating subject for artists and craftsmen. The classical and medieval eras focused on her petrifying gaze, using Medusa's head as a protective symbol on armor and buildings to ward off evil. Renaissance artists like Caravaggio and Bernini captured her wild-eyed visage in their sculptures, emphasizing her grotesque features. Over time, renditions of Medusa shifted, becoming more nuanced and multifaceted. Some interpretations emphasized her doleful transformation from beauty to monstrosity, while others explored her power as a representation of female sexuality and the fear it could evoke.

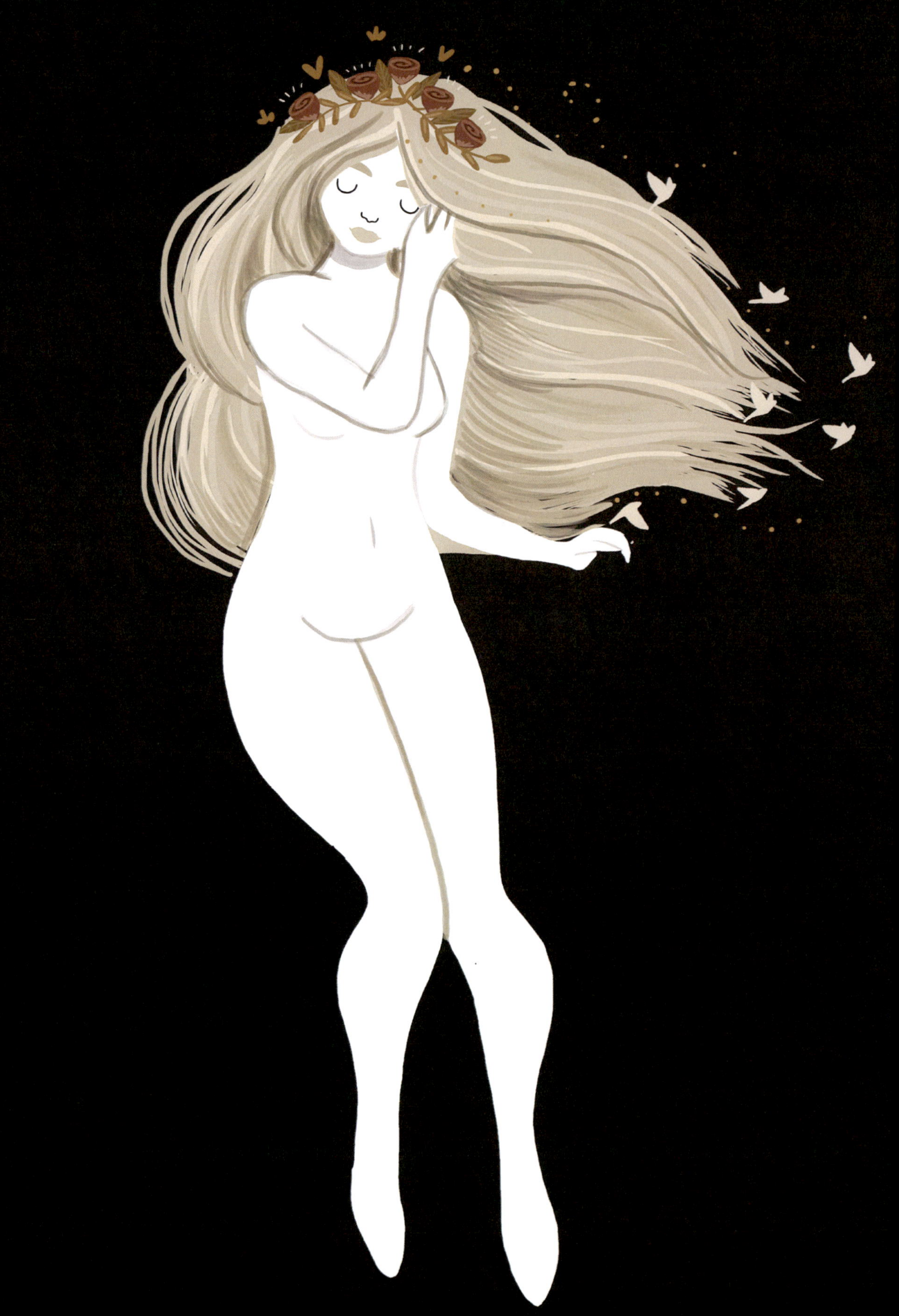

MILDA

"WHEN FLOWERS DRESS IN NEW DRESSES, THE MEADOWS ARE DRESSED IN THEIR ROBES IN MAY. WHEN ALL OF LITHUANIA CELEBRATES THE FEAST OF MILDA…"

—JÓZEF IGNACY KRASZEWSKI, *ANAFIELAS* (1840)

Milda (*mill-dah*), the Lithuanian goddess of love, holds a fascinating yet contentious place in Baltic mythology. Her origins and the authenticity of her worship are subjects of ongoing scholarly debate, yet her legend has endured, becoming emblematic of love, freedom, and national identity. Milda first appeared in historical records in the nineteenth century, notably in Teodor Narbutt's 1835 work on Lithuanian history. Narbutt depicted Milda as a significant deity with temples in major cities, suggesting a widespread following. However, his claims lacked substantial archaeological or folkloric evidence, leading many scholars to question Milda's existence as a pre-Christian goddess.

Some researchers argue that Milda might be a later invention, perhaps a romanticized figure created during the Lithuanian National Revival of the nineteenth century. Others propose that she could represent a hybrid deity that blends elements of various Baltic and Slavic goddesses. Despite the uncertainties surrounding her origins, Milda has acquired a rich tapestry of symbolism and attributes. She is often associated with love, courtship, and marriage, but also with freedom, joy, and spring. Some sources depict her as a beautiful woman driving a chariot pulled by doves, while others emphasize her connection to nature and fertility.

The month of May, a time of blooming flowers and burgeoning love, is often dedicated to Milda. Pagan groups and some Baltic communities continue to celebrate her with rituals, songs, and dances, honoring her as a symbol of love, passion, and the renewal of life. Milda's image has been immortalized in numerous artworks, ranging from romantic paintings to sculptures and folk crafts. Kazimierz Alchimowicz's painting *Milda, Goddess of Love*, for instance, portrays her as a graceful figure reminiscent of the classical Venus. Her name has also been given to a mountain on the planet Venus, solidifying her place in the heavens.

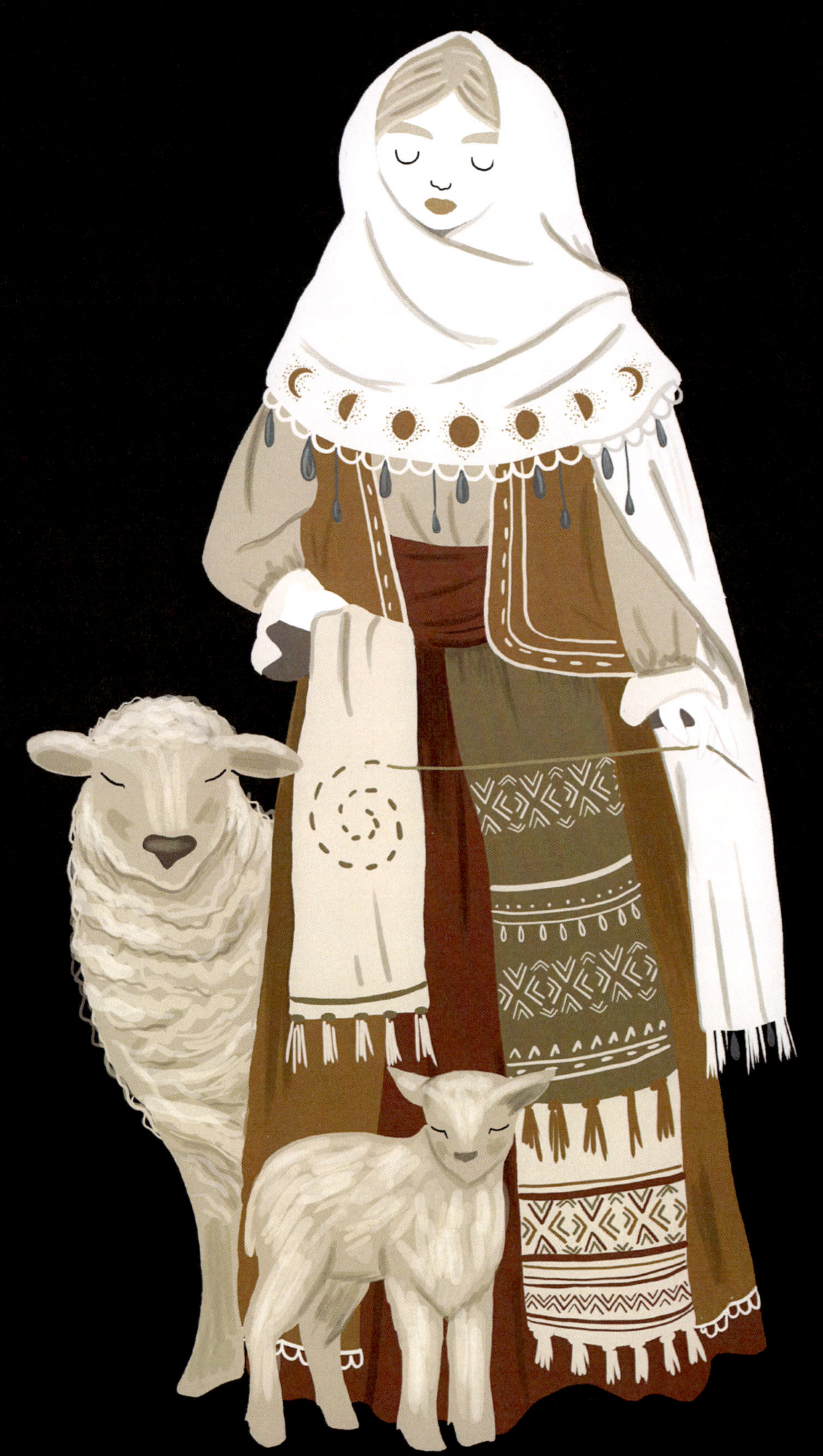

MOKOŠ

"...THE GREAT MOTHER OF PLENTY, OF WOMEN'S DESTINY, AND OF DIVINATION."

—**Linda J. Ivanits,** *Russian Folk Belief* (1942)

Mokoš (*moh-kohsh*) is known as the supreme "moist mother earth" within Slavic mythology, fulfilling a great many roles for people throughout Europe. She is a goddess of fertility and guardian of the fate of women. Of the seven original primordial deities that comprised Slavic mythology, only Mokoš is female. Her role encompassed various aspects of European culture, functioning as a patron of fertility, the protector of sheep and cattle, and the guardian of woven destiny. Much like the Moirai or the Norns, Mokoš spins the thread of fate and determines the future of all things.

As both mother earth and the defender of women, Mokoš remains deeply ingrained in the customs and daily lives of those who worship her. Exemplifying the essence of the earth's fertility, it was deemed taboo to spit on or strike the ground during the months of spring, the time in which Mokoš was said to be "pregnant." On her feast day on May 9, no seeds would be sown, no holes could be dug. Harvest holidays in the autumn honored the divinity that she infused into the earth and the bounty that came of it.

During the Christianization of Europe throughout the early Middle Ages, the worship of Mokoš underwent heavy transformation. She hybridized with Christian figures such as St. Petka, St. Paraskeva Pyatnitsa, and even the Virgin Mary. However, despite the widespread movement to replace archaic gods and goddesses, Slavic women kept the spirit of Mokoš alive. This agitated Christian authorities, who protested the Slavic practices of confessing "sins" to a hole in the ground rather than to a priest and the use of soil during weddings to represent the unification of body and soul.

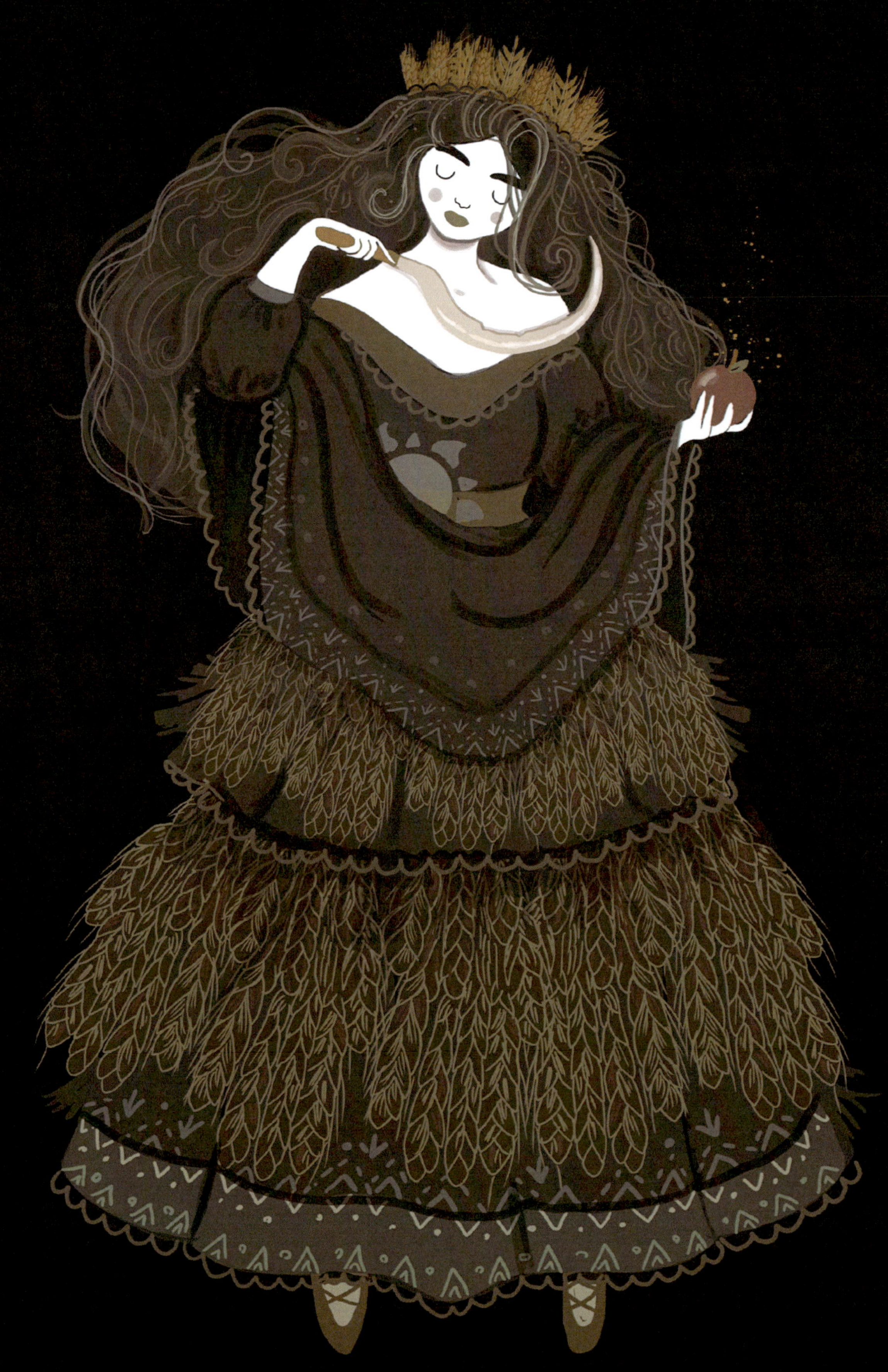

MORANA

"WE CARRY DEATH OUT OF THE CITY, AND BRING IN SUMMER…"

—**ERIKA SUPRIA HONISCH**, "DROWNING WINTER, BURNING BONES, SINGING SONGS: REPRESENTATIONS OF POPULAR DEVOTION IN A CENTRAL EUROPEAN MOTET CYCLE" (2017)

The personification of winter, Morana (*moh-rah-nah*) is the Slavic goddess who brings an end to the farming year. She rules in opposition to Vesna, the goddess of spring, but it is understood that neither could exist without the other. This yearly cycle between them symbolizes the eternal death and rebirth of nature. Key to Morana's mythos is her power over the transition from winter to spring, illustrated by legends depicting her temporary hold over the sun god Dazbog before his emergence signaled warmer weather.

Morana, sometimes referred to as *Marzanna* or *Moré*, is often depicted as a hag or crone, representing the waning of the year and the approach of winter. She is associated with darkness, cold, and the barren landscapes of the dormant season. In some traditions, she is seen as a bringer of disease and misfortune, reflecting the hardships and dangers associated with winter. Though her mythos has led to these negative connotations, portraying Morana solely as a villain overlooks the complexities of her role. Morana typifies the process of decay and decomposition that is essential for new life to emerge. In this sense, she is not only a goddess of death but also a goddess of rebirth and regeneration.

Morana's role in Slavic folklore is made most clear in the various rituals and traditions associated with her worship. One of the most widespread practices is the burning or drowning of an effigy representing the goddess at the end of winter. This act symbolizes the banishment of winter's hardships and the welcoming of spring's renewal. The effigy, often made of straw or wood, is adorned with symbols of winter, such as white cloth or evergreen branches. It is then either set on fire or thrown into a river or lake, signifying the end of Morana's reign and the return of life and fertility to the land.

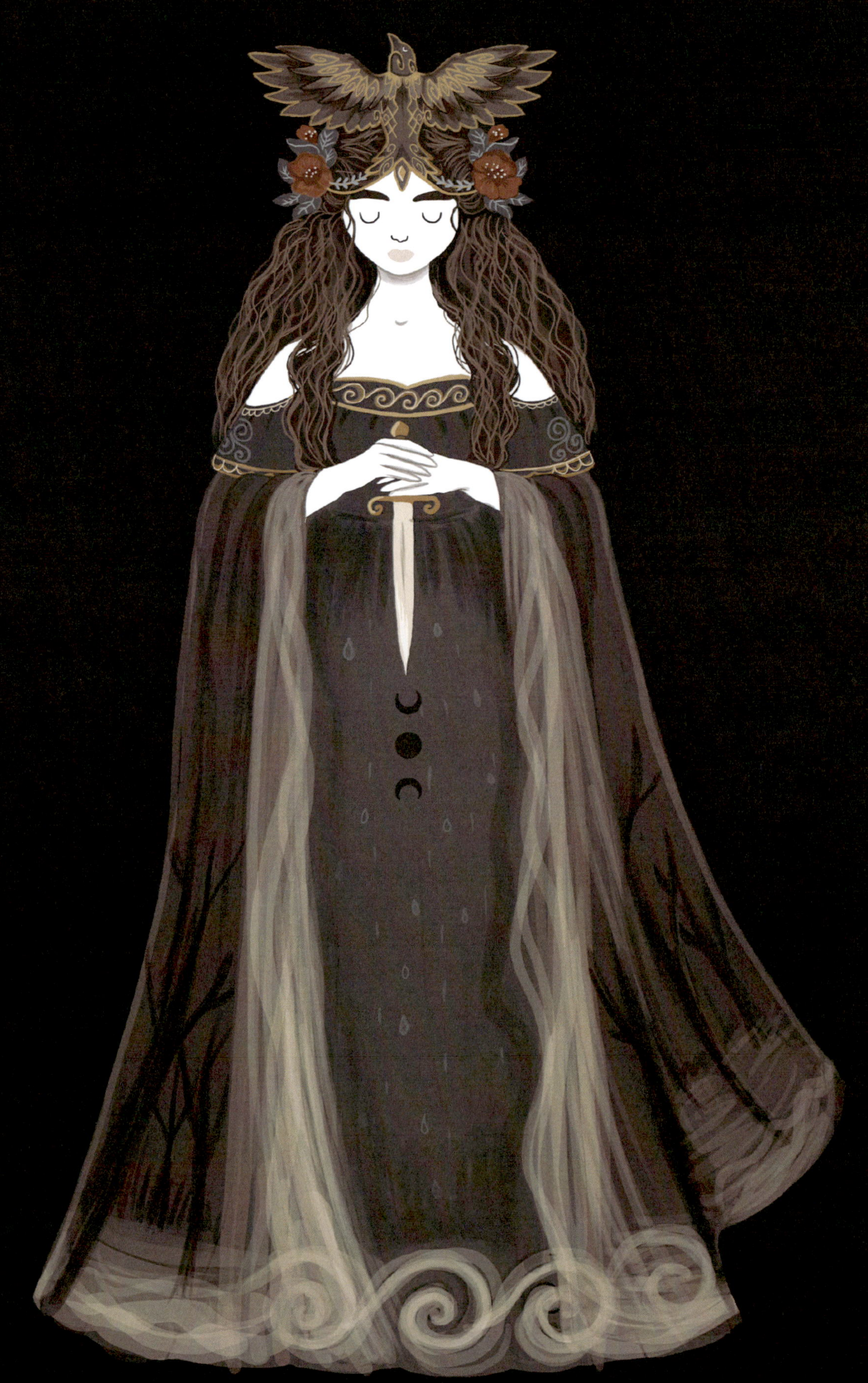

THE MORRÍGAN

"IT IS AT THE GUARDING OF THY DEATH THAT I AM; AND I SHALL BE."

—*ULSTER CYCLE* (FIRST CENTURY AD), "TÁIN BÓ REGAMNA"

The Morrígan (*morh'a-gan*), the "Phantom Queen" of Celtic mythology, commands the tides of war and influences the fates of individuals. As an unrivaled shapeshifter, she often manifests as a young woman, an elderly crone, or even a murder of crows. The Morrígan's diverse roles highlight her command over life's vital forces: she was invoked for military counseling to assure victory and appeared directly to those she favored in battle, yet she also possessed the capacity to provide assistance in matters of fertility, showcasing her unique dominion over both creation and destruction.

Her significant presence is attested to in various Celtic tales, particularly within the *Ulster Cycle*, one of the four great sagas of Irish mythology. In these narratives, the Morrígan frequently interacts with heroes, such as the demigod Cú Chulainn, often assuming different forms to convey warnings of impending defeat or to impart lessons. A striking instance of her prophetic power occurs toward the conclusion of the saga, where the Morrígan is depicted as a hag ritually washing bloodied armor in a river, an act that serves as a powerful omen of imminent death. This event dramatically underscores her role in foretelling and influencing the outcomes of battles.

Celtic mythology places great emphasis on the number three, with ancient Celts often conceptualizing essential aspects of existence in triads. This belief is reflected in the Morrígan's occasional portrayal as a trio of sisters, or the "three Morrígna," rather than a singular deity. While the specific names within the Morrígna varied across the mythos, they generally encompassed a collection of ancient Celtic deities responsible for aspects of life and death for humanity. As a representation of the Triple Goddess in her own right, the Morrígan possesses the capacity to embody each aspect—the mother, maiden, and crone—simultaneously.

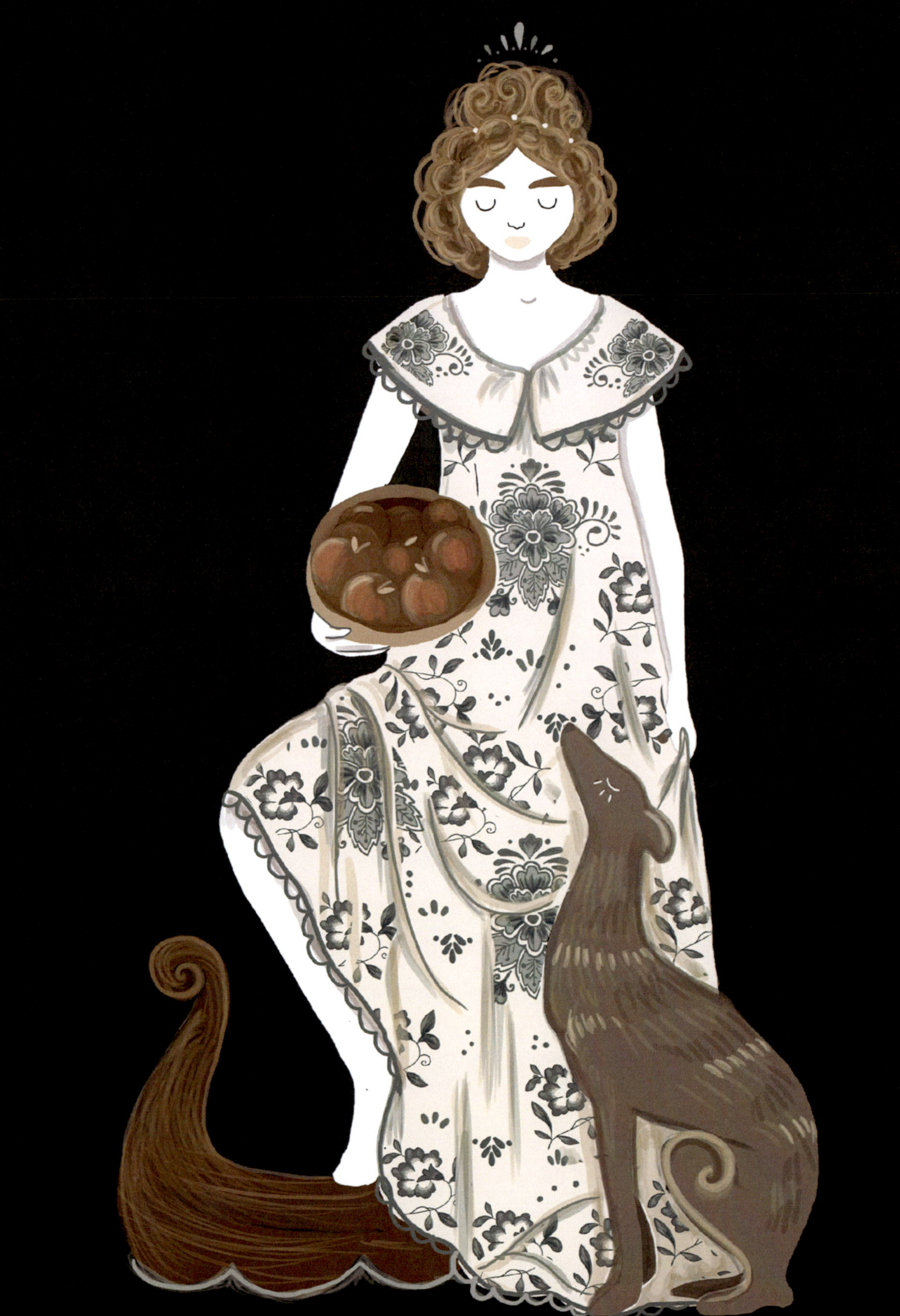

NEHALENNIA

Nehalennia (*neh-hah-leh-nee-uh*), a goddess of uncertain origin, held a significant place in the religious landscape of ancient northern Europe, particularly in the regions surrounding the North Sea. Her worship, primarily corroborated by numerous votive altars discovered in the present-day province of Zeeland in the Netherlands, dates back to at least the second century BC and flourished in the second and third centuries AD. Her name is often interpreted as "she of the mist" or "she of the low-lying lands," alluding to the coastal and estuarine environments where her veneration thrived. Nehalennia is frequently depicted as a youthful woman seated on a throne, often accompanied by a dog. The presence of a ship's prow in some depictions further underscores her association with seafaring and maritime activities.

The majority of votive altars dedicated to Nehalennia were discovered in the vicinity of the Scheldt River estuary, a crucial hub for trade and travel in antiquity. This geographical concentration suggests that she was revered as a protector of sailors, merchants, and travelers, ensuring safe passage across the treacherous waters. The votive altars, often inscribed with personal dedications and prayers, offer a glimpse into the individual and collective aspirations of her worshippers. The recurring motifs of safe journeys, successful harvests, and the well-being of loved ones highlight the goddess's role as a source of hope and solace in a world fraught with uncertainty.

The decline of Nehalennia's cult in the late third century AD coincides with broader shifts in the religious and political landscape of the Roman Empire, including the rise of Christianity. Yet, her legacy endured through the archaeological record, providing invaluable insights into the beliefs and practices of ancient seafaring communities. The rediscovery of her votive altars in the seventeenth century sparked renewed interest in her enigmatic figure, prompting scholarly investigations and artistic representations that continue to this day.

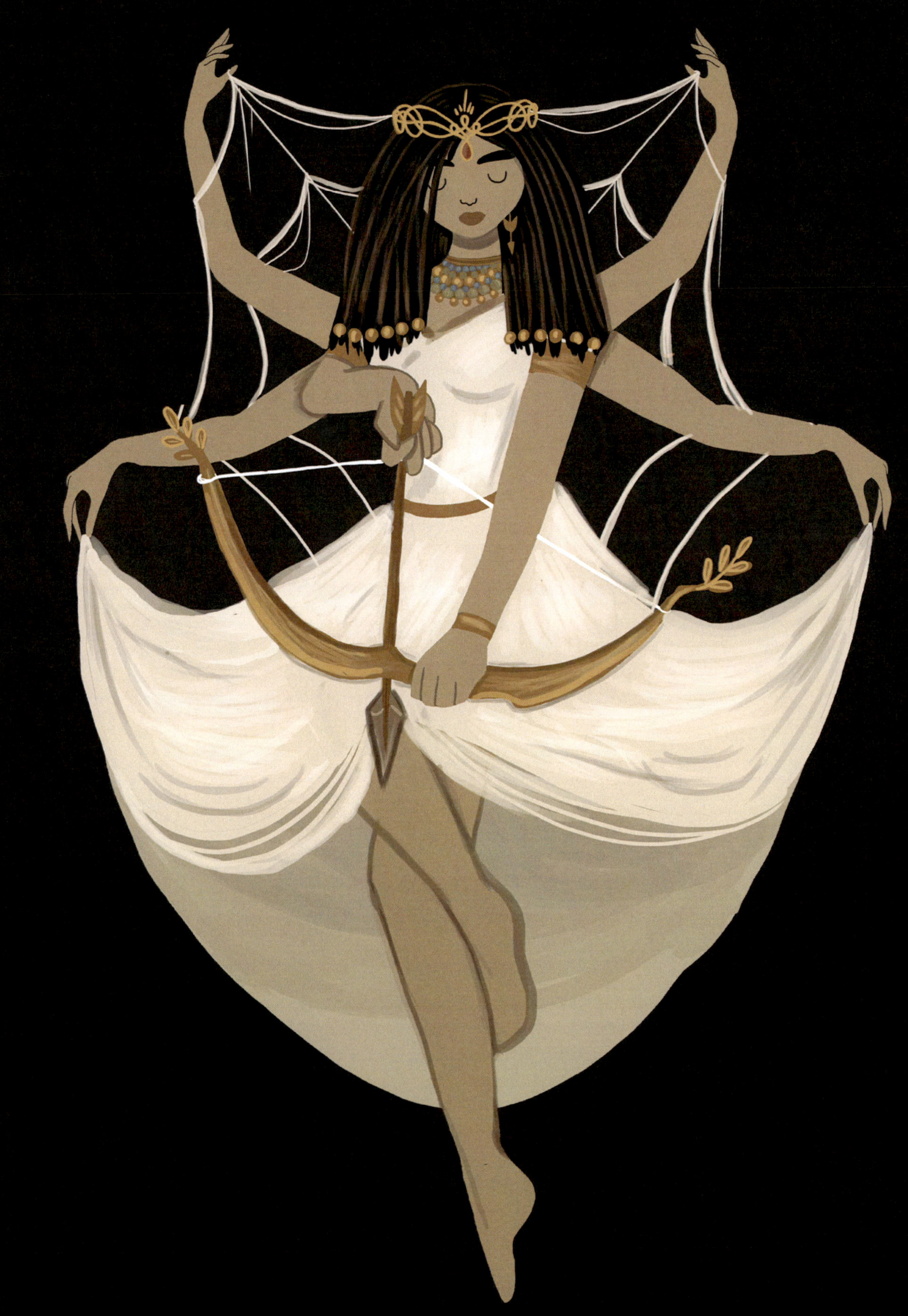

NEITH

"I AM ALL THAT HAS BEEN, ALL THAT IS, AND ALL THAT WILL BE.
NO MORTAL HAS EVER LIFTED MY VEIL."

—**PLUTARCH,** INSCRIPTION FOUND IN SAÏS AND ATTRIBUTED TO NEITH

Neith (*nee-th*), the "First One," is the primordial goddess of creation within Egyptian mythology. It is said that she was never born but instead was generated into being by her own power. In one myth, Neith placed the sky upon her loom and fabricated the entirety of the world into existence; weaving was linked to creation, as the act of interlacing threads mirrored the divine act of bringing order out of chaos. Unsurprisingly, her name may be related to the words "to weave" or "to knit," and for this reason the goddess carries a strong association with spiders. Her worship spanned millennia, from the Predynastic period to the Roman era. The cult of Neith especially flourished in the twenty-sixth dynasty, when the capital of Egypt was located at Sais.

Neith's origins are shrouded in the mists of prehistory, but her name appears on artifacts dating back to the earliest dynasties. She was often depicted as a woman wearing the red crown of Lower Egypt, holding crossed arrows and a bow, symbolizing her martial prowess. Neith's warlike aspect was also deeply ingrained in her character. She was often depicted carrying a shield and wielding various weapons, and her epithet "Mistress of the Bow" highlighted her skill as an archer. In times of war, Neith was invoked as a protector of the pharaoh and the Egyptian army.

In some myths, she was also considered the mother of Ra, the sun god. Neith was also associated with the primordial waters of Nun, from which all creation emerged. This great creator was also believed to protect the deceased in the afterlife, defending them from the dangers that lurked throughout the Underworld.

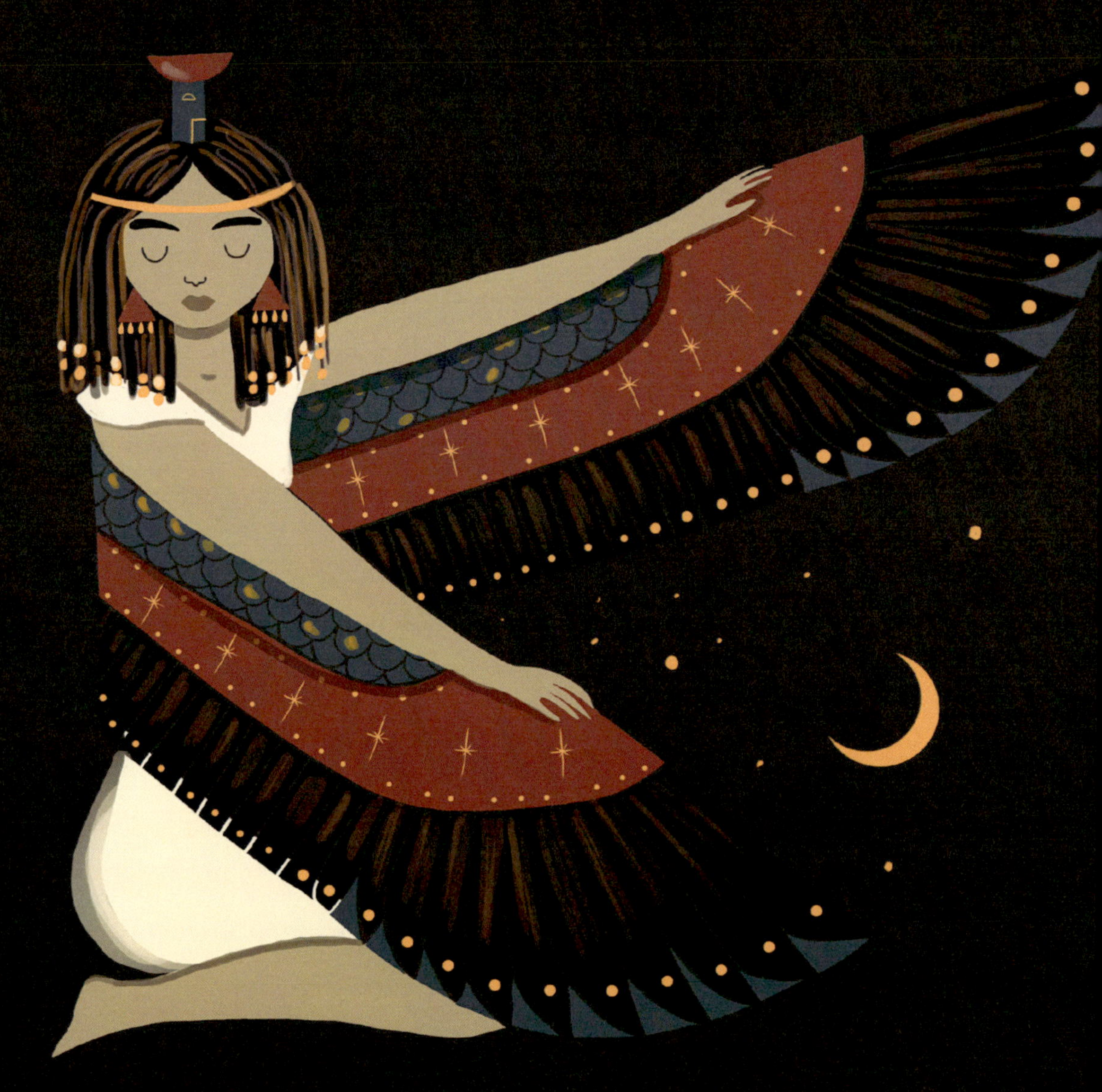

NEPHTHYS

"MY BROTHER, AWAKE! SEE ME, YOUR SISTER, NEPHTHYS,
I HAVE COME SEEKING YOU, WEEPING FOR YOU. DO NOT LINGER THERE!"

—*PYRAMID TEXTS*, UTTERANCE 574

Nephthys (*neff-this*), a lesser-known goddess of ancient Egypt, was a member of the *Ennead*, the group of nine deities who were believed to have created the world. She was the daughter of Geb, the earth god, and Nut, the sky goddess, and her siblings included Isis, Osiris, and Set. Nephthys was often depicted as a woman wearing a headdress that combined the hieroglyphs for a house and a basket, cementing her role as a protector of the home and family.

One of Nephthys's most prominent responsibilities was as a goddess of the dead. She was often depicted alongside Isis, mourning the death of Osiris, their brother, and helping to prepare his body for the afterlife. In this role, Nephthys represented the grief and sorrow that accompany death, but also the hope for rebirth and renewal. Her image was often included on amulets and other objects intended to ward off evil and ensure a safe journey to the afterlife. She was believed to protect the deceased on their trek to the Underworld and to watch over the living, particularly women and children. Nephthys was also invoked in other contexts, such as in magic spells and rituals for protection and healing.

In the later periods of Egyptian history, Nephthys became increasingly associated with Isis, and the two goddesses were often worshipped as a pair. This association reflected the complementary nature of their roles, with Isis representing the creative and life-giving facets of femininity, and Nephthys embodying the darker, more mournful aspects. The worship of Nephthys continued throughout the Greco-Roman period, and she was even adopted into the Roman pantheon as a goddess of mourning. Her function as a goddess of transition was reflected in her association with the liminal spaces between life and death, day and night, and the natural and supernatural worlds.

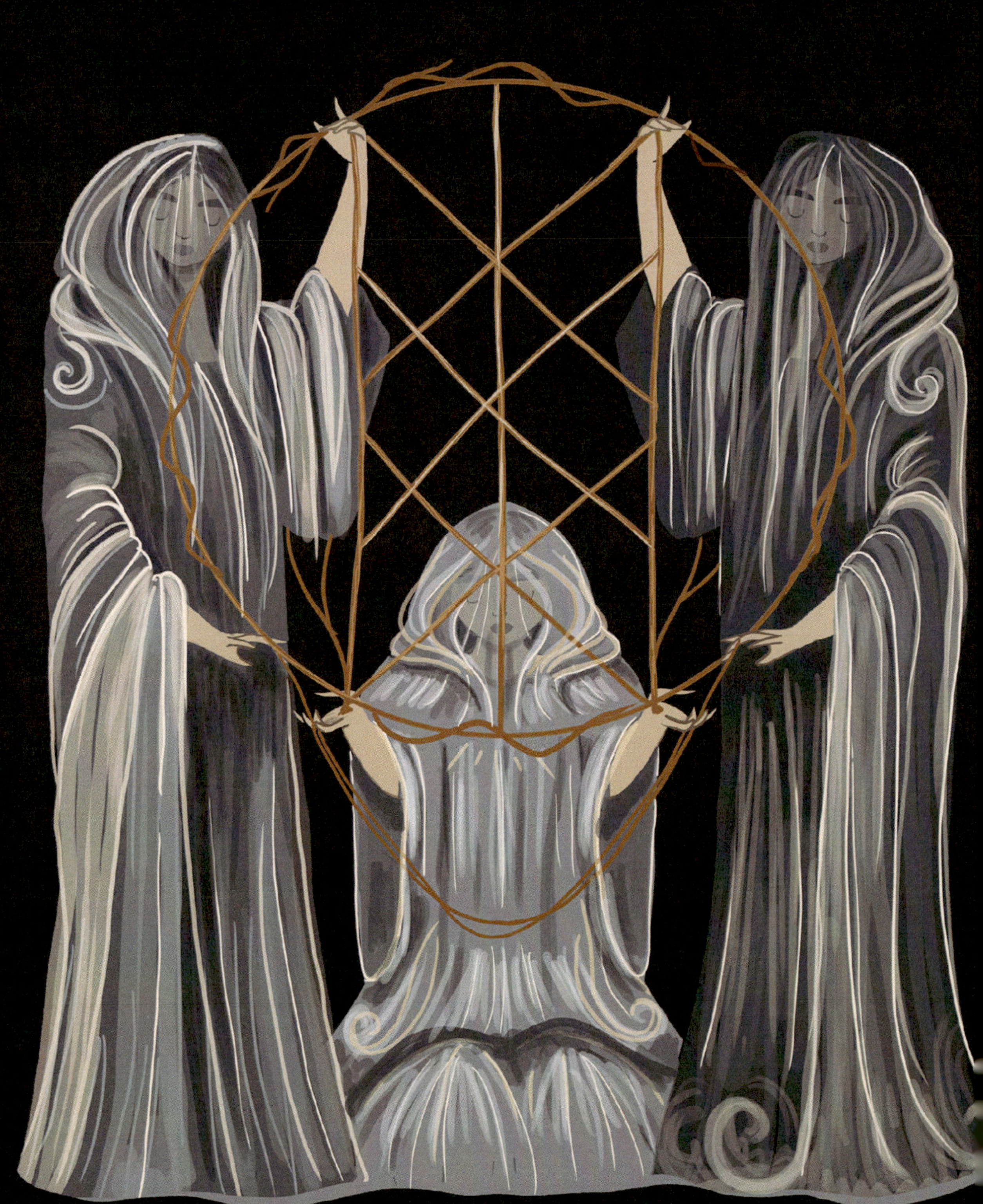

THE NORNS

"THENCE COME THE MAIDENS, MIGHTY IN WISDOM,
THREE FROM THE DWELLING THAT STANDS 'NEATH THE TREE."

—**SNORRI STURLUSON,** *POETIC EDDA,* "VÖLUSPÁ," STANZA 20

The Norns (*nor-nz*), the weavers of fate within Norse mythology, are generally depicted as three sisters: Urðr, Verðandi, and Skuld. Their names signify different aspects of time: Urðr meaning "fate" or "past," Verðandi signifying "present" or "becoming," and Skuld representing "future" or "obligation." These names underscore their connection to the flow of existence and their influence on the unfolding of events. Their influence extended to rituals and ceremonies related to birth, marriage, and death, where their blessings were invoked to ensure favorable outcomes.

These goddesses of fate were revered for their ability to shape the destinies of gods and mortals alike. The Norns reside beneath the world tree, Yggdrasil, where they tend to the well of Urðr, a sacred source of wisdom and knowledge. They are often depicted as spinning the threads of fate on a loom, determining the lifespans and experiences of individuals. Urðr spins the thread of life, Verðandi measures its length, and Skuld cuts it, signifying the end of one's mortal journey.

While their primary role is to shape destinies, The Norns also serve as guardians of cosmic order. They ensure the balance of the universe by upholding the laws of fate and maintaining the natural cycles of life, death, and rebirth.

Revered in Norse society as figures of both awe and fear, The Norns' power to determine one's fortune, whether good or bad, inspired both profound reverence and apprehension. The Norns feature prominently in various Norse sagas and poems, often appearing as wise women who offer counsel and prophecies to gods and heroes. They are also depicted in art, shown as three women of different ages, representing the past, present, and future. The impact of their workings is believed to resonate through both the mortal and celestial spheres.

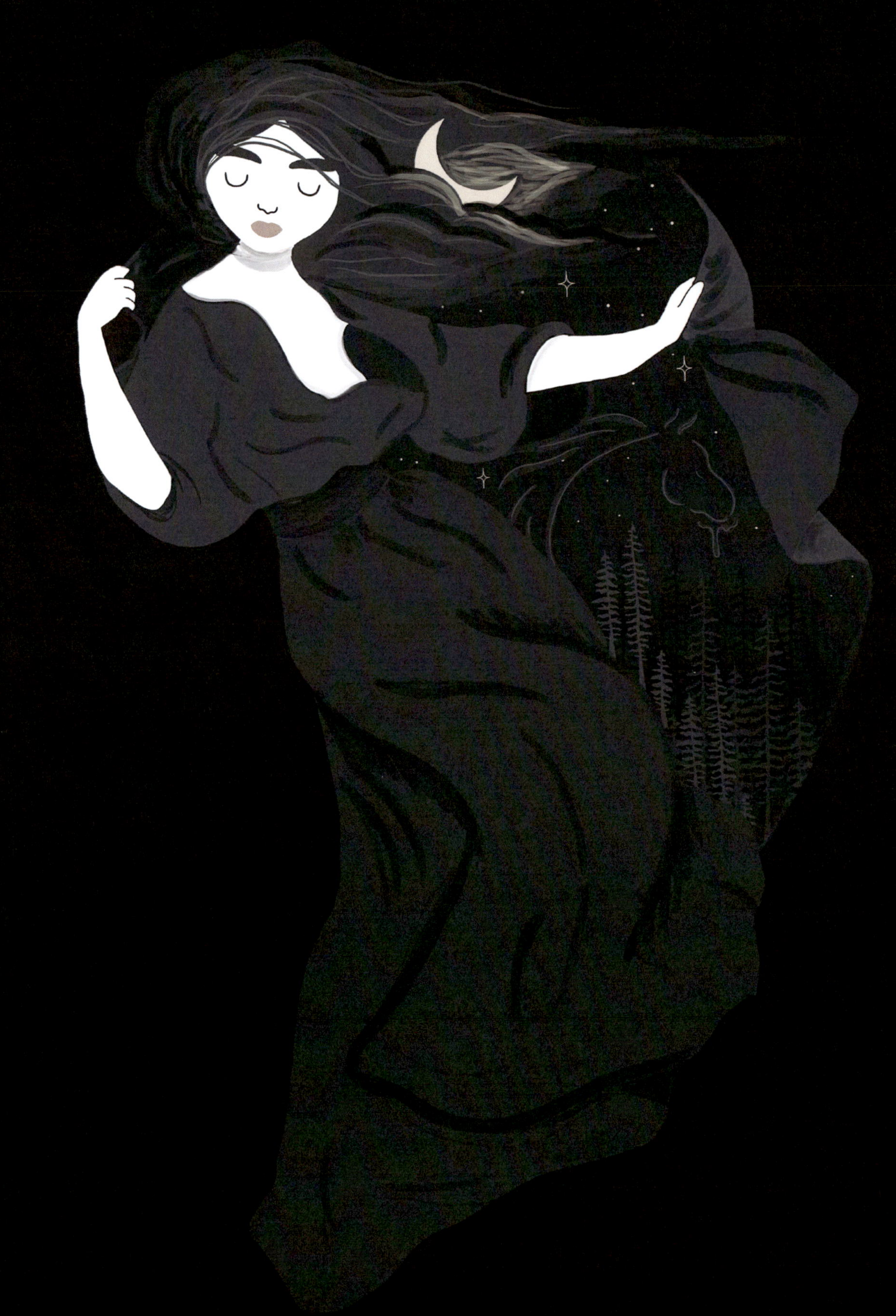

NÓTT

"TO NIGHT AND HER DAUGHTER HAIL! WITH PLACID EYES BEHOLD US HERE,
AND HERE SITTING GIVE US VICTORY."

—**SNORRI STURLUSON,** *POETIC EDDA,* "SIGRDRÍFUMÁL"

As the Norse personification of night itself, Nótt (*not*) governs the midnight hours, facilitating the passage and recollection of time. Her celestial journey is undertaken upon her black horse, Hrimfaxi, the "Frost Mane," whose dripping foam is believed to create the morning dew. Nótt's mythological lineage highlights her role in cosmological creation, as she produced several notable offspring through her various unions. These include Audr, a god of wealth; Jörð, the giantess who, with Odin, would become mother to the thunder god Thor, thus establishing Nótt as Thor's grandmother; and Dagr, the personified "day," who perpetually follows his mother's path each morning to spread light across the earth.

Nótt also embodies a deep connection to both sleep and death. She was believed to bring dreams to mortals, offering them glimpses of future events. In the context of the afterlife, Nótt was seen as a welcoming figure for those who passed away. She is present in significant Old Norse texts, including the *Poetic Edda, Prose Edda,* and the *Saga of the Volsungs.* Over time, the goddess Nótt became synonymous with the concept of "night," frequently appearing as a proper noun within Old Norse texts.

Further mythological accounts provide insight into Nótt's origins and multifaceted nature. The poem *Vafþrúðnismál* discusses her creation through the god Nörvi and her function in guiding humanity's measurement of time. Additionally, *Alvíssmál* includes a dialogue where other names for "night," such as "joy-of-sleep" and "dream-goddess," are revealed, illustrating more of her diverse attributes. In conjunction with figures such as Dagr (day), Sól (sun), and Mani (moon), along with a diverse pantheon of deities representing various aspects of the year, Nótt contributes to the seamless flow of time.

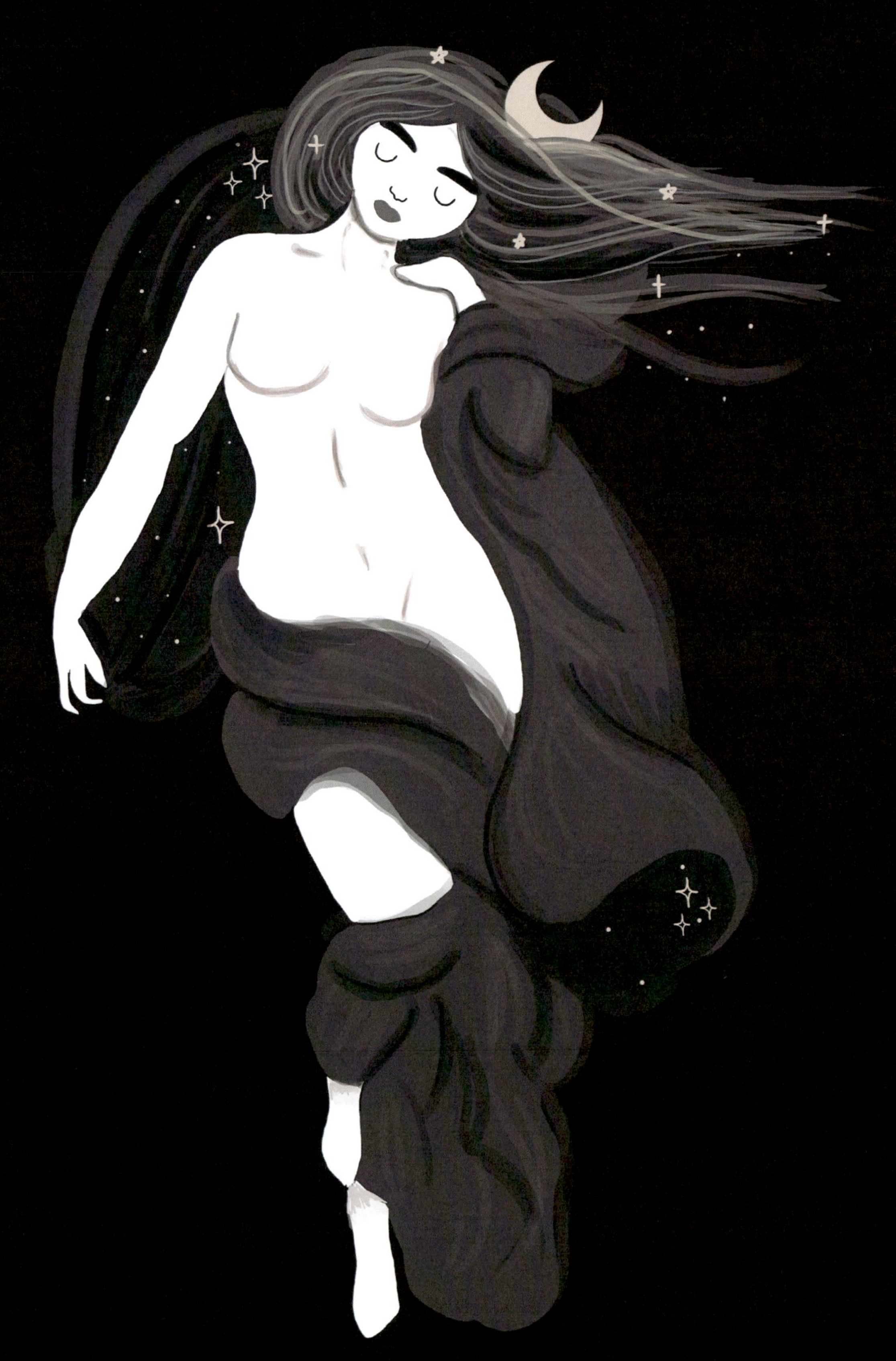

NYX

Nyx (*nix*), the Greek goddess of night, is a primordial deity whose origins can be traced back to the earliest cosmogonies. She embodies the mysterious and enigmatic aspects of darkness and is often associated with the unknown and the otherworldly. In Hesiod's *Theogony*, Nyx is described as the offspring of Khaos, the primeval void from which all existence emerged. Alongside Erebus, the god of darkness, she is the mother of Aether, the "bright upper air," and Hemera, the "day." This familial connection highlights Nyx's role as a foundational figure in the creation of the universe, embodying the primal duality of light and darkness.

A mysterious veiled figure, Nyx can be seen driving her chariot of shadows across the sky. She is also the mother of a brood of dark spirits, including the Moirai (fate), Oizys (suffering), Hypnos (sleep), Thanatos (death), and Eris (strife). Although linked to forces often perceived as negative, Nyx's nature is not intrinsically evil or malevolent. She is a powerful and respected figure, even by Zeus.

In Homer's *Iliad*, Zeus is reluctant to disobey Nyx, indicating her authority and influence over the other deities.

Nyx's role in mythology varies depending on the source. In some accounts, she is described as residing in a cave at the edge of the world, where she instructs oracles and advises the gods. In others, she is depicted as a more active figure, participating in the Trojan War and aiding the Greeks. The worship of Nyx was not widespread in ancient Greece, and there are few surviving temples or shrines dedicated to her. Nevertheless, Nyx's association with the Oracle of Delphi hints that she was likely revered for her own prophetic insights and her profound connection to the mysteries that lay beyond the veil of the ordinary.

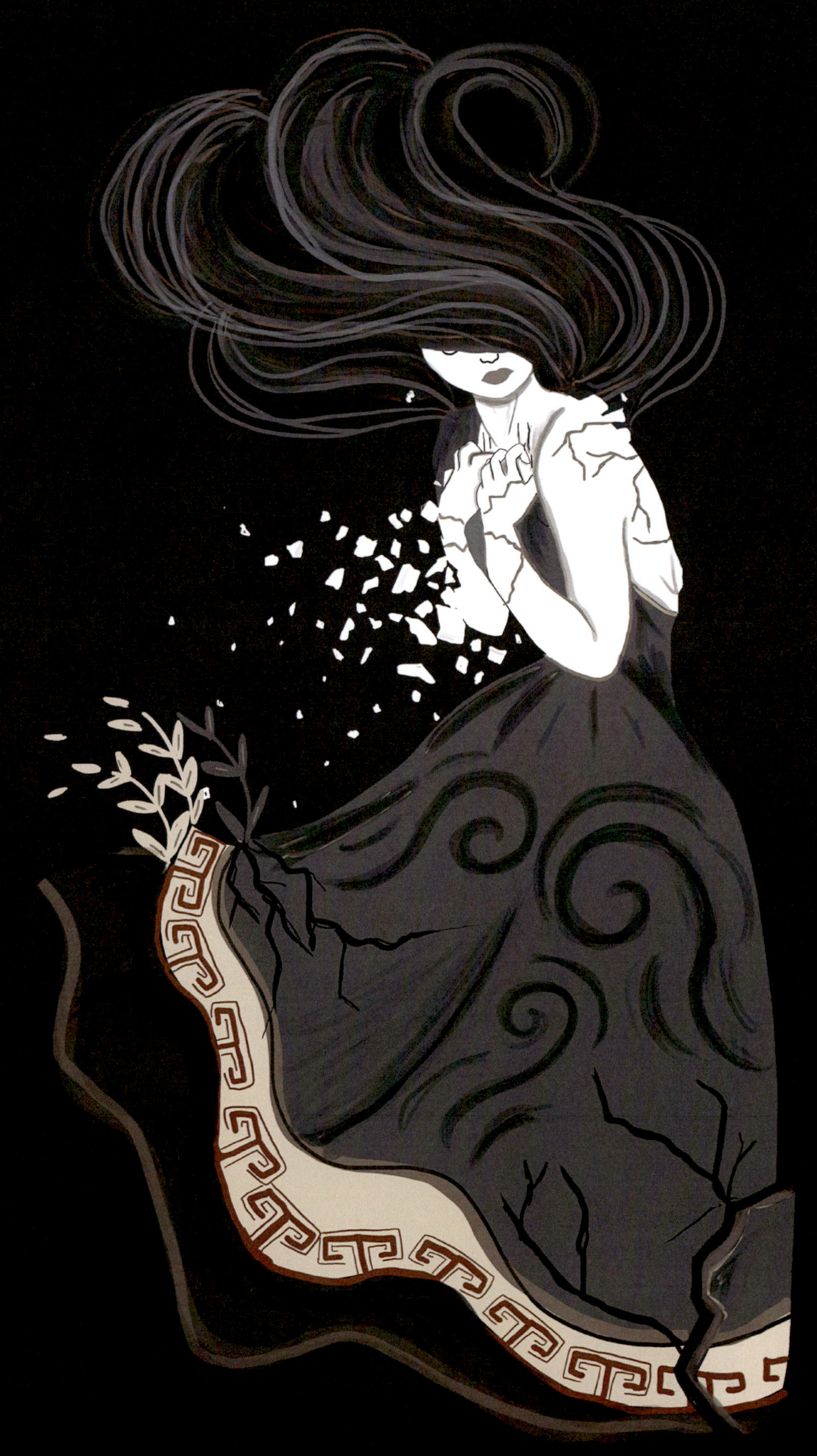

OIZYS

Often overlooked in favor of her more celebrated counterparts within Greek mythology, Oizys (*oy-zee-sis*) represents the darker side of existence, personifying misery, suffering, and hardship. Oizys is primarily known as a daughter of Nyx, the primordial goddess of night, and Erebus, the god of darkness. As such, she is closely associated with the darker forces of the cosmos, embodying the negativity that can permeate human life. In some accounts, Oizys is also considered the sister of Moros (doom), Keres (violent death), Thanatos (death), Hypnos (sleep), and Nemesis (retribution).

The goddess is often depicted as a pale and emaciated figure, her face etched with lines of sorrow and her eyes filled with tears. Her presence is said to bring a sense of heaviness and despair, casting a shadow over even the most joyful occasions. In artistic representations, she is sometimes shown holding a skull or a vial of poison, illustrating the destructive nature of her influence. Although Oizys might be perceived as a purely negative force, her presence in Greek mythology is not without purpose. In a world where gods and goddesses often represent idealized versions of human experience, Oizys serves as a reminder of the harsh realities of life. Her presence acknowledges the inevitability of suffering and the importance of confronting pain and adversity.

In some interpretations, Oizys is also seen as a source of catharsis, providing an outlet for the expression of grief and sorrow. By personifying these emotions, she allows individuals to confront and process their anguish, ultimately leading to healing and growth. In this sense, Oizys can be seen as a paradoxical figure, both a source of suffering and a catalyst for healing, and her presence offers valuable perspective on the complexities of human experience.

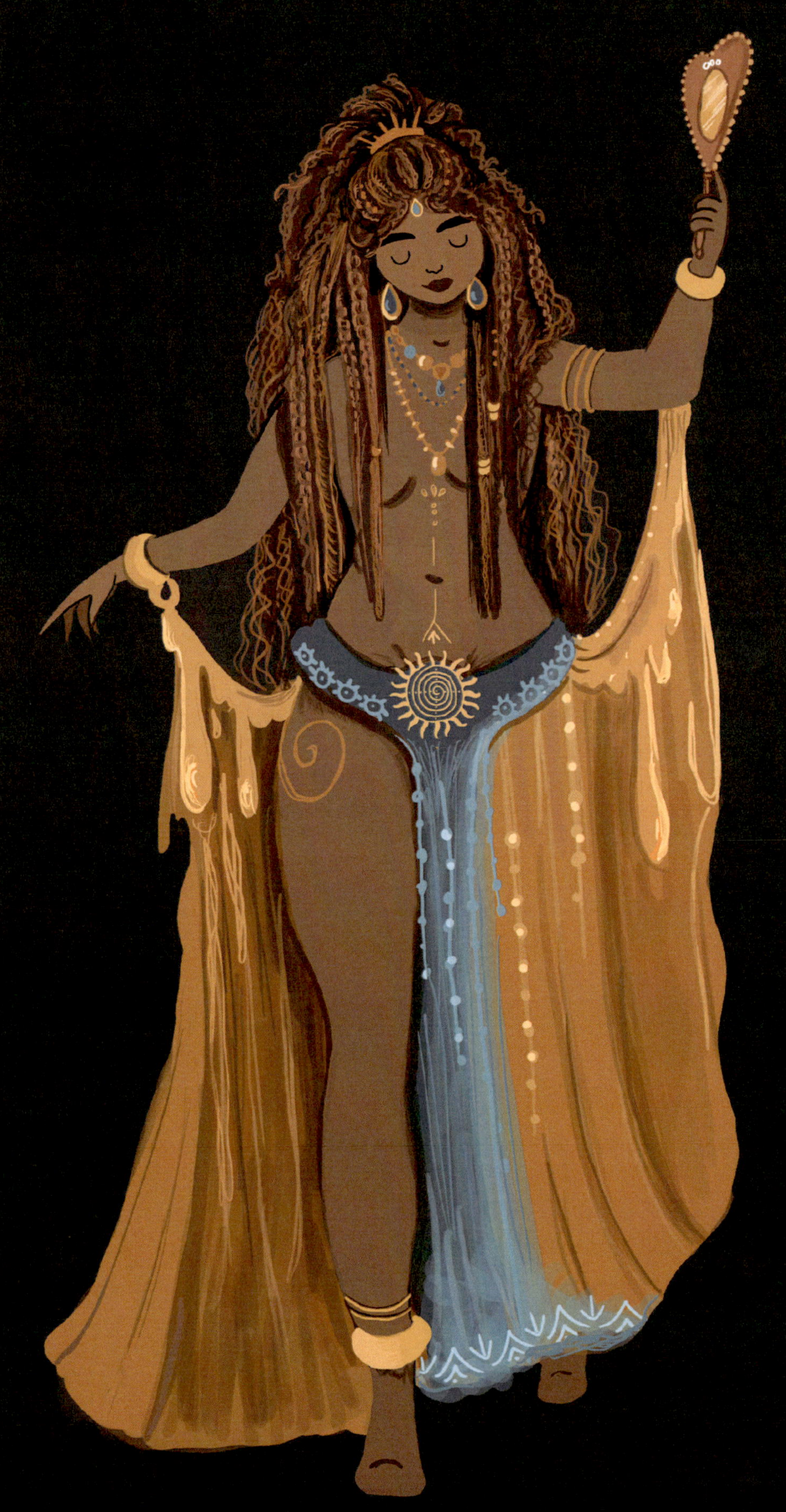

OSHUN

"THERE IS NO PLACE WHERE OSHUN IS NOT KNOWN..."

—THOMAS LINDON, *"ORÍKÌ ÒRÌ À: THE YORUBA PRAYER OF PRAISE" (1990)*

Oshun (*oh-shoon*), also known as the "spirit of sweet water" and the "orisha of the river," is the embodiment of love, beauty, abundance, and divination within the Yoruba religion. She is one of the many orisha, spirits pivotal to Yoruba religions and all beliefs born from it. Oshun governs all things that flow: honey, water, money, and romance. The worship of Oshun dates back to ancient times, with archaeological evidence suggesting her veneration in precolonial Yoruba societies. Oral traditions and mythology cast her as one of the primordial deities, sent by the supreme god Olodumare to shape the earth and establish human civilization. Oshun's association with rivers, particularly the Osun River in Nigeria, reinforces her connection to the life-giving forces of water and the natural world.

Despite being one of over 400 Yoruba orisha, Oshun is generally considered among the most powerful. She is said to watch over sensuality, passion, and romantic relationships. Her association with beauty extends beyond physical attractiveness, encompassing inner radiance, grace, and the appreciation of art and aesthetics. Oshun is also revered as a goddess of fertility, symbolizing both procreation and abundance in all forms. Her connection to prosperity incorporates material wealth, spiritual well-being, and the flourishing of communities.

Oshun's cultural significance extends beyond religious practices. In Yoruba communities, she is venerated through elaborate ceremonies, offerings, and dances that celebrate her attributes and seek her blessings. Oshun festivals, such as the Osun-Osogbo festival, attract devotees and tourists alike, showcasing the vibrant cultural traditions associated with the goddess. Oshun's significance transcends geographical boundaries, reaching the African diaspora through the transatlantic slave trade. In the Americas, particularly in Brazil and Cuba, Oshun was hybridized with Catholic saints, such as Our Lady of Charity, preserving her essence within new cultural contexts.

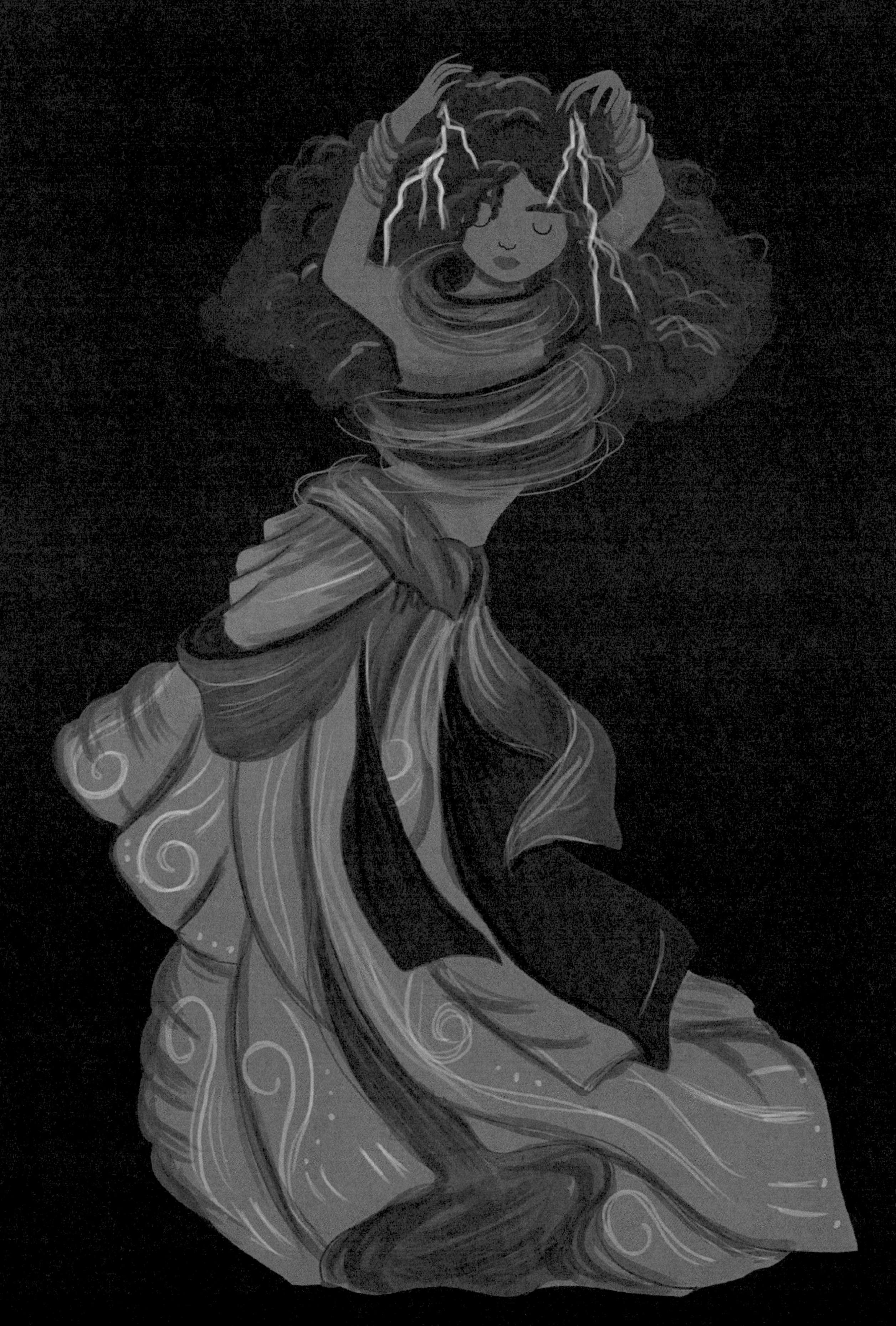

OYA

"TAKE MY RIVERS, ALL OF YOU, & DRINK THEM..."

—HONORÉE FANONNE JEFFERS, "OYA'S RAGE" (2000)

Rooted in the natural world, Oya (*oh-yah*) is one of the most powerful of all the orisha, or venerated spirits of the Yoruba tradition. She governs over thunder, rainstorms, and the winds of inevitable change. Oya is a fierce warrior of justice, standing guard over the realm between life and death. With a wave of her hand, she can conjure hurricanes throughout the Caribbean and tornadoes across West Africa. Oya is revered for her affinity for clairvoyance and the magical arts, and as a powerful orator, she speaks the truth, no matter how hard it may be to hear.

Oya's multifaceted nature in Yoruba mythology is reflected in her diverse associations. The color maroon, often linked to her, signifies change and potent energy. The significant Niger River is also tied to her, representing her power over vital waterways and transitions. Complementing these aspects, Oya is frequently portrayed as a formidable warrior, wielding a sword or other weapon, and is celebrated in legends for her leadership of armies in times of conflict. In some Yoruba communities, women held positions of power and authority within Oya's priesthood. These priestesses were responsible for leading rituals, interpreting prophecies, and providing guidance to the community.

The origins of Oya's worship can be traced back to ancient Yoruba society. As Yoruba history was largely preserved and conveyed orally through generations, the precise date of her emergence remains elusive. However, archaeological evidence and oral traditions suggest that Oya has been venerated for centuries. Oya was worshipped alongside other orishas like the similar Shango, the god of thunder and lightning, and Oshun, the goddess of love, fertility, and rivers. Each orisha has a specific role to play in maintaining balance and harmony within the natural and spiritual worlds.

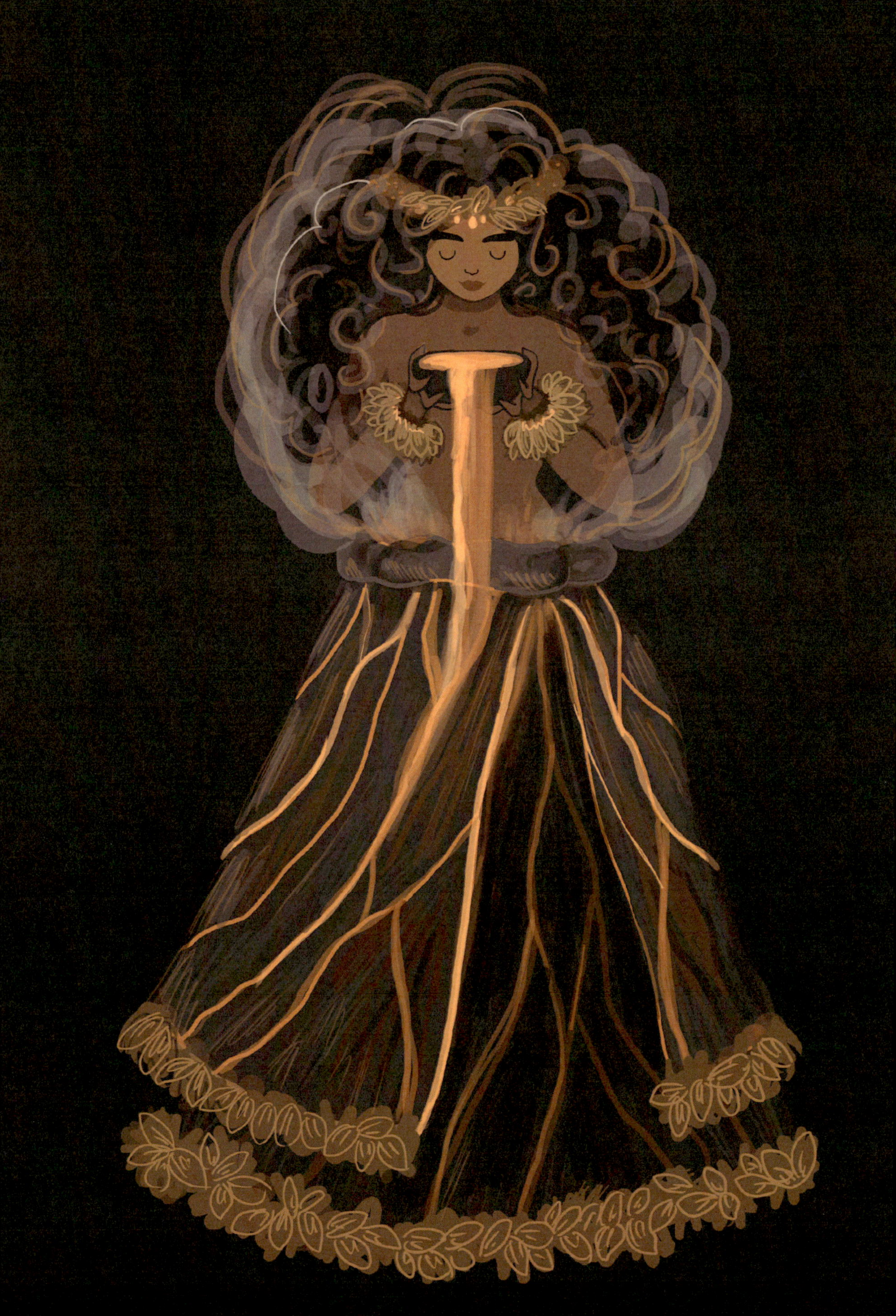

PELE

Deep within the Kīlauea volcano resides Pele (*peh-leh*), the Hawaiian goddess of fire, lightning, and dance. Traditional Hawaiian chants proclaim Pele to be "she who shapes the sacred land" and the "earth-eating woman," emphasizing her powerful connection to the Hawaiian landscape. While Christian missionaries sought to abolish indigenous Hawaiian religions, her legacy endured in secret among rural communities before experiencing a significant revival during the Second Hawaiian Renaissance of the 1970s. Revered as both a creator and destroyer, her presence is deeply intertwined with the geological dynamism of the Hawaiian Islands.

Pele's mythological origins are steeped in Polynesian oral traditions, where she is identified as the offspring of Haumea, an ancient earth goddess, and Kane Milohai, a creator deity. Her numerous siblings each embody a different natural force. Accounts often describe Pele's fiery temperament and volcanic nature as causing conflict within her family, leading to her eventual exit from her original homeland. These narratives detail her voyage across the Pacific Ocean, during which she tested various islands by digging fiery pits with her magic staff, pāoa. She ultimately found her new home on the Big Island of Hawaii, specifically within the Halemaʻumaʻu crater of Kīlauea volcano. This active volcanic landscape, characterized by continuous eruptions and dramatic lava flows, has become synonymous with Pele's powerful and enduring presence.

The historical worship of Pele is inextricably linked with the social and political structures of ancient Hawaiʻi. The *Aliʻi*, or ruling chiefs, held Pele in high regard, recognizing her immense power and seeking her blessings for their communities. This reverence for Pele carried practical implications for traditional land management and resource allocation. Volcanic eruptions, while inherently destructive, also provided fertile soil and other natural resources, profoundly shaping the way the Hawaiian people interact with their environment. The ongoing volcanic activity of Kīlauea serves as a constant, tangible reminder of her pervasive influence.

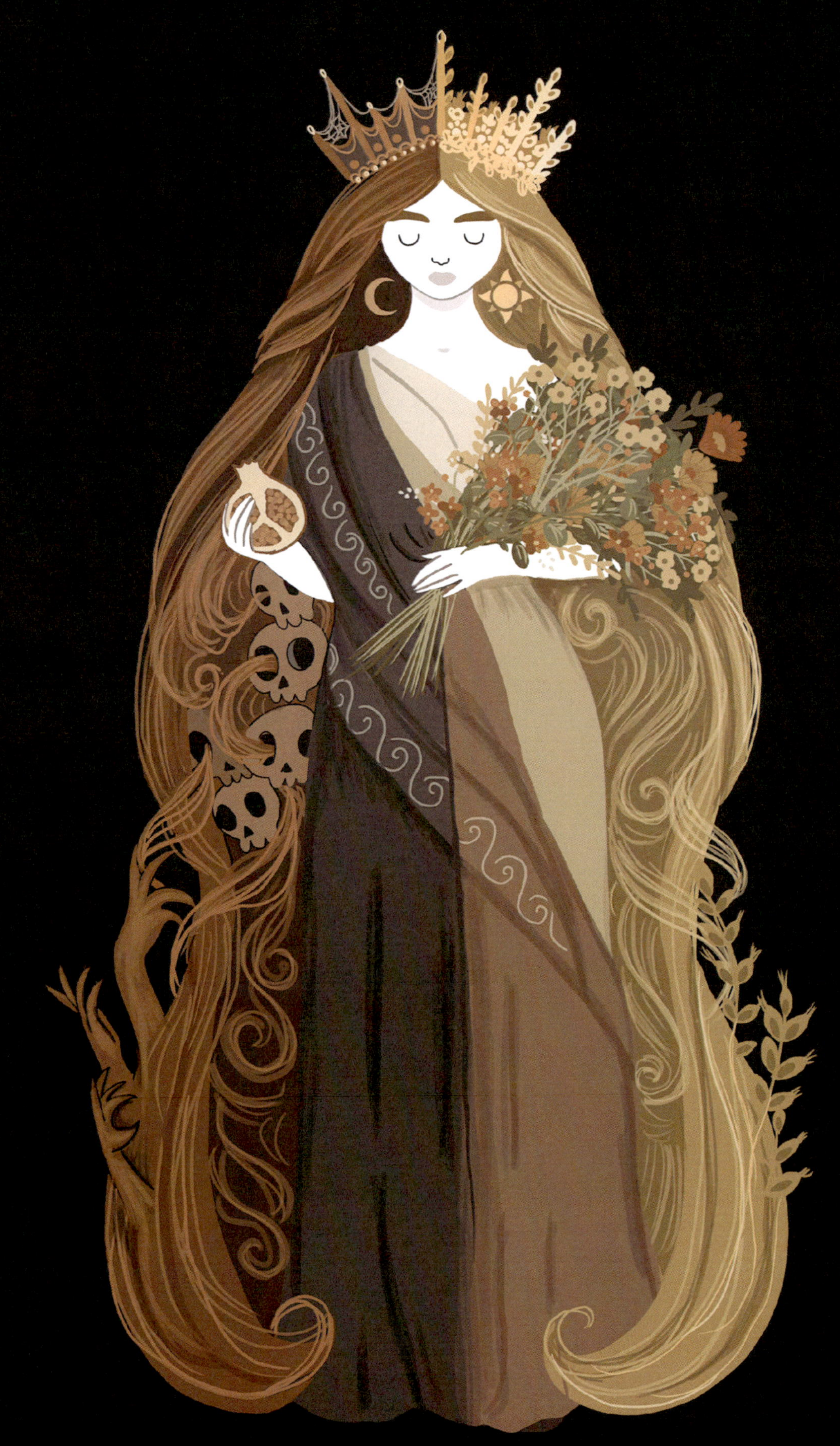

PERSEPHONE

"Pluto's honor'd wife, O venerable Goddess, source of life."

—**Orphic Hymns**, Hymn XXVIII ("To Persephone")

In the realm of Greek mythology, Persephone (*per-seh-fuh-nee*) stands as a captivating figure, serving as an embodiment of the cyclical nature of life, death, and rebirth. She is the daughter of Demeter, the goddess of agriculture, and Zeus, the king of the gods. Beyond her more widely known name, Persephone was also referred to as *Kore*, meaning "maiden" or "girl." Her mythology features themes of abduction, loss, and resilience, illustrating her unique navigation between the worlds of the living and the dead.

Persephone's most famous myth, concerning her abduction by Hades, the god of the Underworld, is central to understanding her dual nature. This pivotal event, which occurred while she was gathering flowers, directly triggered Demeter's profound grief. As a consequence of this sorrow, the land became barren and lifeless, leading to widespread famine. Though Zeus initially permitted Hades to claim Persephone, the suffering of humanity compelled him to intervene, orchestrating her retrieval. However, due to her consumption of pomegranate seeds while in the Underworld, Persephone became permanently bound to a cyclical return, requiring her to spend a certain number of months each year with Hades.

This recurring cycle, directly reflecting Persephone's presence in each realm, is understood as the origin of the seasons. Her time on earth corresponds with the blossoming of spring and the bountiful harvest of summer. Conversely, her return to the Underworld ushers in the waning warmth of autumn and the icy grip of winter. Her yearly journey signifies the transformative power of nature and the constant ebb and flow between growth and decay. The myth of Persephone was also central to the *Eleusinian Mysteries*, a secret religious cult that flourished in ancient Greece for centuries. The annual initiation rites, held in the city of Eleusis, were believed to offer participants deeper understanding and a glimpse into the afterlife.

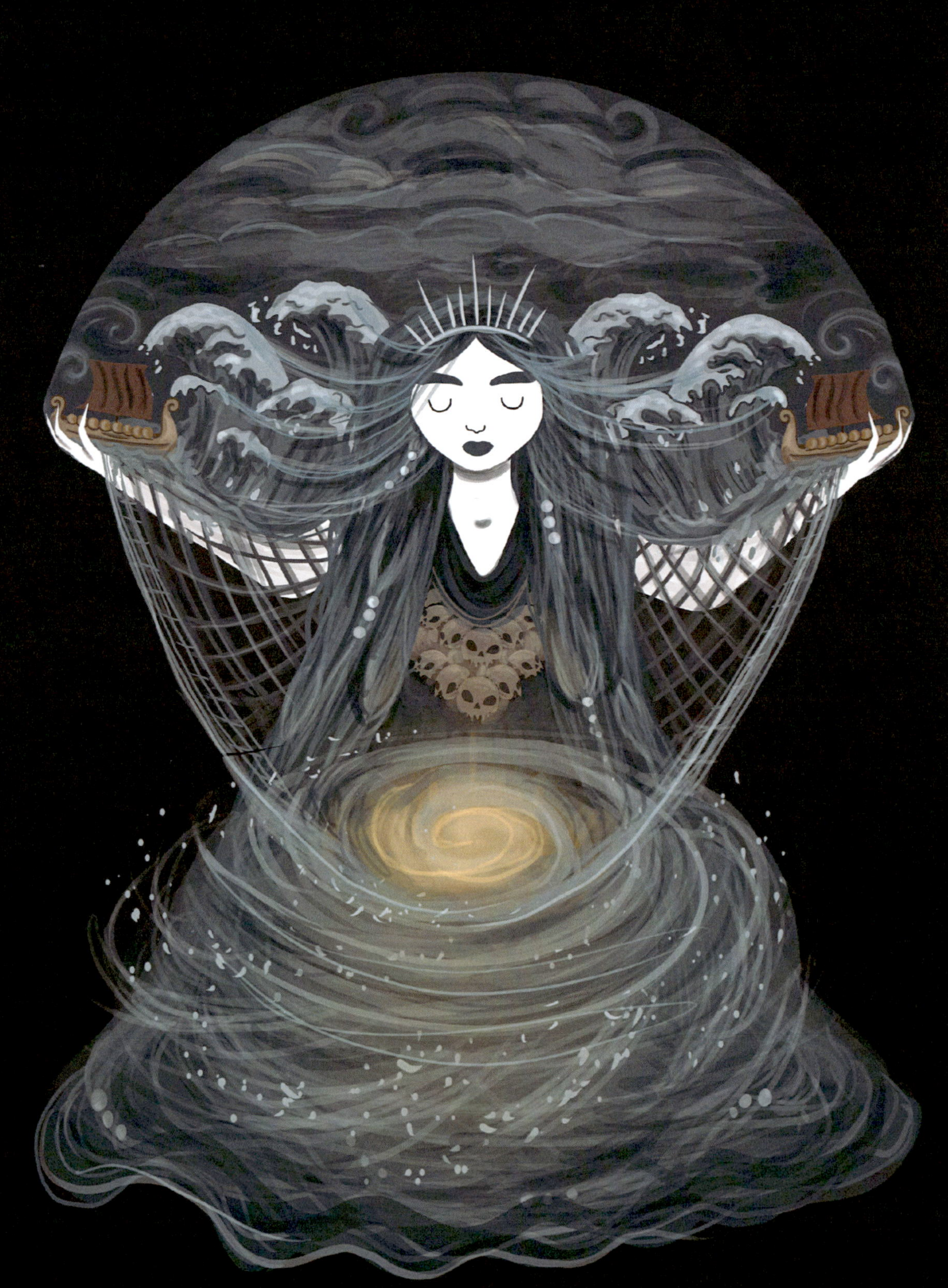

RÁN

"THEN THE SHIP OF THE BATTLE-BOLD HERO BROKE ASUNDER
BENEATH THE BILLOWS OF RÁN."

—**SNORRI STURLUSON,** *POETIC EDDA,* "HELGAKVIÐA HUNDINGSBANA II," STANZA 38

The unpredictable and often perilous nature of the sea is embodied by Rán (*rahwn*), a prominent figure within Norse mythology. As the goddess of the ocean's depths, she holds dominion over the fates of seafarers, so her power is both revered and feared by those who traversed the waves. Her name, derived from Old Norse, translates to "robbery," "theft," or "plunder," reflecting her association with the sea's destructive power. Some legends tell that Rán emerged from the primordial chaos that preceded the creation of the world.

The formidable Rán is often depicted with a net, used to seize unsuspecting sailors and pull them down to her abode beneath the water, where the souls of those lost at sea find their eternal rest. While her actions may seem cruel at first glance, they are a reflection of the sea's inherent dangers and the possibility of death for those who venture into its domain.

In Norse mythology, Rán is married to Ægir, a jötunn, or giant, who also personifies the sea. Together, they have nine daughters who represent the ocean waves. The relationship between Rán and Ægir is described as complementary, with Ægir epitomizing the sea's calmer aspects and Rán manifesting as its more turbulent and destructive forces. Despite her fearsome reputation, Rán was not solely a figure of dread. Her influence extended beyond the realm of the sea, as she was also associated with wealth and abundance. This connection arose from the belief that Rán hoarded the sea's vast treasures, including gold and precious jewels, within her underwater home. In some accounts, gold is even referred to as "Rán's fire." Fishermen and sailors would offer sacrifices to Rán, hoping to appease her and ensure safe passage across the oceans.

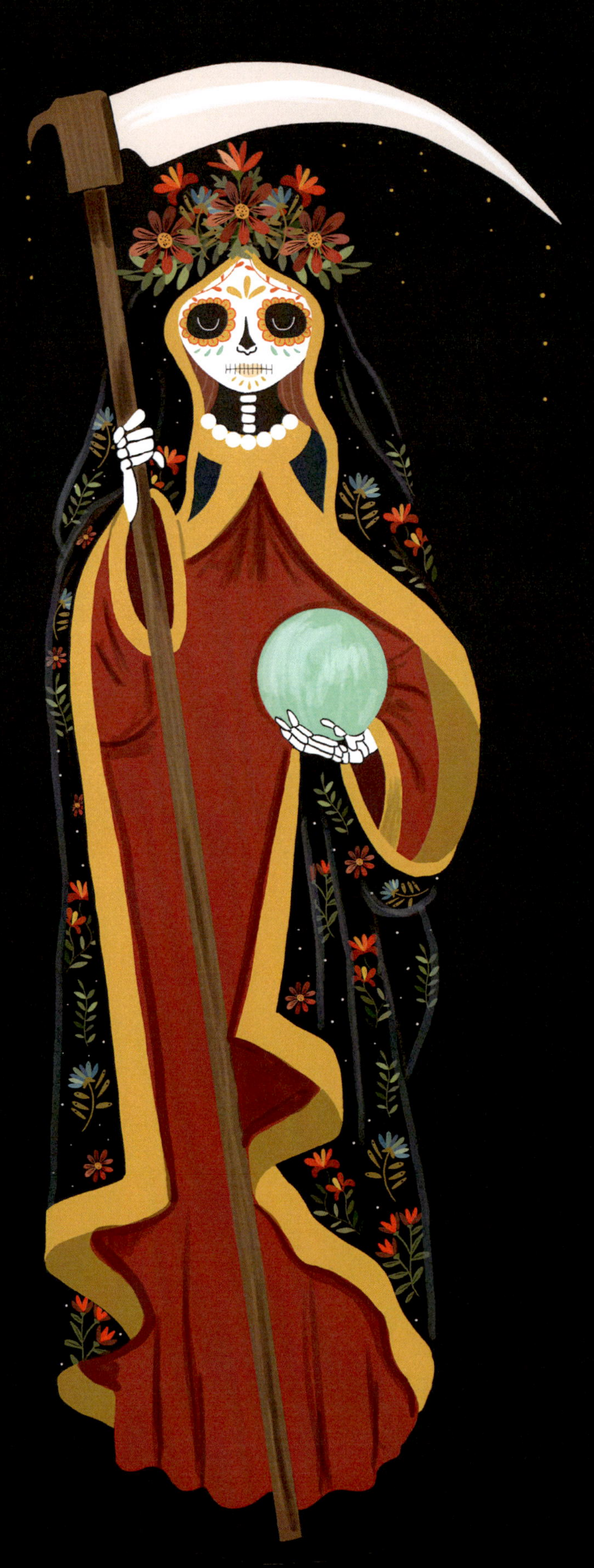

SANTA MUERTE

"HOLY DEATH…PLACE US IN A CELESTIAL SPHERE WHERE WE'LL ENJOY DAYS WITHOUT NIGHTS FOR ALL ETERNITY."

—JOHN THOMPSON, "SANTÍSIMA MUERTE: ON THE ORIGIN AND DEVELOPMENT OF A MEXICAN OCCULT IMAGE"(1998)

Known as *Nuestra Señora de la Santa Muerte*, or "Our Lady of the Holy Death," Santa Muerte is a highly revered deity within Mexican neo-paganism and folk Catholicism. She is the personification of death itself, often depicted as a female skeleton beneath a robe of ever-changing color, holding a scythe in one hand and a globe in the other. The followers of Santa Muerte also associate her with healing, protection, and safe passage to the afterlife. While this depiction is relatively recent, her roots can be traced back to ancient traditions and beliefs surrounding death and the afterlife.

The concept of a deity or figure representing death is not unique to Santa Muerte. Throughout history, many cultures have personified death in various forms. While these figures share similarities with Santa Muerte, her modern manifestation is a product of Mexican culture and history. It is believed that her following emerged during the colonial period, likely due to a mixing of indigenous beliefs and Catholicism. Over time, Santa Muerte evolved, incorporating elements from various traditions, including European folklore and African spirituality. Her devotees come from all walks of life to seek her assistance with protection, healing, and financial well-being.

Santa Muerte's popularity has surged in recent decades, particularly in Mexico. However, her growing popularity has not been without controversy. The Catholic Church and some evangelical groups have condemned her worship, labeling it as blasphemous and demonic However, many of her devotees argue that these negative portrayals are inaccurate and misrepresent their faith. She is a figure who understands their struggles and offers solace in the face of adversity. Her veneration is a testament to the enduring human need for spiritual connection and the power of faith to transcend cultural and religious boundaries.

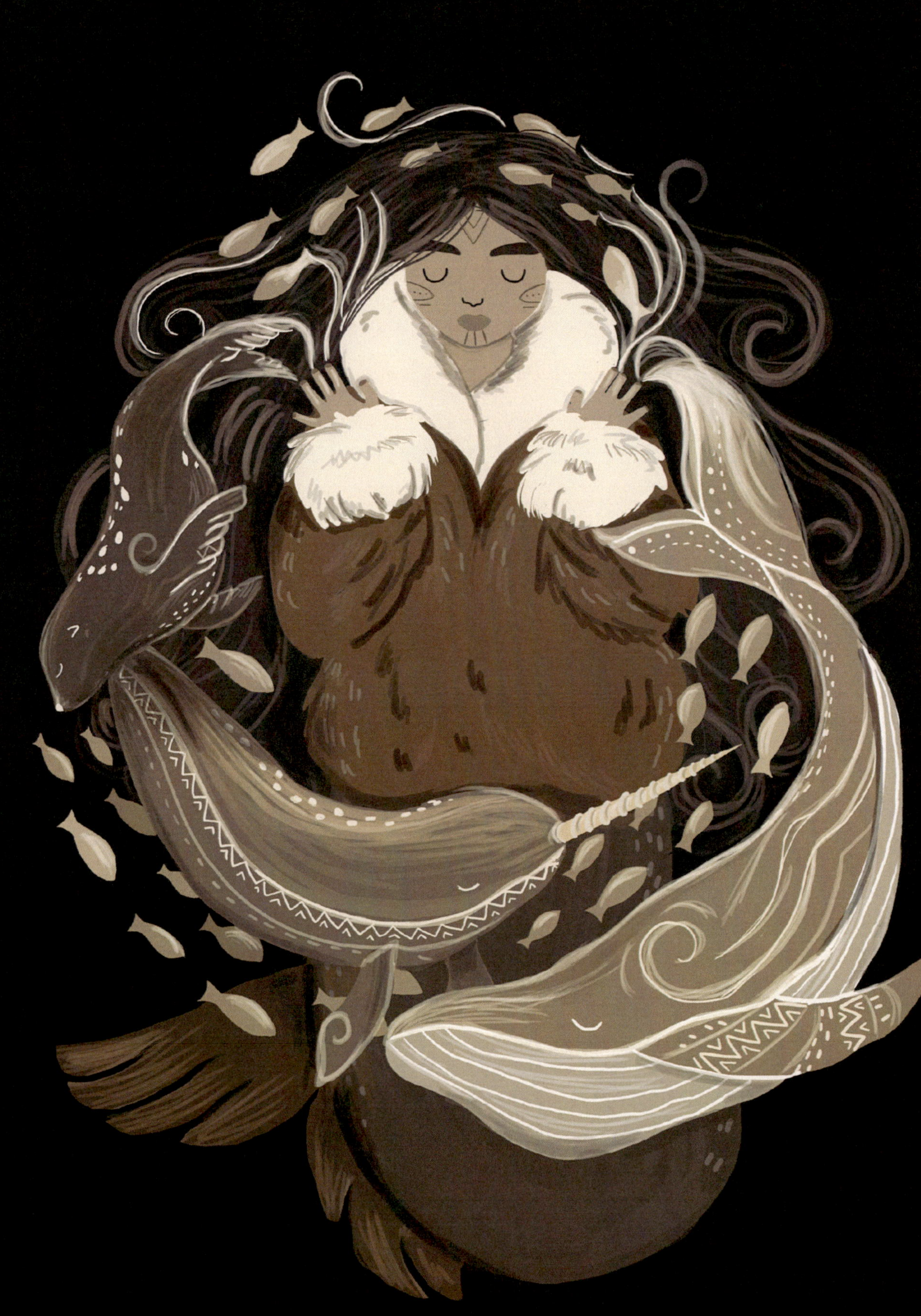

SEDNA

"FROM THE DIFFERENT JOINTS OF HER FINGERS COME THE SEA-MAMMALS..."

—MARGARET LANTIS, "THE MYTHOLOGY OF KODIAK ISLAND, ALASKA" (1938)

Sedna (*sed-nuh*), the revered goddess of the sea and marine animals in Inuit mythology, is known to her followers as the "Mother of the Sea." The Sedna myth, transmitted through generations of Inuit oral tradition, encompasses several variations, but they all depict a young woman named Sedna whose transformative experiences lead to her becoming a powerful deity residing in *Adlivun*, the Inuit underworld.

The various origin narratives of Sedna consistently illustrate her profound connection to the sea and marine life. In some accounts, her transformation into a sea goddess is directly linked to her father's actions. One version describes his enraged response to her dissatisfaction with suitors, resulting in him casting her into the sea and severing her fingers as she attempted to reenter his boat. These fingers became the first seals. Other traditions portray Sedna as a giant, whose aggressive actions lead to her being thrown overboard by her father, Anguta. Again, her fingers are severed and become various marine mammals. Through this process, she descends to rule the underwater realm.

The Sedna myth serves multiple crucial purposes within Inuit culture. It functions primarily as an explanation for the origins of marine animals, while the narratives emphasize the importance of respecting these animals and the critical need for balance between hunting and conservation. Depending on the telling, Sedna's mythos sometimes functions as a cautionary tale, highlighting the severe consequences of greed, disobedience, and the mistreatment of family members. Her ultimate fate acts as a stark warning against such behaviors, underscoring the vital importance of social harmony and respect for elders. Ultimately, Sedna's story reflects the harsh realities of life in the Arctic, where survival is intrinsically dependent on a close, respectful relationship with the environment and its resources.

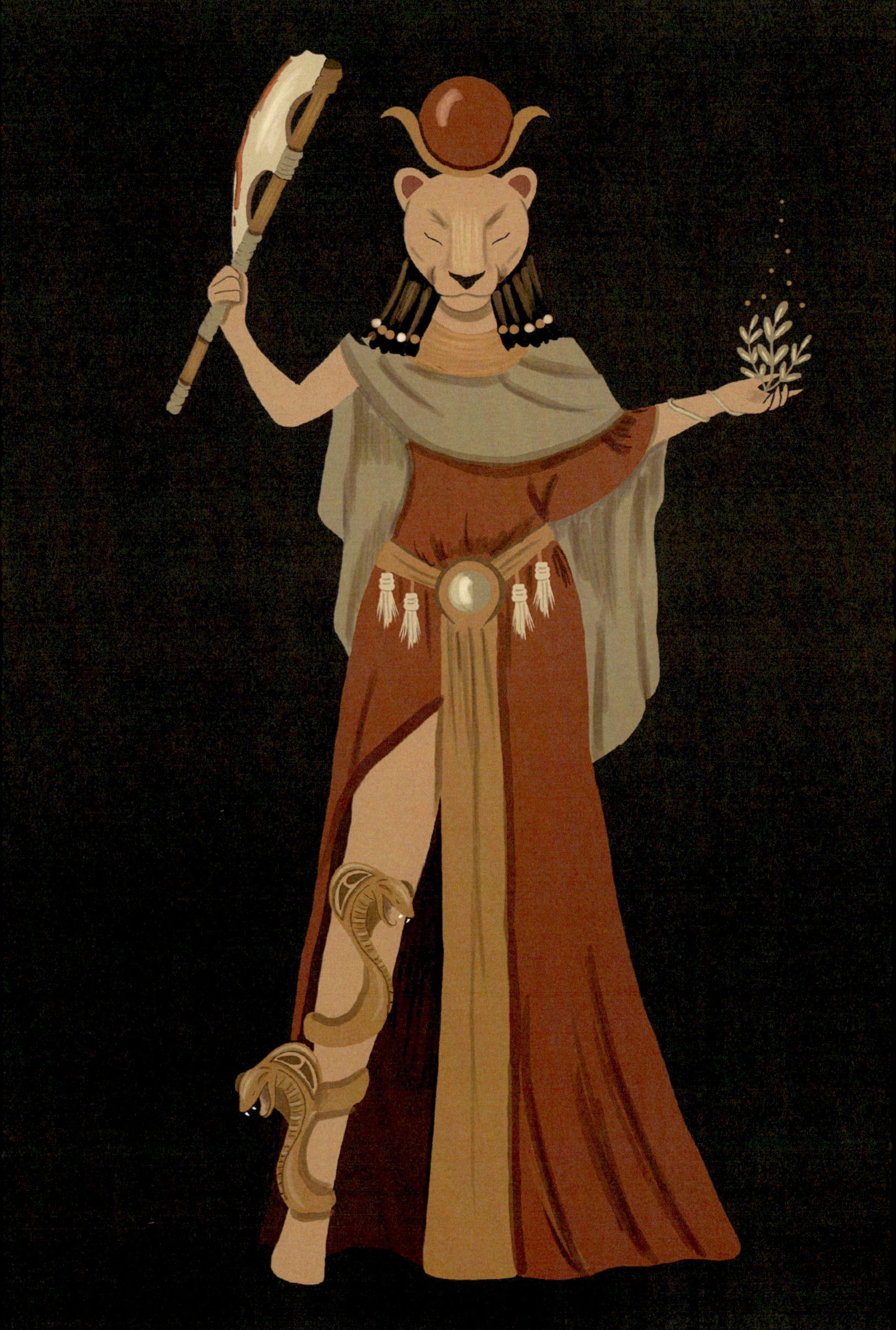

SEKHMET

"O SEKHMET, GREAT OF MAGIC, MIGHTY OF POWER."

—*BOOK OF THE DEAD,* CHAPTER 17

Within Egyptian mythology, Sekhmet (*sehk-met*), the great warrior lioness, wielded immense power over warfare, justice, and healing. Even amidst the extensive pantheon of ancient Egypt, with its deities experiencing cyclical worship, Sekhmet remained a vital and enduring presence for those who invoked her. Due to the wide-ranging aspects of her mythos, she was known by many titles, such as "One Before Whom Evil Trembles" and "She Who Mauls." As a solar deity, Sekhmet was normally depicted adorned with both the solar disk (Aten) and the Uraeus, a stylized, upright cobra denoting royalty or divine authority.

Sekhmet's origins are inextricably linked to the sun god Ra, particularly through a key myth illustrating her dual nature as both punisher and protector. According to this narrative, Sekhmet was brought into existence from the fiery gaze of Ra, unleashed to chastise humanity for its disobedience against Ma'at, the goddess of cosmic order and justice. This initial act of divine retribution saw Sekhmet unleash immense destructive power, nearly annihilating humankind. However, the myth concludes with Ra's intervention, where he appeased her bloodlust with a cunning ruse involving beer mixed with red ochre, effectively halting her rampage and preserving humanity.

While Sekhmet's primary function was as a goddess of war and destruction, she served another vital role as a healer. Specializing in both blood ailments and the menstrual cycle, the goddess was routinely invoked for aid, particularly concerning women's reproductive health. Historical practices, such as the pharaoh Amenhotep III's placement of over 600 Sekhmet statues within his temple (circa 1386–1349 BCE), illustrate her renown as a healer as well as a fierce warrior.

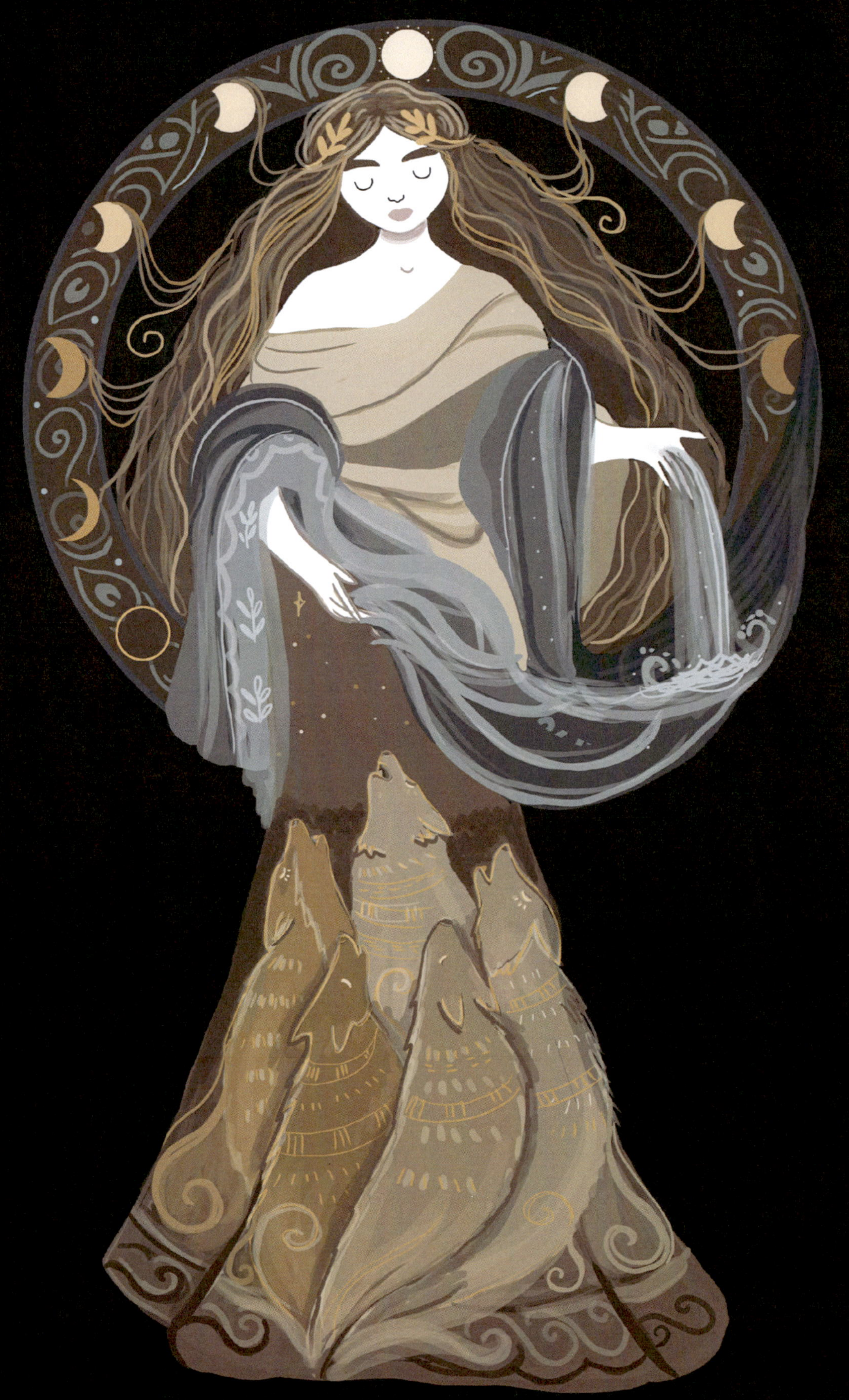

SELENE

"ROSY-FINGERED SELENE AFTER SUNSET, SURPASSING ALL THE STARS...THE DEW IS SHED IN BEAUTY, AND ROSES BLOOM AND TENDER CHERVIL AND FLOWERY MELILOT."

—**SAPPHO,** FRAGMENT 96

Born of Titans and sister to both "Dawn" and "Sun," Selene (*suh-lee-nee*) is the moon incarnate within the rich tapestry of Greek mythology. Together, this triumvirate of celestial deities orchestrated the daily cycle of light and darkness. Although other goddesses also held lunar associations, Selene alone was distinguished by Greek poets and historians as the direct personification of the moon in both its physical and spiritual forms.

Selene's mythological activities frequently illustrate her connection to the night sky and its influence. Legends describe her nightly immersion in the sea before ascending to the sky on her chariot, a symbolic representation of the moon's rise above the horizon and its effect on the tides. Her mythology also includes a prominent, albeit tragic, love story involving the mortal shepherd Endymion. Selene was deeply captivated by Endymion's beauty, leading her to visit him during his slumber. Recognizing the disparity between her immortality and his human lifespan, Selene, out of a profound inability to endure his eventual demise, ultimately employed her divine power to cast an everlasting sleep upon him. This act secured his eternal life as her lover, transforming a fleeting connection into a perpetual bond.

The name Selene derives from the Greek word *mene*, signifying both "month" and "menstruation," a linguistic connection that deeply roots her identity in the cyclical rhythms of time and the feminine body, both already highly linked to the moon. Within certain interpretations of the Triple Goddess archetype, Selene embodies the nurturing and generative "mother" phase, a role that signifies the fullness of creation, fertility, and mature power. She is positioned alongside Artemis, who represents the youthful, independent "maiden" aspect, and Hecate, who embodies the wise, transformative "crone" phase, thereby highlighting Selene's multifaceted symbolism within Greek thought as the cosmic nurturer.

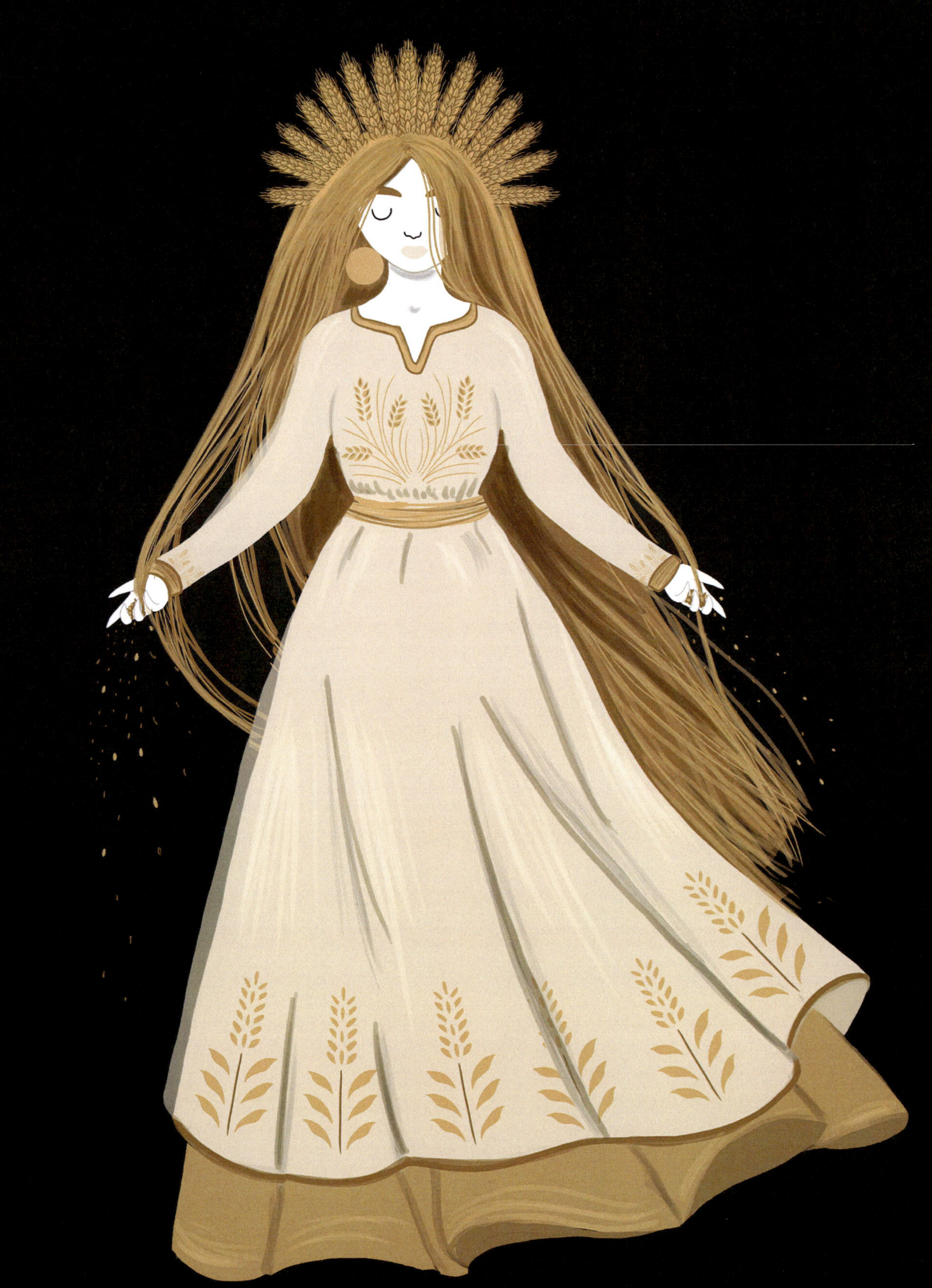

SIF

A prominent member of the Ásynjur, the major goddesses of Asgard, Sif (*siff*) is regarded as the goddess of fertility, family, and the earth. Her most notable feature is her long, golden hair, which is frequently described as resembling fields of wheat ready for harvest, solidifying her agricultural associations. While the precise origins of Sif's worship remain unclear, she is believed to have been a popular pre-Christian goddess among the Germanic people. Her significance in Norse mythology is primarily inferred from various sources, including the *Poetic Edda* and *Prose Edda*, both compiled in the thirteenth century by Snorri Sturluson.

Sif's core symbolic importance is famously highlighted in a key myth involving the trickster god Loki. In this narrative, Loki's mischievous act of cutting off her golden hair directly challenges Sif's representation of fertility and natural abundance. Thor's subsequent outrage over this act is a central element of the tale, compelling Loki to undertake a quest for a magical, dwarven-made replacement. This event is pivotal in revealing the cultural importance placed upon Sif's beauty and her association with the vital forces of fertility and the earth.

As a key motif in her narratives, Sif's hair functions as a powerful symbol of the earth's fertility, its golden sheen directly representing the ripened bounty of grain fields. The act of its removal within the myth exemplifies a disruption of the natural order and agricultural prosperity, thus explaining her husband Thor's fierce reaction and the demand for its restoration. Moreover, this specific tale involving Sif and Loki is renowned for indirectly leading to the creation of several other powerful and famous artifacts in Norse mythology. In his efforts to appease Thor and rectify his mischief, Loki commissions the dwarves to craft not only Sif's replacement hair but also other treasures vital to the Aesir, including Thor's hammer Mjolnir and Odin's spear Gungnir.

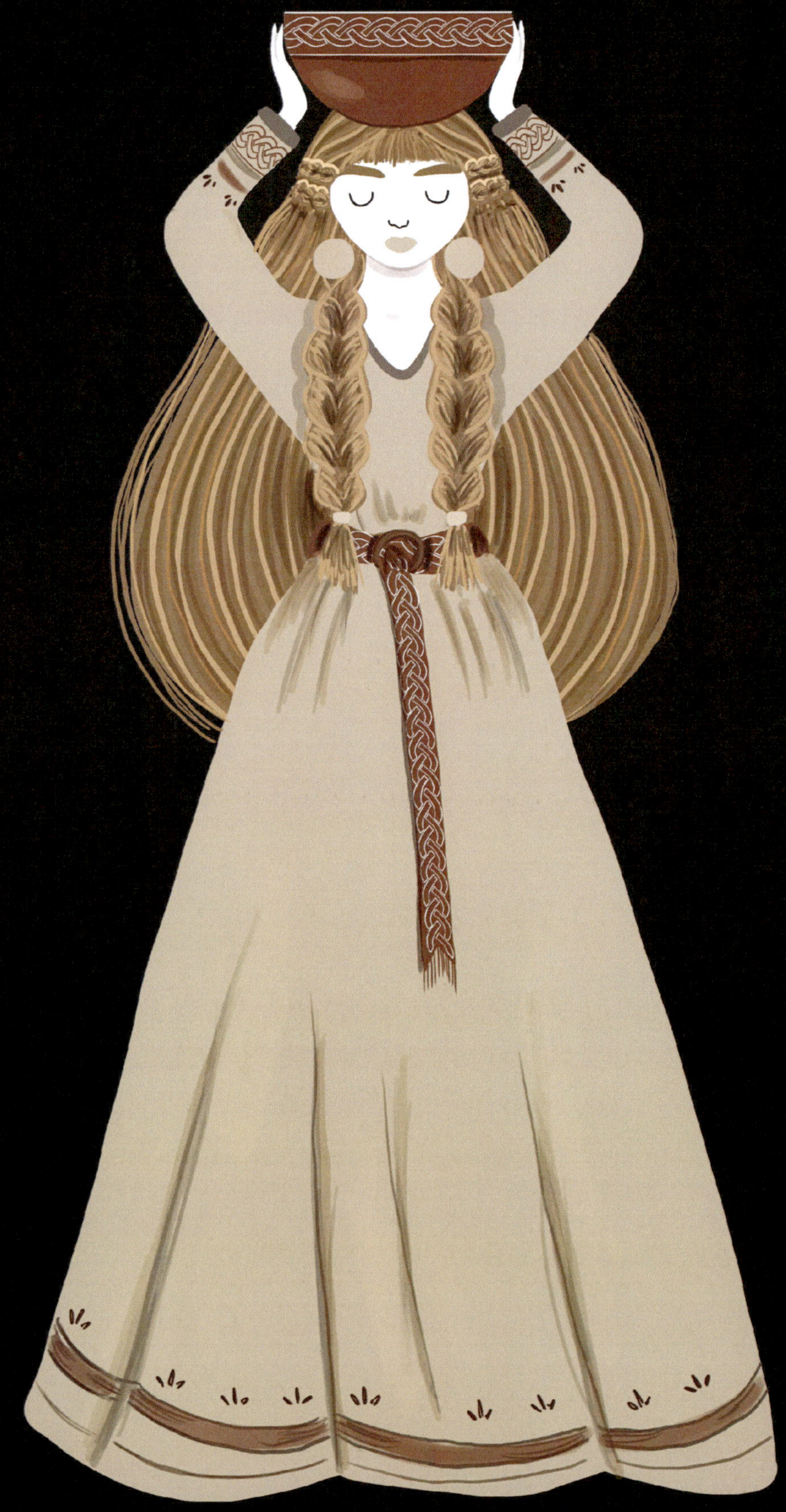

SIGYN

"…HIS WIFE STANDS BY HIM AND HOLDS A DISH UNDER THE VENOM;
BUT WHEN THE DISH IS FULL, SHE GOES AWAY TO EMPTY IT."

—**SNORRI STURLUSON,** *PROSE EDDA*, "GYLFAGINNING," CHAPTER 50

Despite the notoriously fragmented nature of Norse mythological sources, sufficient information has survived to provide background on the goddess Sigyn (*sig-in*), the deity of fidelity, nurturing, and grieving and the wife of the trickster god Loki. After Loki orchestrated the death of the god Baldur, she played an integral, albeit passive role.

Sigyn's unwavering loyalty and nurturing nature are prominently illustrated by her actions in response to Loki's punishment. Following Baldur's demise, Loki was condemned to a cave, where a snake's venom was set to drip upon him as unending torment. In a profound display of devotion, Sigyn remained steadfastly by his side, continuously holding a bowl to catch the corrosive venom and offer him momentary respite. This portrayal highlights her admirable and tragic loyalty, often interpreted as either a subservient act or a powerful demonstration of strength and resilience in the face of immense suffering.

Sigyn's presence in the *Poetic Edda*, a collection of Old Norse poems, is more subtle, with fleeting but significant mentions. For instance, she appears within the *Völuspá*, a pivotal poem that vividly recounts the chain of events culminating in Ragnarök, the prophesized apocalypse. Even these brief references underscore her enduring presence within the cosmic narrative of destruction and renewal. Beyond these primary sources, narratives featuring Sigyn are relatively sparse. However, Old Norse poetry further solidifies the connection between Sigyn and Loki through *kennings*, or poetic circumlocutions; these often refer to Loki as "Sigyn's husband" or "the burden of Sigyn's arms." Additionally, her name has been linked to the Old Norse words *sigr* ("victory") and *vina* ("friend"), suggesting a translation of "friend of victory," an interpretation that aligns with her role as a steadfast supporter of Loki, despite his association with chaos and trickery.

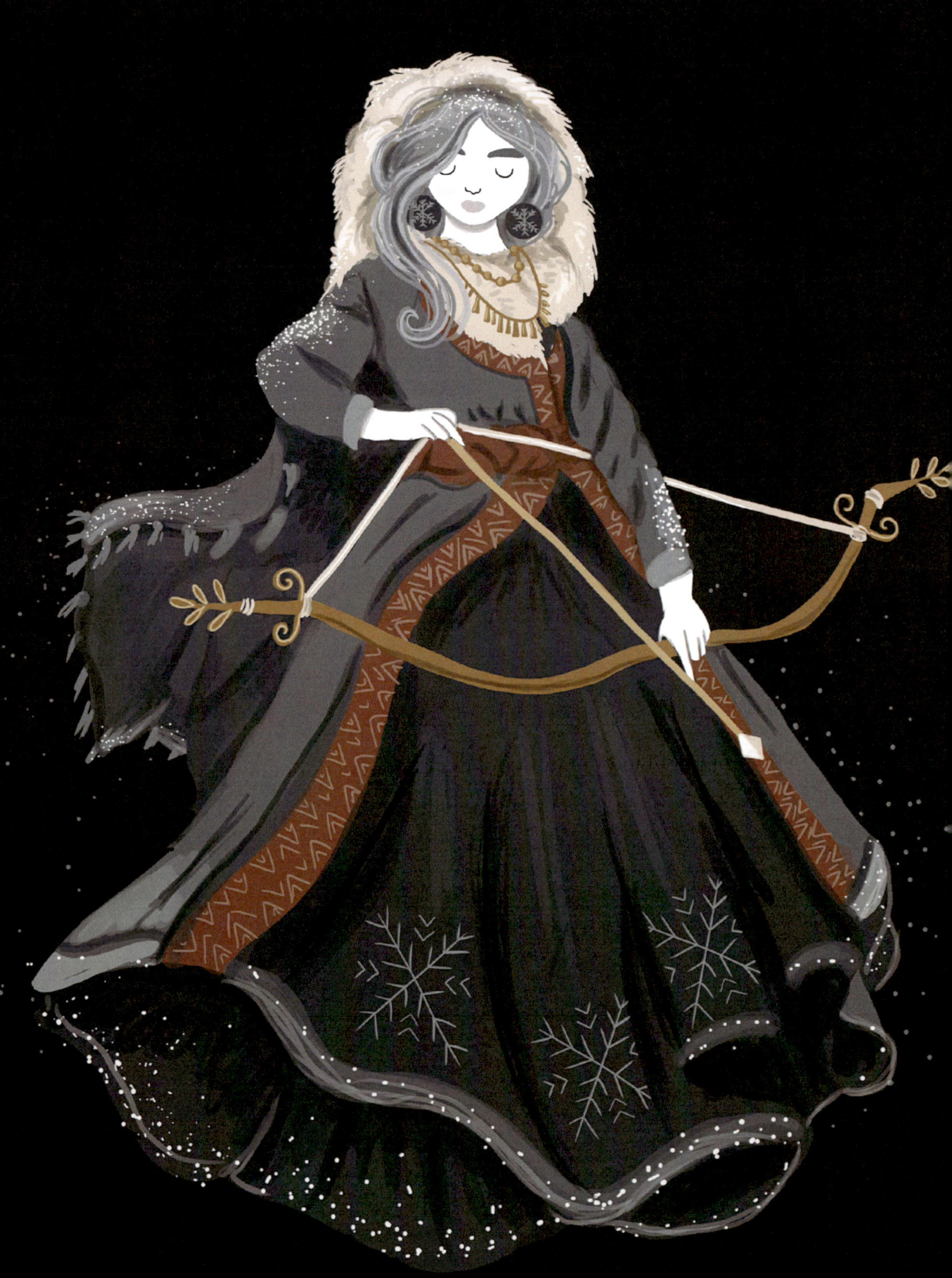

SKAÐI

"She went with armed men to Ásgarðr after the death of her father…and the Aesir offered her atonement and reconciliation."

—**Snorri Sturluson,** *Prose Edda,* "Gylfaginning," chapter 23

The Norse goddess Skaði (*ska-thee*) is intrinsically linked to the untamed northern landscapes, dwelling high upon mountaintops where snow perpetually lies, and is frequently depicted with her characteristic bow and snowshoes. Her name, identical with the Old Norse term for "harm" or "damage," likely reflects her lineage from the frost giants; however, she is primarily understood as a benevolent winter patroness. Skaði thus embodies both the harsh beauty and the unforgiving power inherent in these cold environments.

Skaði's mythological origins frequently highlight her independent and formidable nature. As the daughter of the giant Þjazi, whose death occurred at the hands of the gods in retribution for his abduction of Iðunn, Skaði sought recompense from the Aesir. Mythological accounts detail the gods' attempt to appease her by offering a husband from their ranks, under the unique condition that she choose him solely by observing his feet. This led to her betrothal to the sea god Njörðr, a union that ultimately proved ill-suited due to their contrasting domains—Skaði's preference for the mountains versus Njörðr's affinity for the sea. Despite the eventual dissolution of this marriage, Skaði's presence among the Aesir symbolized a fragile peace between the gods and giants, a truce frequently undermined by underlying tensions.

As an adept huntress and skier, Skaði powerfully personifies dominion over winter environments and the tenacity required for survival in harsh conditions. Her strong mountainous associations further cement her link to the untamed wilderness and the elemental power of nature. Skaði's narrative, particularly her interactions with the Aesir, offers a compelling lens through which to examine the intricate and often paradoxical relationships between the gods and giants in Norse mythology. While the overarching mythos frequently depicts them as adversaries locked in existential conflict, Skaði's presence in Asgard serves as a constant reminder of this nuanced interplay, where cooperation and conflict exist in a delicate and shifting balance.

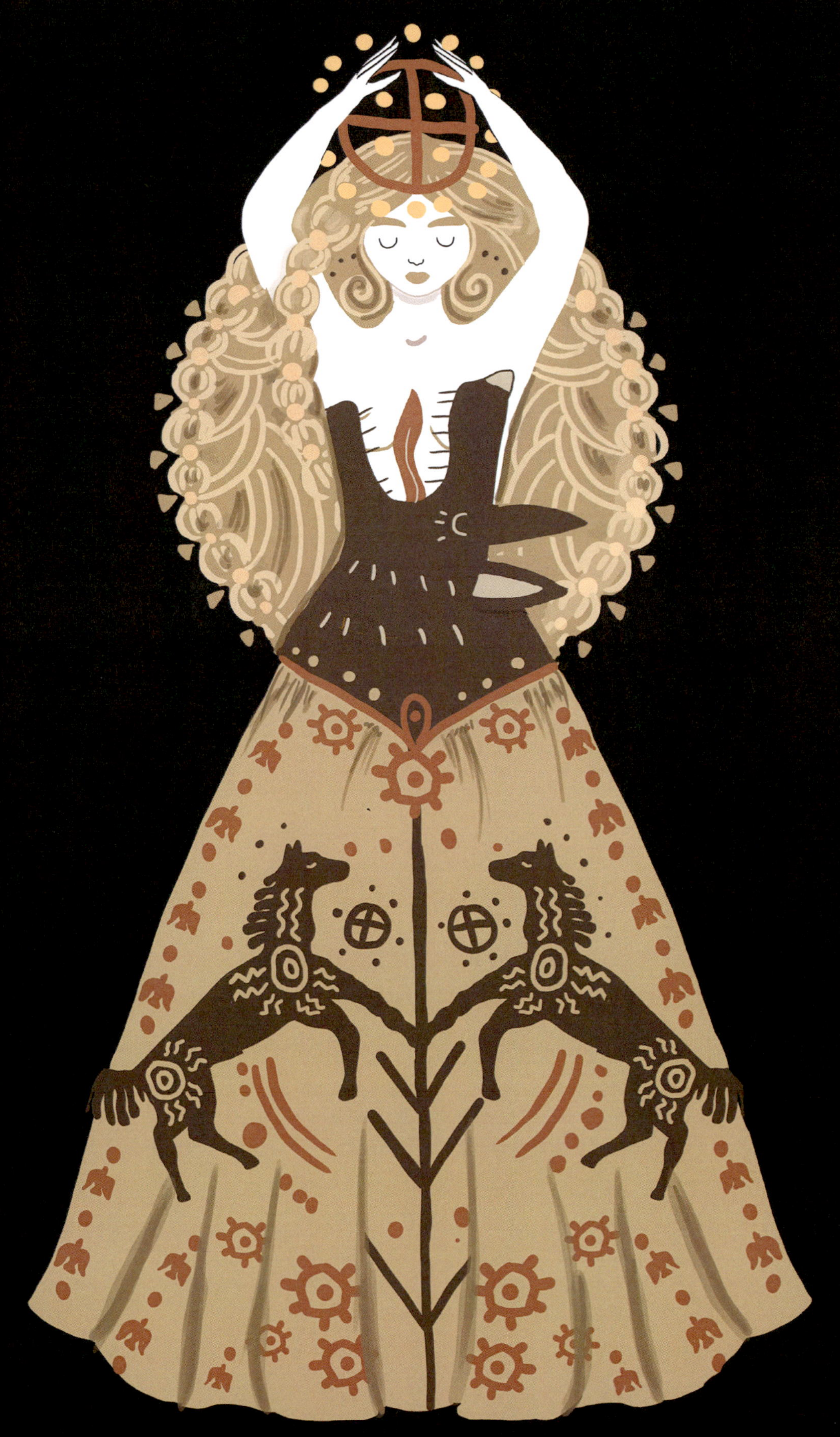

SÓL

—**Snorri Sturluson,** *Prose Edda*, "Gylfaginning," chapter 11

Sól (*sohl*), the Norse personification of the sun, drives her golden chariot across the sky, bringing daylight forth from the celestial heights. Known as the eternal "bright bride" of the sky, a title found throughout both the *Poetic Edda* and the *Prose Edda*, her journey is guided by her swift steeds Árvakr ("Early Riser") and Alsvið ("Swift"). She is accompanied by her brother, Mani, the personified moon, who follows to usher in the night. Sól and Mani are perpetually pursued by the monstrous wolves Sköll and Hati, offspring of Fenrir, symbolizing the constant threat of cosmic destruction. The duration of daylight is attributed to the distance Sól maintains from the relentless pursuit of Sköll.

Sól's destiny, in keeping with the fundamental Norse tenets of balance and duality, is intrinsically linked to the inevitability of *Ragnarök*, the prophesied end of the cosmos. In this cataclysmic event, Sól is destined to be engulfed by Sköll, while Mani is similarly fated to be consumed by Hati. This act of destruction is a powerful signal of Ragnarök and paves the way for a new cosmic beginning, with Sól's daughter then assuming her mother's celestial role.

Sól is mentioned at various points throughout the *Poetic Edda* and the *Prose Edda*, and her worship may even trace back to the Nordic Bronze Age. Archaeological findings, such as rock carvings and the Trundholm Sun Chariot, venerating the sun demonstrate the distinct role Sól played for Bronze Age Scandinavians. While Norse mythology does not position a solar deity as its central focal point, Sól's significant cultural regard is evident in her name being the origin for the word *Sunnudagar* ("Sunday").

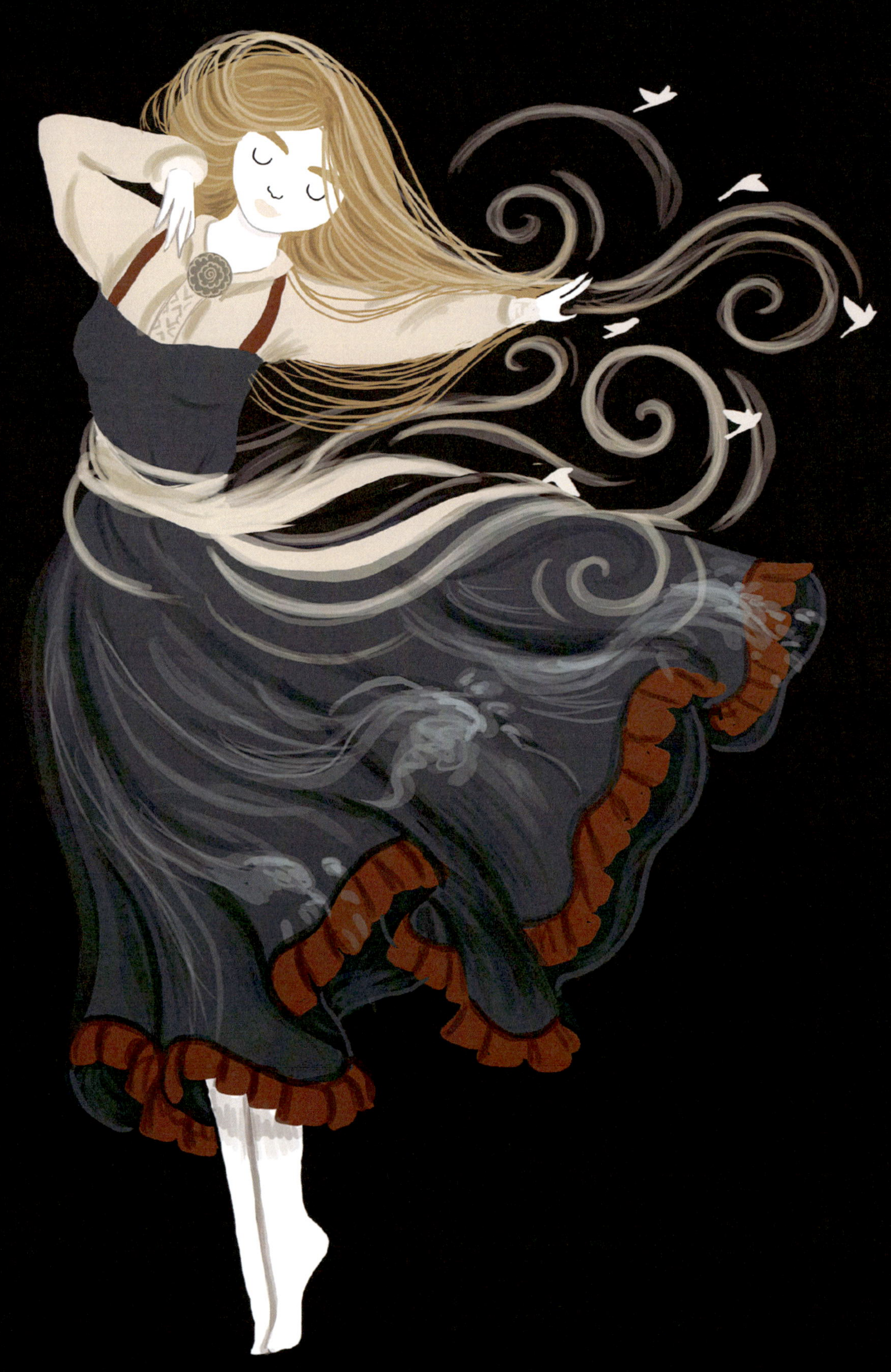

TUULETAR

"WITH HER SPORT THE ROLLING BILLOWS, WITH HER PLAY THE STORM-WIND FORCES..."

—**ELIAS LÖNNROT,** *KALEVALA* (1835)

As the Finnish deity of wind and air, Tuuletar (*too-leh-tar*) personifies both the raw, untamed power and the unpredictable capriciousness of nature. Tuuletar's origins can be traced back to the pre-Christian era in Finland, a time when animistic beliefs were prevalent. The ancient Finns believed that natural phenomena were governed by spirits and deities, and Tuuletar was considered one of the most powerful among them. Her name, derived from the Finnish word *tuuli*, meaning "wind," reflects her association with the element of air and its manifestations.

Tuuletar was often depicted as a beautiful woman with long flowing hair that resembled the wind's movements. She was believed to reside in the sky, where she controlled the winds and weather patterns. Tuuletar's moods were believed to manifest in the shifting winds, ranging from gentle breezes to violent storms. This mirroring of her emotional state made her a figure evoking both awe and apprehension among those who worshipped her.

Tuuletar's significance in Finnish mythology also encompassed agriculture, navigation, and even warfare. Farmers appealed to her for the blessing of good weather and abundant harvests, while sailors entrusted their voyages to her favorable winds. Warriors believed that Tuuletar could influence the outcome of battles by directing the winds to their advantage. Despite her significance, Tuuletar's presence in Finnish mythology gradually diminished with the advent of Christianity. The old pagan beliefs were replaced by Christian doctrines, and Tuuletar, along with other Finnish gods, was relegated to the realm of folklore and legends. However, her legacy continued to survive in various forms, including folk tales, proverbs, and place names. There has been a notable revival of interest in Tuuletar recently, particularly among individuals seeking a deeper connection to their Finnish heritage.

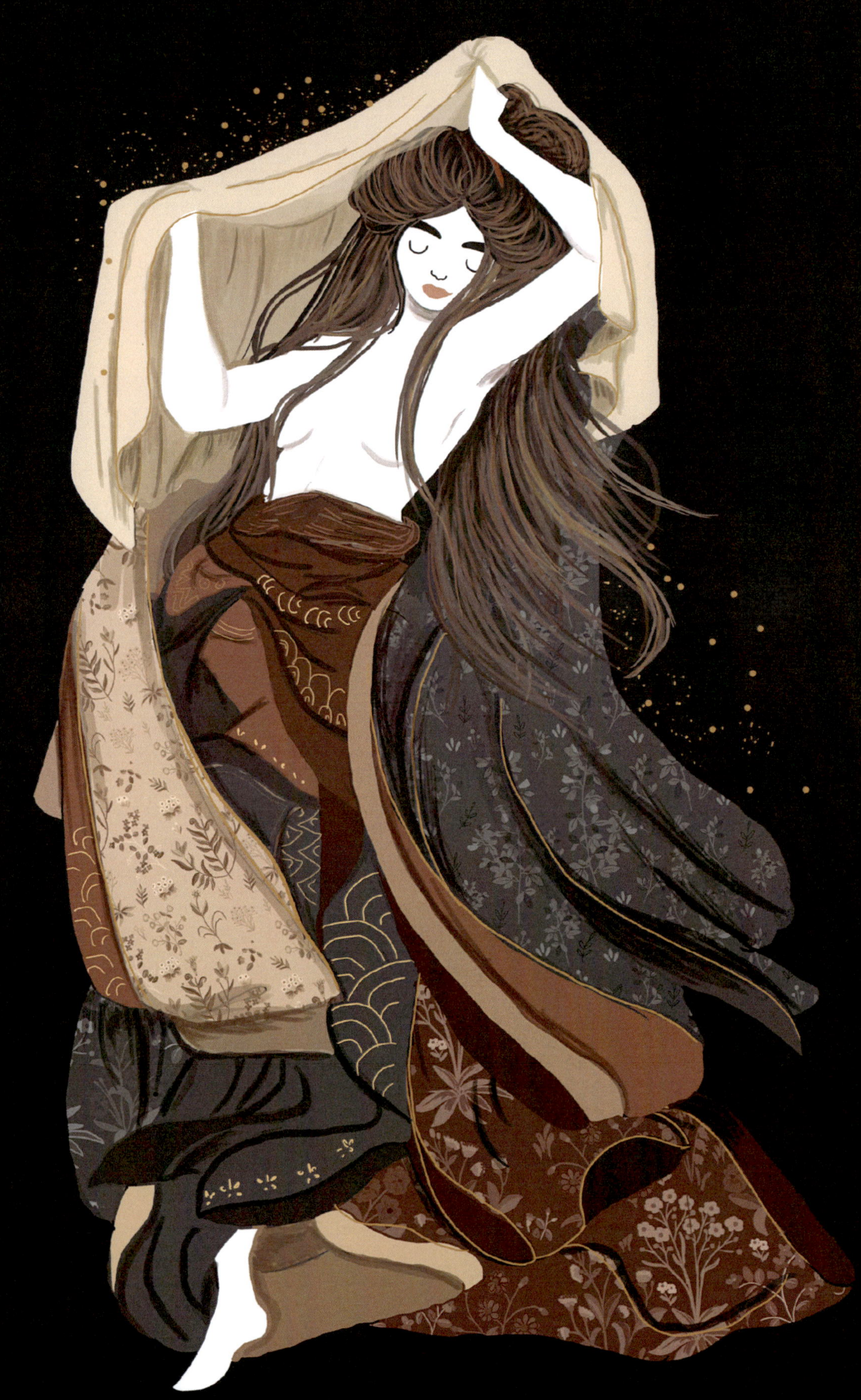

UZUME

"THEN THE EIGHT HUNDRED MYRIAD DEITIES ALL TOGETHER RAISED A SHOUT OF
LAUGHTER,
SO THAT THE PLAINS OF HIGH HEAVEN WERE SHAKEN."

—*KOJIKI,* BOOK 1

Ame-no-Uzume-no-Mikoto, often shortened to Uzume (*oo-zoo-meh*), is a prominent figure in Japanese mythology and the Shinto religion. Revered as the goddess of dawn, mirth, revelry, and the arts, she plays a crucial role in the myth of Amaterasu, the sun goddess. Uzume's legend holds significance not only for its religious implications but also for its reflection of ancient Japanese culture and societal values. Her most famous act, coaxing Amaterasu out of the Heavenly Rock Cave, serves as a pivotal illustration of her power to restore light to a world plunged into darkness. Uzume's renowned joyful and inventive nature manifested in a spirited dance and comedic display outside the cave, generating sufficient mirth and curiosity to prompt the solar deity's emergence and the dispelling of the cosmic darkness.

This central myth highlights Uzume's strong association with dawn and light, as her actions represent the banishment of darkness and the sun's reappearance. Furthermore, the narrative emphasizes her significant role as a mediator and peacemaker, demonstrating her capacity to resolve the conflict between Amaterasu and Susanoo that had precipitated the sun goddess's withdrawal. Beyond her mythological significance, Uzume maintains a unique place in Japanese culture, where she is often depicted as a cheerful and energetic figure embodying the spirit of celebration and joy.

The cultural value placed on humor and creativity is vividly evident in Uzume's legend. The *kagura*, a sacred Shinto theatrical dance still performed today, is directly rooted in the myth of Uzume's iconic dance outside Amaterasu's cave. These dances, traditionally offered to the kami (Shinto deities), serve various purposes, including ritual purification, entertainment for the gods, and the transmission of ancient myths and legends.

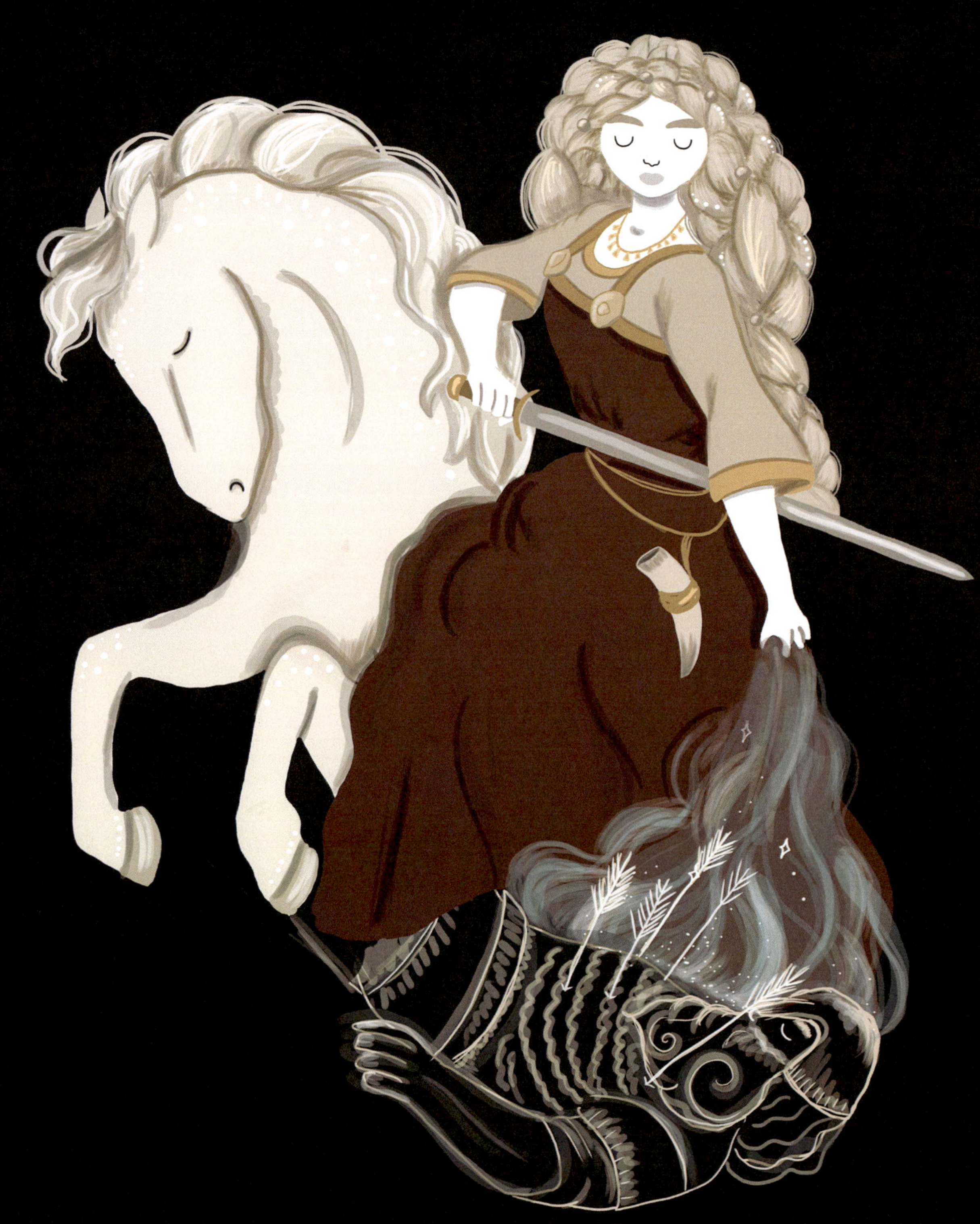

VALKYRIES

"SHIELD YOURSELF NOW, YOU CAN SURVIVE THIS STRIFE...THOSE MIGHTY WOMEN MARSHALLED
THEIR POWERS, AND THEY SEND SHRIEKING SPEARS."

—*LACNUNGA* (TENTH CENTURY AD), "WIÐ FÆRSTICE"

Valhalla and Fólkvangr were the ultimate destinations that all warriors strived for upon their deaths in battle. Freyja received half the dead to take to Fólkvangr, while the other half were selected to aid Odin in Valhalla in preparation for Ragnarök. It is this half that is escorted by a group of war-maidens called the Valkyries (*val-kih-reez*). As Odin's emissaries, these warrior deities were dispatched to every battlefield to guide the worthy slain into the majestic halls of Valhalla. The Valkyries acted as a vital link between the mortal realm of battle and the divine realm, where preparations were underway for the end times.

These Valkyries, often envisioned astride winged steeds and descending from the celestial realm in armor shimmering with sunlight, were later mythologized as the genesis of the Aurora Borealis, or the "Northern Lights." The word "Valkyrie" can be traced from the Old Norse word *valkrja*, consisting of *val* which meant "to choose" and *kyrja* which meant

"the slain on the battlefield." The Valkyries may have even had a say in who was to die in battle (somewhat akin to the Norns) and often showed favor toward particular warriors or disdain for others.

Several of these shieldmaidens would eventually become revered in their own right, such as Brynhildr the "bright battle," Sigrún the "victory rune," and the renowned healing goddess Eir. The precise number of Valkyries serving under the command of Odin remains elusive within Norse mythology, as no definitive count is ever provided in early accounts. Instead, our understanding of their numbers is gleaned from the various individual names of Valkyries that appear across the *Poetic Edda* and the *Prose Edda*, as well as occasional references to groups of these warrior maidens. This piecemeal evidence has led scholars to generally accept a fluid range, suggesting anywhere between six and forty individual Valkyries.

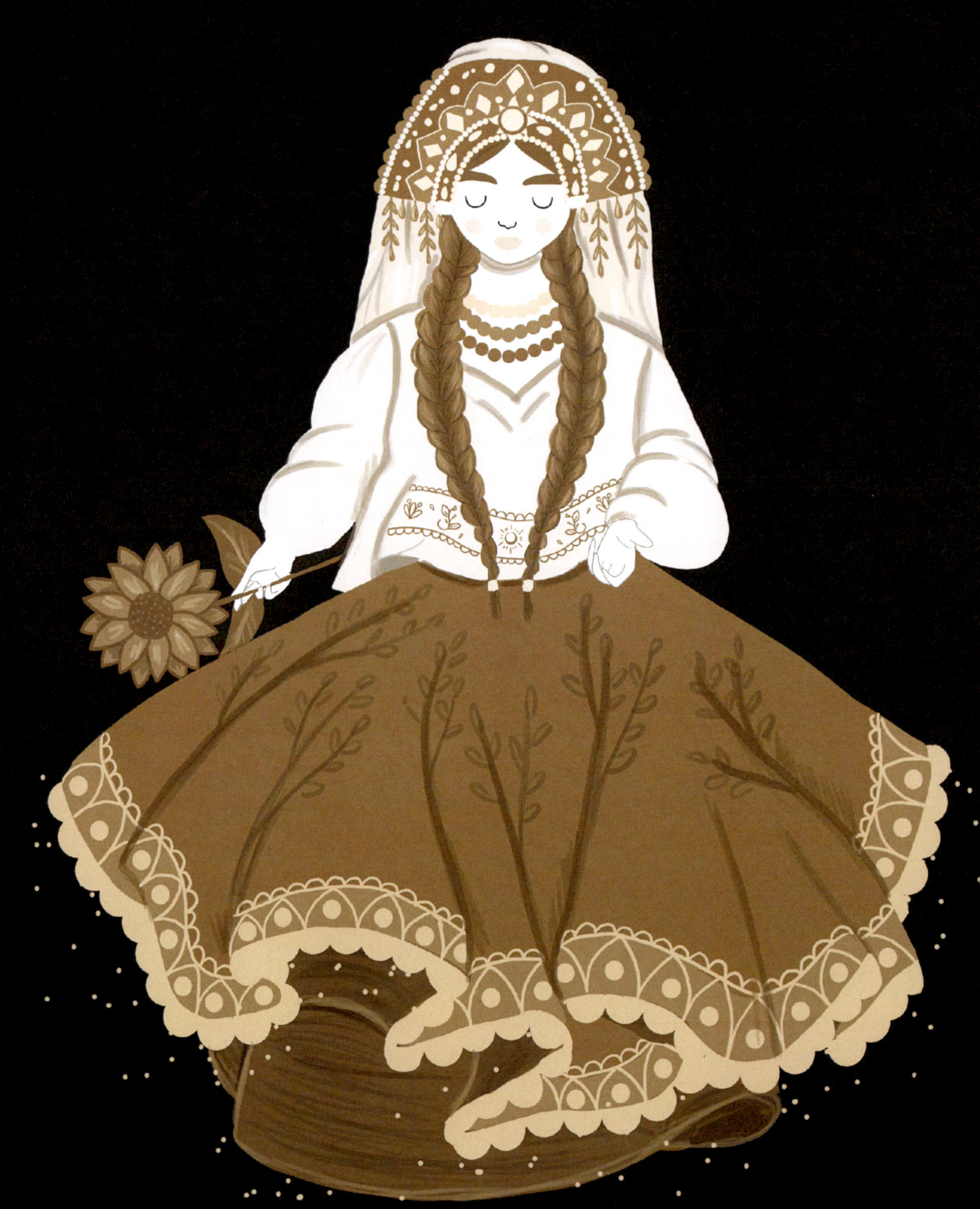

VESNA

"I AM ENJOYING THE BREATH OF THE EVER-WAVING SPRING, ON THE BOSOM OF RURAL QUIET!"

—RICHARD F. GUSTAFSON, "THE METAPHOR OF THE SEASONS IN EVGENIJ ONEGIN" (1962)

Vesna (*ves-nuh*), the Slavic personification of spring renewal, is associated with several seasonal rites that are still observed across various parts of the world. In stark contrast to Morana, the goddess of winter, the arrival of Vesna embodies the rebirth of abundance and life. Traditional songs and chants are performed to encourage the goddess to chase away the bitter freeze of the winter months to expedite the arrival of spring. Though an ally to her followers, it was understood that light couldn't exist without dark, implying the equal importance of both goddesses.

Underscoring her intimate connection to the season of rebirth through a name etymologically linked to the proto-Slavic term for "spring," Vesna's arrival was eagerly anticipated by early Slavic communities who relied on agriculture for sustenance. As the snow melted and the days grew longer, Vesna's presence was felt in the budding trees, blooming flowers, and the return of migratory birds. Though depictions of Vesna vary across Slavic regions, she is often portrayed as a young, beautiful woman adorned with flowers and greenery, sometimes carrying a staff or branch symbolizing the burgeoning life of spring.

To hasten her arrival, a customary ritual involved either burning or symbolically "drowning" an effigy representing Morana, the embodiment of winter's dormancy and eventual demise. This act of banishment was often performed while carrying a similar effigy fashioned in the likeness of Vesna. These welcoming rituals for Vesna frequently involved communal singing and dancing, the lighting of bonfires symbolizing the sun's increasing power and warmth, and the offering of symbolic gifts intended to invoke her favor and ensure a fertile season. These offerings typically included the first flowers of spring, painted eggs representing new life and potential, and honey, signifying sweetness and abundance.

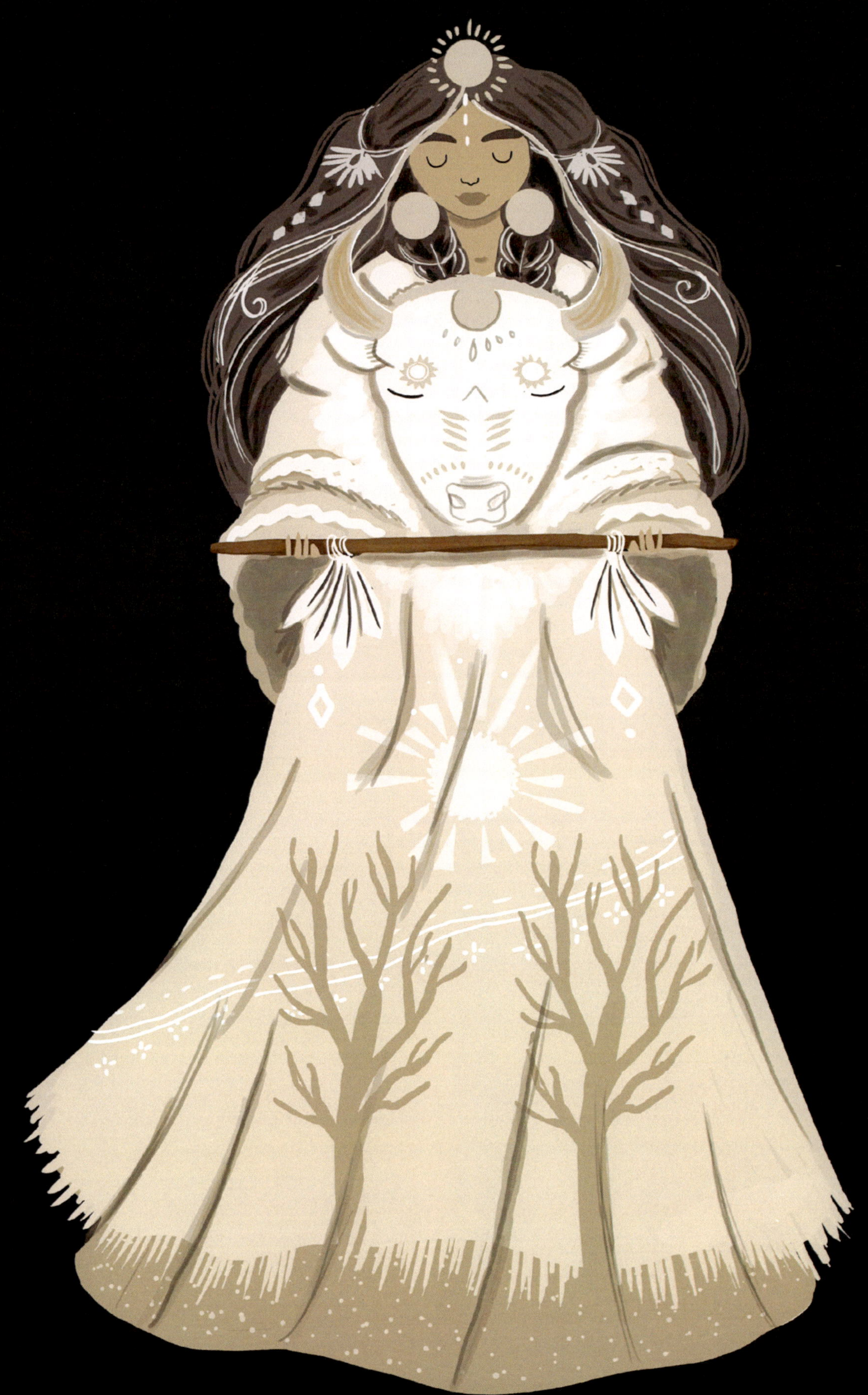

WHITE BUFFALO CALF WOMAN

"HIS BONES LEFT A LEGACY OF THE SACREDNESS OF WHITE BUFFALO CALF WOMAN'S SPIRIT..."

—SKYBLUE MORIN, "WHITE BUFFALO CALF WOMAN'S SPIRIT" (1993)

The White Buffalo Calf Woman (also known as the White Buffalo Maiden) is an ancient goddess central to the Lakota religion. She serves as their primary deity, notably bestowing upon the Lakota people their "Seven Sacred Rites," as well as the čhaŋnúŋpa, their sacred ceremonial pipe. These vital ceremonies, which include rituals for purification, child naming, healing, and marriage, are believed to ensure a future of harmony and balance for her people. The čhaŋnúŋpa itself possesses profound symbolic features: its red stone bowl represents the earth, a buffalo head carved into the pipe signifies the animal kingdom, the wooden stem connects it with nature, and twelve eagle feathers symbolize the birds of the sky.

The foundational legend of the White Buffalo Calf Woman illustrates her role as a pivotal spiritual guide during a period when the Lakota people faced dire hardship and a fractured relationship with the sacred. Narratives describe her miraculous appearance to scouts, and she imparted the importance of purity in heart and mind. Upon entering the camp, this sacred figure gifted the people with the ceremonial pipe and offered the essential knowledge of the Seven Sacred Rites, which also include practices such as the sweat lodge, vision quest, and sun dance, which remain vital to Lakota spirituality. This event established her as the central conduit of spiritual law and traditional practice.

Upon concluding her teachings, the White Buffalo Calf Woman is depicted as departing, with her symbolic transformation through the white, brown, and black buffalo representing the cyclical nature of life and the interconnectedness of all beings. The prophecy of the White Buffalo Calf Woman's return persists as a cherished hope within Lakota tradition, with the rare birth of a white buffalo calf serving as its sacred harbinger, signifying renewal and spiritual awakening.

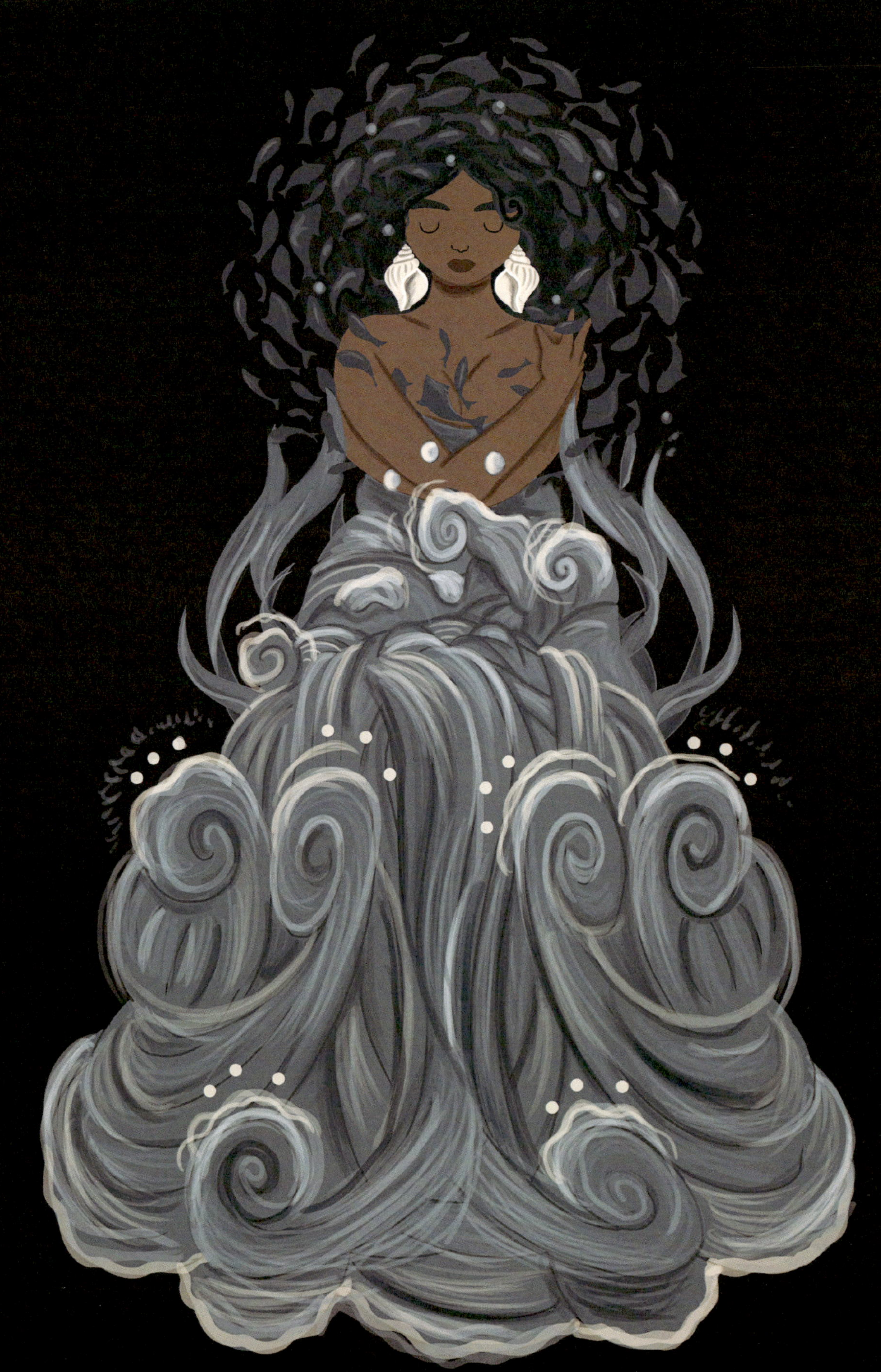

YEMAYA

Yemaya *(yeh-mah-yah)*, also called Yemoja and Yemanja, is the primordial mother of all Yoruba Orishas and the patron deity of life-giving waters. Orishas are sacred spirits based in West African tradition, with several religions that branch out from the Yoruba foundation adopting their own versions of the deities. Yemaya is strongly protective of her children but keeps a particularly watchful eye over women and all that pertains to their health and well-being. In an ancient legend, it was said that when Yemaya's waters broke, a great flood covered the earth to create rivers and streams, as well as the first mortals.

Yoruba mythology recognizes Yemaya as the powerful goddess encompassing the ocean, motherhood, fertility, and protection. Her name is believed to derive from the Yoruba phrase *Yey Omo Eja*, meaning "Mother Whose Children are the Fish." This reflects her profound association with the abundance of the seas. Yemaya is often depicted as a beautiful woman adorned in blue and white, her colors symbolizing the depths of the ocean and the purity of water.

During the transatlantic slave trade, Yoruba deities, including Yemaya, were transported to the Americas alongside their followers. In the face of cultural suppression, enslaved people found ways to maintain their spiritual practices by hybridizing their deities with Catholic figures. Yemaya, with her association with water and motherhood, was often mixed into the worship of the Virgin Mary, particularly Our Lady of Regla in Cuba. The goddess became a central figure in *Santería*, a religion that emerged in Cuba, blending Yoruba beliefs with Catholic practices. In Santería, Yemaya is revered as the queen of the sea, the protector of women and children, and the source of love and compassion. Likewise, in *Candomblé*, a related Brazilian religion, the veneration of Yemaya is profoundly embedded in the spiritual lives of adherents.

ABOUT THE AUTHORS

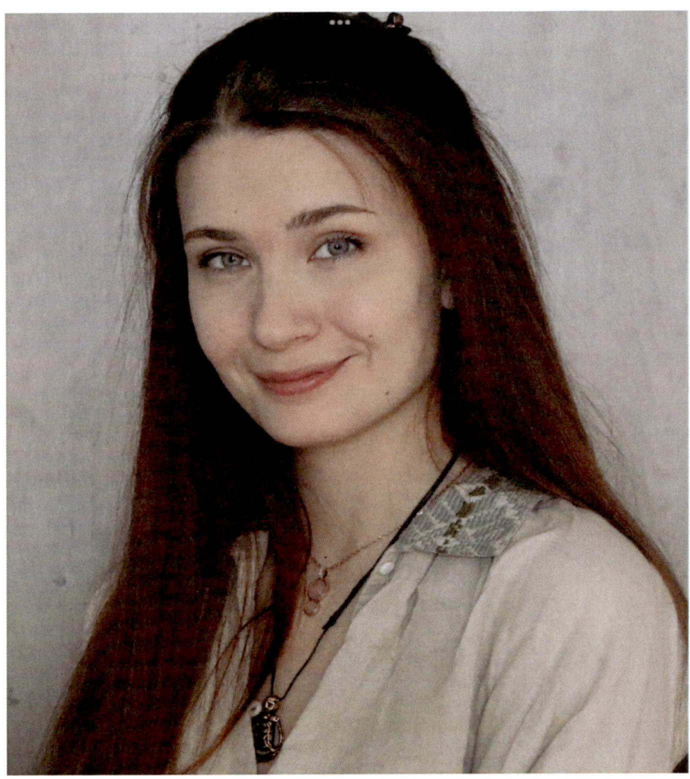

Anette Pirso is a self-taught illustrator and storyteller. Her work focuses on visual storytelling, cultural preservation, and the female religious symbol. She has illustrated for books, companies, and private clients, and held a lecture and exhibited at Castlefest (NL). Her previous books are *The Divine Feminine* and *Femme Folk Oracle Deck*. Her online platform includes over 165,000 followers on Instagram (@Anetteprs), where she shares original illustrations and narratives. Her work has been featured in feminist, historical, and metaphysical art circles. She is from Tallinn, Estonia, and lives in Edinburgh, Scotland.

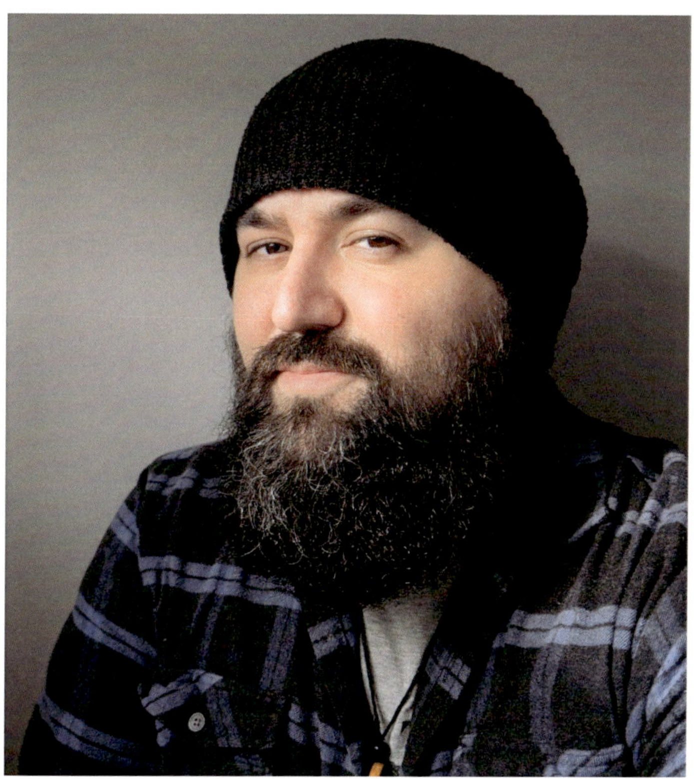

Israel Gonzalez is a writer of poetry and prose, often weaving intricate mythological themes with unrequited romance and highly structured rhyming patterns. His work is heavily influenced by his deep appreciation for classic literature, Pre-Raphaelite artwork, and alliteration. Although currently based in Rhode Island, Israel draws inspiration from his Mexican American heritage with the aim of making mythology both accessible and enjoyable for everyone. Israel has collaborated on several successful projects with illustrator Anette Pirso, where they join their love of mythology and the divine through art and writing, resulting in beautifully balanced endeavors.

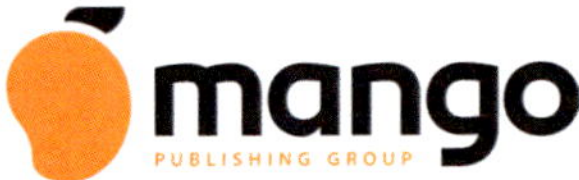

Mango Publishing, established in 2014, publishes an eclectic list of books by diverse authors—both new and established voices—on topics ranging from business, personal growth, women's empowerment, LGBTQ studies, health, and spirituality to history, popular culture, time management, decluttering, lifestyle, mental wellness, aging, and sustainable living. We were named 2019 *and* 2020's #1 fastest growing independent publisher by *Publishers Weekly*. Our success is driven by our main goal, which is to publish high-quality books that will entertain readers as well as make a positive difference in their lives.

Our readers are our most important resource; we value your input, suggestions, and ideas. We'd love to hear from you—after all, we are publishing books for you!

Please stay in touch with us and follow us at:

Facebook: Mango Publishing
Twitter: @MangoPublishing
Instagram: @MangoPublishing
LinkedIn: Mango Publishing
Pinterest: Mango Publishing
Newsletter: mangopublishinggroup.com/newsletter

Join us on Mango's journey to reinvent publishing, one book at a time.